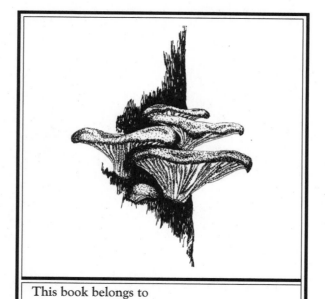

This book belongs to

Backyard Almanac

Larry Weber

Illustrations by Judy Gibbs

Pfeifer-Hamilton Publishers
210 West Michigan Duluth MN 55802-1908

Pfeifer-Hamilton Publishers
210 West Michigan
Duluth MN 55802-1908
218-727-0500

Appointment with Nature series
Backyard Almanac

Printed in the United States of America
10   9   8   7   6   5   4   3   2   1

Editorial Director: Susan Gustafson
Graphic Design: Sally Rauschenfels

Library of Congress Catalog Card Number: 95-74734

ISBN 1-57025-071-5

For Fran,
My companion in critter watching
and the adventure of life.

Acknowledgments

A project like this requires much help and would not have happened without the kindness and generosity of many people. I say thank you to all who were genuinely interested and encouraging in this endeavor. Special thanks go to Julie Ball, Kathy Hermes, Tom Diener, Karen Snyder, John McGee, and other colleagues at The Marshall School for giving me the time and space to complete this task. Judy Gibbs labored tirelessly over the illustrations, demonstrating her skills as a professional artist and naturalist. Susan Gustafson, Kathy DeArmond-Lundblad, Sally Rauschenfels, Sr. Mary Richard Boo, and others on the upbeat Pfeifer-Hamilton staff kept me stimulated while Gene Johnson and his crew at Computers Don't Byte solved many computer problems. Steve Adams at University of Minnesota-Duluth helped me locate quotable quotes. Stephanie Hemphill and Lisa Bartell allowed me a time to babble about critters on KUMD. Mike Savage and Peter Leschak provided me with inspiring and useful writing workshops.

Through their books, many local and state authors provided much-appreciated information. For more information about the northland, I recommend books by Laura Erickson, Jerry Wilber, Mark Stensaas, Kim Eckert, Barney Oldfield, Evan Hazard, Olga Lakela, John and Evelyn Moyle, and Jim Gilbert.

Thanks also to the many students that I've known over the years who have taught me to take a closer look at critters. The biggest thank you of all goes to Fran who listened to, read, and reread hundreds of entries through the year and kept me going.

Introduction

Many people believe that to look at nature they must travel to distant wild areas. No doubt those places provide wonders for the wanderer, but our backyards also offer natural adventures. In this book, I use the word backyard in both literal and figurative ways. A plot of land near our homes, often quite small, is the literal definition, and though we may expect it to be nearly devoid of wildlife, a plethora of critters live there for all or part of their lives. Figuratively, I define the backyard as any region close enough for us to visit frequently. A nearby park, meadow, roadside, vacant lot, swamp, pond, or even a large expanse of wild woods and water may fall into this category. Though some critters discussed in this book are found in wild settings, most live near our homes.

As I write these words while sitting in my backyard, I am visited by bees, moths, butterflies, and spiders. The late spring floral display is near at hand, and the avian songsters proclaim their territorial rights. Baby birds calling for a meal catch the interest of a passing hungry raccoon.

Written as a daily look at nearby nature, this book includes an entry for each day of the year. From year to year, what is written for a particular date may pertain just as well to nearby dates, but the seasonal phenology is accurate. Each month displays its natural identity, and a close examination of nature's calendar reveals this pattern. Thoreau was such a master of nature observation that his friend Emerson said about him: "He thought that, if waked (sic) up from a trance, in this swamp, he could tell by the plants what time of the year it was within two days." The essays and illustrations in this book are meant to whet your appetite for a close look each day at your own special place.

As we near the end of the twentieth century, the growing human population along with the destruction of wild lands, makes our backyards even more important to us and to wildlife. As you watch the seasons change, I hope this book will help you appreciate the treasures you have close to home. With a keen sense of observation, each walk in the woods or hour in the backyard will be one of more interest. In the words of naturalist John Burroughs, "If you want an adventure in nature, take the same walk that you took yesterday, and do so again tomorrow."

Good critter watching!

Larry A. Weber
1995

January

January

Look carefully on bare branches for cocoons—hibernating sleeping bags.

1 Cocoons abound in the winter woods. Though not always large or attached to trees, these hibernating sleeping bags are most obvious to us when good sized and fastened to bare, open branches. They have been placed there by moths and a host of other insects, but not by butterflies. The pupa of a caterpillar that will eventually become a butterfly, and which is correctly termed a *chrysalis*, consists of uncovered skin. Cocoons, on the other hand, are composed of materials such as silk and they cover the sleeping larvae.

Some of the largest cocoons are those spun by giant moths of the silkworm family (not related to the oriental silkworm). In their caterpillar stage, they are often seen feeding on our yard or garden leaves. Eventually they will emerge as large green or brown moths with feathery antennae, familiar to us as the beautiful moths of luna, polyphemus, promethea, and cecropia.

In the fall, the cocoons we see are made of leaves and threads; with this insulation, the critters sleep through the winter and arise as moths in the spring. They not only survive the cold, they need it. Cocoons gathered in fall and kept at room temperature through the winter will not develop.

Notes

January

2 Often, the first signs of life on frigid winter mornings appear at backyard bird feeders, where chickadees, ignoring the cold, are actively greeting the day. Looking just as they did the previous summer, their small gray bodies feature black caps and bibs.

Black-capped chickadees form small flocks to cope with winter, using bird feeders as regular places to gather. After cold winter nights spent alone in tree hollows, they arrive at dawn and stay until dusk, even braving snowstorms. If the day is severe, they look like chubby puffballs, fluffing their feathers to trap body heat. But if the day is clear and mild, they may sing the "fee-bee" song associated with spring.

Wintering chickadees gobble sunflower seeds, suet, and peanut butter to maintain a daytime temperature of 104 degrees, caching uneaten seeds in nearby and distant trees to provide security just in case we forget to fill the bird feeder. We might think that chickadees could not survive winter without us, but on a diet of seeds, acorns, and insects, these northland forest residents can do well on their own.

If you want to see black-capped chickadees at your bird feeder, be sure to keep it filled with their favorite treats. You may need the chickadees' cheerful antics as much as they need the food you provide.

Notes

January

The elusive boreal chickadee may only be seen if you are an alert hiker in a coniferous forest.

3 We could live in the northland for years and never encounter the boreal chickadee. This small neighbor—formerly known as the brown-capped chickadee—looks much like its more common black-capped cousin, with whom it maintains a friendly relationship. The boreal, however, shies clear of bird feeders and backyards. Instead, its slow, wheezy "chick-day-day" call sings out from the coniferous forests it loves and in which it makes its meals of balsam, spruce, and birch seeds—as well as any unfortunate insects who catch its bright eye.

A northern bird by preference, the boreal chickadee tends to wander in severe winters, ranging across the continent from the Atlantic to the Pacific. In our locale, where diverse diets and habitats are available, we are privileged to enjoy both the boreal and the black-capped members of this sprightly family.

Notes

4 Certainly the bark of trees would not afford ample winter shelter for us, but for many species of bark beetles, it does just fine. The insects, adult or larvae, are not likely to be seen by an observer, but in winter their tunnels are clearly visible under the bark of living or dead trees. The beetles may be specialized not just to particular trees, but even to certain parts of those trees. One kind may live in the trunk, another in the branches, and perhaps another in logs on the ground. There they spend much of their lives in tunnels that take on shapes unique to the species; the wood beneath the bark holds their engraved signatures.

Mating occurs in the adult chamber, and females proceed to lay eggs along the walls of this cavity. Hatching larvae strike out independently, tunneling away from the adults at right angles and engraving a long-legged centipede pattern in the subsurface tree wood. Their excavations, enlarging as the larvae grow, terminate when the larvae reach pupation; holes tell of subsequent emergence into adulthood.

Woodpeckers, although they probably don't actually see these insects, find them for winter food. No doubt the hungry birds can tell from the exterior of the tree what is happening in the interior.

No matter how sharp your eyes are, woodpeckers will probably find bark beetles more efficiently than you can.

Notes

January

Snow can insulate in the same manner as a down sleeping bag.

5 To most of us, snow means cold. We forget that it can function as an insulator as efficiently as can a warm winter coat or sleeping bag. Insulated clothes keep us warm by providing air spaces around our body and by recycling the heat we ourselves generate. Those of us who have crawled into a thick down sleeping bag on a winter's night can attest to the fact that the bag is not warm until our body heats it.

Dry, powdery snow acts much the same way, influencing the temperatures both above and beneath it. Snow reflects sunlight, as we can see on clear winter days, and the air above the snow stays cold. The blanket of snow on the ground is filled with open spaces, and though it settles, a good deal of air remains trapped. Geothermal heat from deep inside the earth is captured here, causing ground temperatures below the snow to be relatively mild. A snow cover of two feet can result in a remarkable difference: zero degrees above the snow may be thirty-two degrees beneath. Tunneling and burrowing critters find the warmth to their advantage; meadow mice, for example, may be quite comfortable during the cold of January.

Notes

January

6 Survival in northland winters often depends on using what is available to cope with circumstances. Critters wintering here demonstrate this ability: whether they face a change of diet, habits, or denning site, they adapt to the scene.

Such is the case of the ruffed grouse, who take advantage of January's deep snows to ward off the chill of a cold snap. The birds need enough snow to bury themselves under a three or four inch cover. Flying straight into the snow, they proceed to form burrows. The typical scenario involves plunging into the snow, burrowing a few feet to create a shelter, and then exploding out the next day. Their tracks and wing marks on forest snow are a common winter sight to those of us who walk the woods in January. Prolonged inclement weather can keep these grouse holed up for several days of hungry safety.

Not only is the burrow a shelter from predators, but snow also acts as an insulator for the grouse, allowing them to spend the night in a climate perhaps thirty degrees above the outside air temperature. When proper snow for burrowing cannot be found, birds form "snow-bowls" on the surface or settle into conifers for the night.

On a walk in the winter woods, look for the tracks and wing marks of ruffed grouse.

Notes

January

As you walk through and look at the tall pines, listen to the wind softly sighing through them.

7 January offers us a great opportunity to get acquainted with evergreen trees. Some ten kinds of evergreens native to the northland are adapted to endure the winter with their leaves still intact. Several of these have thin leaves called needles, but best known are the pines. Although some other types have been planted here, eastern white pine, red pine, and jack pine remain the three native northland species. Each of these three has cones and needles in groups, but if we look more closely, the types are easy to distinguish.

Eastern white is our only pine with needles in clumps of five. Needles grow to approximately four inches in length and last two years. Cones up to six inches long are the longest produced by northland pines.

Red pine needles grow in pairs, may be six inches in length, and persist four years. The cones are short: only two inches. Its reddish bark gives this tree its name, although it is sometimes called Norway pine, after Norway, Maine.

Jack pine, the smallest of the trio, also has paired needles, but their length is shorter: one and one-half inches. The needles last for three years. The two-inch cones on the jack pine are usually curved and remain closed unless they are opened in a forest fire.

Notes

January

The cedars that may decorate your yard also thrive in swamps.

8 In the northland winter landscape, an evergreen more rounded than others can be seen along edges of swamps and streams. The white cedar copes with the dry cold of winter in a way of its own. A conifer, cedar has needles, but not the long thin leaves seen in pine, spruce, or balsam. Instead, its needles form as tightly locked scales that completely cover the tips of its twigs. Shorter than one-fourth inch, these overlapping structures do what thin needles do for other conifers—keep it from drying out and limit snow build up.

Thick growths of cedar are common in or near poorly drained swamps, but they do not live in the wetter or more acidic wetlands. Spruce, tamarack, black ash, poplar, aspen, and alder share the habitat with white cedars. Animals share this space too, and dense cedar stands provide sheltered food yards for wintering deer while birds find safety deep within the thick boughs.

The flat-growing twigs and branches make this evergreen a favorite ornamental shrub in yards. Tiny half-inch-long cones, formed in fall, are hard to see in the foliage.

Notes

January

The flock of small birds in your pine or spruce trees may have the X-shaped mouth of the crossbill.

9 Adaptation to habitat and food are best seen in a bird's feet and bill. The two species of northland crossbills illustrate excellent examples of the latter. Upper and lower mandibles cross, and the bird's closed X-shaped mouth looks deformed. In both the red- and white-winged crossbills, this strange beak is well suited to help the birds to tear open cones and extract seeds of various conifers. January is usually a good time to see flocks of crossbills feeding in our local coniferous trees. Look for crossbill males, who have red bodies with dark wings, and females, who are more yellow in hue. White-wings display the white wing bars which their red cousins lack. Flocks of red crossbills can be recognized by their "jip" cry and white-wings by a "chip" or "chet" call.

Both kinds of crossbills range through the boreal forests of Canada, usually remaining the entire winter. If the cone crop is poor, they will wander considerable distances southward.

Red crossbills prefer the large cones of the pines, while white-wings go for spruces. In dire straits, however, crossbills will eat the cones of many kinds of evergreens.

Notes

10 Even in the cold of January, the rapidly moving water of some large rivers will not freeze. Such sites are worth our attention. There you might see the goldeneyes—ducks that breed in the lakes of boreal forests, but winter here.

These midsized ducks get their name from their yellow eyes, but the male possesses even more colorful features: a green head, white cheek patch, and a great deal of white showing on his black-and-white body. Females are gray with a brown head.

Rising mist from the waters on these winter days can make viewing difficult, but ducks dive and feed in apparent comfort. The water temperatures are warmer than those of the air, and the ducks' well-insulated feathers keep the wet bodies from losing much heat.

While some goldeneyes winter as far south as the Gulf, with freeze-up, most of the northland's goldeneyes move only a short distance south or gravitate to large bodies of water. Nevertheless, if there is open water in our rivers throughout winter, some goldeneyes are bound to be there.

Walk along the open water of large rivers or lakes to look for goldeneyes.

Notes

January

The tiny, black, moving specks that catch your eye may be dwarf spiders.

11 We would expect that in January, if we were to see spiders at all, they would be indoors. Sheltered there, whether in the basement or the garage, they often remain alive for the duration of winter. On some winter days, however, we can see spiders not only outside, but walking on the snow. Most common of those we spy are the tiny dwarf spiders.

On a cloudy day with temperatures in the upper twenties, a few of these critters climb from the leaf litter beneath the snow up the plant stems for some moving and searching. Normally, one-fourth-inch-long spiders would not be noticed as we pass by hiking or skiing, but their dark bodies scurrying on the snow surface show up easily, and we can even see their eight legs clearly.

Why are they here on a January day? Two possible answers appear obvious. They are looking for mates or food. But because the spiders are nearly always alone, mating seems unlikely, and if they need food, hunting sites are much better under the snow than on it. We must conclude, then, that on some particular days, dwarf spiders simply find surface movement easy, and they wander until evening temperatures send them once again beneath the cover of the snow.

Notes

January

12 At four inches long, the gray short-tailed shrew is large among shrews. With pointed head, small eyes, and short tail, it is neither a mouse nor a mole, although it is often called both. This tiny carnivore, probably our most common shrew, remains under the snow all winter, but does little other burrowing.

Under the safe snow blanket, the little shrew keeps hidden from its many predators while seeking their prey in meadows and woods. Little influenced by extreme cold, the world underneath the snow cover is alive with many critters, and the shrew itself is able to satisfy its own demanding appetite. Not only is it active all through the winter, it also functions by day or night in its quest for food. It devours insects (often as larvae), worms, snails, seeds, acorns, grass stems, and mice.

Occasionally conditions will bring the shrew to the surface, where we can see its tiny walking (not hopping) tracks. The short-tailed shrew almost always travels alone, and we can often find its tracks in the new, light snow of midwinter as it cautiously crosses our sidewalks.

After a light dusting of new snow, check for the tiny tracks of short-tailed shrews.

Notes

January

The large black bird that leaves its meal of road kill to escape your approaching automobile is probably a raven.

13 The croaking call of one of nature's toughest birds, the raven, is often heard on the biting cold days of January. Larger cousins of the crow, ravens survive the coldest and bleakest conditions, and when many other animals go hungry or starve, the adaptable ravens endure.

Ranging in North America throughout the west and north, these dark, twenty-four-inch-long birds may live in habitats as varied as coastal areas, canyons, deserts, and northern boreal forests. Much of their range overlaps with that of the crow, but ravens can be distinguished by their size; their thick, heavy bill; their long wedge-shaped tail; and the hoarse "cr-r-ruck" or "prruk" of their call, as contrasted with the "caw" or "cah" of the crow.

Winter survival depends on the birds' not being finicky, and in January they feed on almost anything. During winter, these highly intelligent birds flock and with powerful wings continuously survey the region. Word of any possible food quickly spreads among the hungry birds. Preferring fresh carrion, they readily take road kill, rob traps, and will even eat droppings. As adaptable as they are, ravens cope successfully with the severity of the season.

Notes

January

14 Although the redpolls of the far north have been with us since October or November, we may not have seen them. These tiny birds have stayed hidden in alders, birches, or weedy meadows. Here they have been feeding on available seeds, even shaking them hungrily from plants when none have scattered on the snow.

By midwinter, flocks of common redpolls, with a few hoary redpolls, arrive at northland bird feeders. Redpolls are gregarious and will form flocks of thirty or more, feeding on the ground as readily as on feeders. Once they get word of obtainable food, especially thistle seeds, these active little birds remain with us and brighten much of our winter. Eventually flocks get restless, begin singing mating songs, and finally leave us in March or April for the long flight north.

Common redpolls derive their name from the bright red foreheads of both sexes. Males may also carry some red on their chests. Most of the body is streaked, but they have a dark throat, wings, and tail. Hoary redpolls are similar except for their much whiter body. Both of these five-inch-long birds often give rising "swee-ee-eet" calls from their perches.

Add thistle seeds to your bird feeder to attract redpolls.

Notes

January

It's muskrat houses rather than muskrats that you are most likely to see on a winter walk in the marsh.

15 Their name to the contrary, muskrats—common residents of swamps, marshes, and slow streams—are actually a kind of mouse. A foot long with a naked nine-inch-long tail, they are certainly very big mice. Not likely to be recognized as mice, they could be mistaken for swimming beavers. The latter are much larger, however, and have flat tails, while muskrat tails are laterally compressed.

Muskrats remain active all winter, but since much of their activity is under ice and at night, we are not likely to see them. We do, nevertheless, see signs of their presence. When enough materials, such as cattails, are available, they build dwelling lodges that look like small beaver houses. Unlike those of the beaver, muskrat lodges are only three feet high and are constructed of herbaceous plants. Built in the fall, the lodges are strong and large enough to house a family for the winter. If not enough plants are obtainable, the muskrats dig bank burrows of comparable size.

Surfacing to breathe air, muskrats are able to swim under ice to gather plants for winter food. Tracks which include a dragged tail tell us of occasional wanderings over the winter ice.

Notes

16 Both woody and nonwoody (herbaceous) plants are frequently subject to swelling growths called galls. These galls were not easily visible when leaves were still cloaking them, but now we may see them easily. Many trees such as the poplar, willow, aspen, maple, basswood, and oak have them, but so do some bushes—for example, the blackberry, blueberry, and rose. The insects which cause these hard plant swellings often winter inside them.

On their stems, blackberry plants commonly hold swellings several inches long and much thicker than themselves. Rabbits and hares that eat the rest of the plant avoid these hard growths. Blueberry galls also persist into the winter. In summer, they begin on the green stems, enlarge, and grow to a big C-shape. Now, in January, the leaves are gone and the quarter-sized galls can be seen at the snow surface.

Rose bushes hold several kinds of galls. Globular galls, looking like poorly formed balls, may cover the stem. Nearby, on small branches and appearing to be spiny burs the size of marbles, other galls may be seen.

All four of these types of galls are caused by tiny wasps, less than one-fourth inch in length, who lay eggs in the stems of the plants.

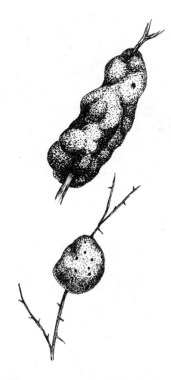

Slice open a gall and look for an immature insect inside.

Notes

January

Goldenrod is so common that you may easily find and identify all three types of goldenrod galls.

17 Throughout the summer, we saw swellings on goldenrod stems. By far the most common are the ball galls, but the stem also develops elliptical galls and bunch galls grow on top. On stems protruding from the snow, all three can be seen now.

The elliptical galls may be unique. In spring, the larva of the goldenrod-gall moth hatches and digs into the stem. There it stays, causing swelling, and feeds until pupating in midsummer. The adult emerges in late summer and vacates the gall for winter but spiders and wasps that parasitized the larva remain for winter. Or, if the cavity is empty, other critters may move in.

Both the ball galls and bunch galls are occupied all winter. Ball galls develop from gall fly eggs in June; there are often two or three on a single stem. Larvae cause the swelling, then feed and spend winter in the gall, emerging in spring. The grub may be used as bait for ice fishing or by downy woodpeckers for a snack.

Bunch galls look like big buds on top of the plant. Caused by midges, they apparently are found only on Canada goldenrod. A single larva is inside, but in the tight-fitting outside scales, other critters find shelter.

Notes

January

18 Last summer cattails stood up to nine feet tall in the marsh. In the midst of these long green leaves, flowers formed on a middle stalk. Male flowers were at the top, releasing large amounts of yellow pollen that drifted down to female flowers below. Thus fertilized, the cigar-shaped spike called a cattail formed. Flowering completed, the long brown structure of densely packed seeds stood staunchly through fall and early winter. Now, in the dry air, it breaks open, and fluffy seeds emerge to be dispersed by the wind. By mid-January, many cattails have lost seeds to the wind, but others still hold them intact.

Passing by marshes and swamps in the winter, we see just how common the cattail is. The stately plants stand high above the snow, even in death. Only the brown container of hard-packed seeds remains alive in the part of the plant we see. Its large network of rootstock, or tubers, is, however, also very much alive and holds the starchy food essential to spring growth. Unfortunately, hungry marsh animals like muskrats or beavers often feed on these tubers and rob the stored food before spring even begins. As a result, the fluffy stored seeds become very valuable for propagating the cattail.

By January, it may be too late to gather cattails for winter flower arrangements.

Notes

January

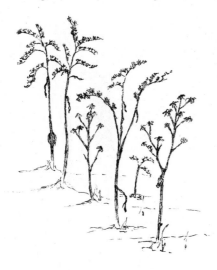

A walk through a snow-covered meadow will give you a close look at the skeletons of goldenrods and asters.

19 Yellow goldenrods and blue and white asters filled the meadows last September. During their lengthy bloom, they attracted the attention of almost every kind of insect available for pollination, then faded to form the fluffy seeds that caught rides on the wind. In the ensuing months, autumn winds did their part and many of these meadow plants now stand bare and empty of seeds. Others, however, wait with the patience of plants for winter gusts to disperse their offspring.

The several kinds of goldenrods growing in the northland have flowers of the same color, and so in summer we must distinguish them by their height, shape, and habitat. Now with the yellow blossoms long gone, we can still recognize the skeletons of those sturdy plants by these more lasting traits.

Asters get their name from the starlike appearance of the flowers. In January, with seeds gone from many of the plants, the empty seed containers, called receptacles, look even more like stars. Because of their varied shapes, asters are hard to distinguish from each other in winter. Habitat is our best clue.

Notes

January

20 After the fall mating season, white-tailed deer form groups that stay within a limited area for the duration of the winter. They become familiar with the site, pack down a series of trails, and change their feeding habits. Snow has covered the herbaceous food that was available for much of the year, and now the deer reach for branches in order to browse on the buds and foliage of various trees. These include deciduous trees like maple, ash, aspen, birch, and dogwood as well as conifers like balsam, pine, and cedar. Browse gives them less nutrition than does their regular plant food, and during the early winter, bucks drop their antlers. Deer lack a complete set of incisors and so use molars to bite, leaving a more ragged pattern than other browsers on branches.

Their hollow hairs provide insulation and keep the white-tailed deer warm; but, unfortunately, because the deer sink in deep snow, they cannot travel well. Cedar swamps, which offer food, warmth, and shelter, are often selected as winter yards. Winter deer are less active here, but form a hierarchy within their groups. Winter mortality may result from this herd order, with the young and weak more likely to perish before spring.

On a cross-country ski through a cedar swamp, you might discover a deer yard.

Notes

January

To differentiate these wingless winter crane flies from spiders, count only six legs.

21 Mid-January is one time we expect to see no insects, but during mild days on the snow of mixed forests, they are common. Among them are the wingless winter crane flies which live under the snow through much of the winter. They have no wings, but like all true flies, they possess wing-stubs called halteres. These dark winter insects appear only in cold months and are so specialized that they stay under snow on days too cold or too warm. However, when temperatures hover between twenty and thirty degrees, especially on cloudy days, they climb to the surface for a mate-finding walk. Insects reproduce only when mature, and for most of them this means summer. For these strange insects, however, it is winter. Usually alone, they keep moving until they encounter another crane fly. They mate immediately, right on the surface of the snow.

In the summer, crane flies, with their wings and long legs, are often misidentified as giant mosquitoes, although they do not bite. Wingless winter crane flies are often called spiders when seen walking across the snow—despite the fact that they have six legs, not eight.

Notes

January

Astonishingly, you can collect living insects from winter pond waters that are just above freezing temperature.

22 During January, few of us except ice fishers use a shovel and an ice auger to dig through fifteen inches of snow and drill through an equal amount of ice to see what is happening with critters in the winter pond. Those who do drop in for a winter visit get another perspective on pond ecology.

Since late October, the pond has been frozen over, and since mid-November, a snow cover has shrouded this winter scene. By the time we come by for a look, pond residents have spent the last two months in dark water just slightly above freezing. Here they compete with each other and the rotting plants for the little oxygen that is available.

The pond greets us with a gasp of putrid gases. Methane and hydrogen sulfide, formed during decay and trapped under ice, rush out in a gust of aquatic bad breath. We do not expect to see much life in these conditions, but when we examine collected water, we find snails, scuds, water fleas, immature insects, and several adult insects: water boatmen, back swimmers, diving beetles, and a giant water bug. All these tiny predators and air breathers have found conditions adequate for survival, even in the biting cold of a northern winter.

Notes

January

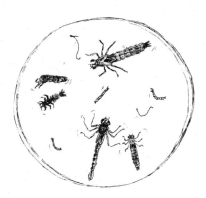

Experiment by taking a container of pond water into your warm house. Can you see any larvae? Will adult insects develop?

23 Although adult insects are found in the winter pond, they are outnumbered by the young. Myriads of immature insects—larvae and nymphs—survive these dark days to emerge as adults in spring. This dim, cold place is very much alive.

About one-inch long and looking vaguely like a cricket, dragonfly nymphs (often called naiads) reign as the largest and fiercest of the pond's young insects. With a long, flat, extending lower lip, they grasp prey of any kind. Water forced from the abdomen gives them a propulsive movement.

Damselfly nymphs are smaller and thinner than their cousins, and though they, too, are predators, they choose small critters as their victims.

Larvae of many kinds are a small but vital part of winter pond life. Caddis fly larvae use bits of plants and gravel to construct cases or houses around their bodies. With their head and six legs projecting, they move among bottom plants and feed on algae. Little red midge larvae—bloodworms—survive winter in the bottom mud consuming decaying matter. Larvae of phantom midges or phantom gnats have a body so clear that only their eyes and floating air sacks can be seen as they swim through the pond.

Notes

January

24 Bogs and swamps are frozen now and filled with deep snow. Walking and snowshoeing here is difficult, but by passing through on ski or snowmobile trails, we get a chance to see winter in this unique habitat. Tamarack and black spruce abound here, and among the shrubs of leatherleaf and Labrador tea we can glimpse tracks of the mobile residents. Also living here and hanging from many trees, especially dead spruce, is long greenish-gray material known as beard lichen or old man's beard. If we look closely, we notice that this plant is composed of a couple of layers.

A lichen, it has the algae-fungi relationship found in all lichens, but—unlike others—old man's beard does not grow flat on trees or rocks. Holding on to tree branches, it grows there without hurting them, using live or dead branches for support, not for food. In some northland bogs, nearly every dead spruce or tamarack is draped with this stringy, gray lichen. Old man's beard hangs here all year, but is most easily seen during the winter.

Winter is the best time for you to seek out old man's beard lichen deep in a bog.

Notes

January

Examine tree trunks for yellow lichen basking in winter sunlight.

25 Yellow lichen, a crusty, yellow-gold plant, has been on the tree bark all year, but now with the leaves gone, a snow pack around the base of each tree, and cold sunlight penetrating the woods, we see this lichen much more clearly.

Some of the hardiest of all organisms, lichens are abundant here and serve as a testimony to our healthy home in the northland. The tough material can endure severe conditions (it lives in both the arctic and antarctic), but with limited covering over their thalloid bodies, lichens do not survive dirty air.

Friendly coexistence between resident algae and fungi allows lichen—whether on trees, rocks, or ground—to live. Using chlorophyll, algae make food, while the spongy fungi hold moisture.

Yellow lichen is most common on the bark of deciduous trees. In winter, these trees give the lichen a chance to get sunlight and stay above the snow. Exposed to sunlight, the lichen is also exposed to cold; however, during mild weather conditions, it grows slowly and can live for decades.

Notes

January

The bright coat of the red fox stands out cheerfully against white snow.

26 Red foxes are with us all winter; we regularly spot their straight-lined trails in our backyards. Fox populations have spread into urban and suburban areas, and they appear to thrive there. Though not normally burrowers, they often occupy the underground dens of woodchucks or badgers, preferring openings on south-facing hillsides. Denning by day and hunting by night, they cope well with winter. Occasionally we can see them searching for mice and rabbits at dusk or dawn; only extreme cold or storms keep them shut in.

Now in late January, mating season is starting and the foxes become more active. Monogamous and perhaps mating for life, they do not struggle for mates as many other creatures do, but they become possessive of their home territories. Fox trails now begin to show more use, and at selected sites, patches of yellowish urine decorate the snow. The aromatic urine, with an odor similar to that of skunks, is used as a marker and an indicator to unmated foxes that this territory is taken.

After a gestation of fifty-two days, the female fox bears four to eight pups in late March.

Notes

January

You are most likely to see a barred owl in your yard during bitterly cold January weather.

27 The barred owl, perhaps our most common owl, gets its name from the lines or bars on its upper chest and striped belly. These birds are brownish-gray and about twenty inches long. They do not have the distinctive ears or horns found on some owls; instead, they possess a rounded head. Unlike other winter owls, they do their hunting at night.

We find barred owls ranging over most of eastern North America, living in river bottoms, swamps, and dense coniferous or mixed woods. They are nonmigratory and can search out enough small mammals and birds to survive winter in the northland; although during hungry times in January, barred owls may appear in our yards and stay for days, watching for careless feeder birds.

In late winter, they give their distinct series of loud hoots as breeding season nears. These calls, often translated as "who-who-who-cooks-for-you, who-who-who-cooks-for-you-all," are occasionally given all winter, making us aware of the proximity of this nocturnal raptor. We can also recognize favorite roosting sites by the presence of disgorged pellets of undigested prey under the trees.

Notes

January

28 Except for its obvious loss of yellow flowers and green leaves, the tansy plant looks much as it did last summer. A rigid stem with flat flower clusters maintains its shape, but now the hardy plant is brown. The three-foot tall stem that held composite flowers (now seeds), stands defiantly above January's deep snow. You can see the leaves on the stem, curled and dried, but still present. At the base of the plant, under snow, is a rosette of green leaves indicating that this perennial is already prepared for spring growth.

Some flowering plants develop seeds that can be carried by wind, the seeds of others are transported by animals. The opportunistic tansy, however, has seeds capable of being dispersed by both wind and animals. The abundant seeds are small and flat enough to be blown in the wind, but birds such as redpolls and sparrows use them as tasty winter food as well. Hungry birds shake the plants to dislodge seeds onto the snow. Those that are not eaten will germinate in the spring.

Equipped with underground rootstock, green rosettes, and hardy seeds, the tansy handles winter weather well indeed.

Tansy seeds, though enjoyed by birds, may not be appropriate for your bird feeder. You probably won't enjoy the tansy plants that emerge under the feeder in spring.

Notes

January

Shake a standing mullein to release the tiny black seeds.

29 With a thick, solid stem, large woolly leaves, and standing six feet tall, mullein dominated summer meadows and roadsides. Tiny yellow flowers got overlooked, but these robust plants of empty wastelands could not be missed.

Now, in winter, when the meadow landscape is snow-covered with only a few dead sticks of summer flowers emerging, the mullein again is obvious. The large leaves are gone, but the stem stands straight, holding its spiked flower heads of seed capsules through the winter. Most of the giants have just one spike, but a few branch on top to look like roadside candelabra. Up to two feet long, the spikes are filled with round pods containing numerous small black seeds. Though the plant remains standing, winds and wandering animals can shake the stem causing seeds to fall onto the snow where they are eaten by small birds and mammals.

Mullein is a biennial, and this tall tough growth took two years to form. One-year-old plants may be nearby, but as a flat leafy rosette buried beneath the snow, they do not show up like their older siblings.

Notes

January

Although bears may appear in your yard during warmer months, in January they are deep in the forest.

30 It is late January, and although still far from spring, an event we usually associate with spring takes place in many northland dens: black bear cubs are being born. Two or three babies compose a usual litter, and since each is only seven inches long and weighs in at ten ounces, they are merely a handful.

We last saw the bruins in November, when they left tracks in the new, wet snow. Since then, the confines of a four-foot den have been their home. The most common denning site is beneath an overturned tree, but bears also bed down in hollow trees, sheltered caves, dense thickets, or even under conifers. Here they spend an incomplete hibernation with waking periods and even some moving, but seldom do they leave the sleeping sites.

After a seven-month gestation, the sow gives birth to cubs during a drowsy, waking time in late January. Helpless and with their eyes closed, the young sleep and nurse until they emerge with their mother in the spring. Her thick layer of fat has helped her through hibernation, pregnancy, and nursing. The young of this year will stay with her for two years: next winter's sleep will not be interrupted by the birth of cubs.

Notes

January

A walk along an open stream during January thaw could give you a glimpse of an emerging caddis fly.

31 Often referred to as caddisworms, the caddis flies are better known in their immature stages than they are as adults. It is as larvae that they make portable cases or houses that they carry with them while feeding on algae. Species live in both ponds and streams: those in ponds construct shelters from plant matter, while stream residents use small gravel. The young spend winter in water, and larvae stay in their cases to form the pupa stage.

By midwinter, the northland has had frequent snows and cold snaps, but nearly every year we experience a respite during which temperatures rise to freezing or above for a few days—a phenomenon known as the January thaw. It is then, apparently, that in the open water of some streams, a few caddis flies climb out and become adults. The half-inch-long, gray-brown insects with large folded wings, long antennae, and big eyes are obvious on the white snow. In these mild midwinter days, they walk instead of flying and appear not to eat. Many insects have short adult stages consisting of almost nothing other than mating. Perhaps that is what is happening with these winter caddis flies. With more cold sure to come, they will not be likely to live long.

Notes

February

February

The remains of a winter picnic might entice a gray jay to join your party.

1 Gray jays, which live throughout the boreal forests, are also called Canada jays, camp robbers, or whiskey jacks. Nonmigratory, they have only a limited movement in the northland during most years. Winter survival is accomplished because they eat a wide variety of foods. Boldly, they approach campsites and, living up to the camp-robber name, steal anything that looks edible. Unfortunately, they eat items like soap that are not nutritious.

The same size as their blue jay cousins, they are mostly gray with a light underside and head. Gray jays have been described as giant chickadees. The young are a dark, sooty color. We will not confuse gray and blue jays, but they can be mistaken for the masked northern shrike.

Winter ski or camping trips are made more interesting with visits from gray jays. Many times these forest birds have accompanied trappers and other north country travelers. Unlike blue jays, these quiet birds give only soft "whee-ah" notes as they survey opportunities in the winter scene. Although basically forest dwellers, occasionally these birds will visit yards and feeders.

Notes

February

When weather forecasters announce that the groundhogs have seen or not seen their shadow, you'll know that they never saw the light of day.

2 Probably few animals get as much attention while asleep as the groundhog or woodchuck. Through a series of superstitious stories and misidentification, this critter has been given powers that it neither possesses nor needs. While we look to this marmot for a sign of the coming spring, it continues the sleep of winter.

Northland woodchucks usually go into hibernation during October. Curled in a ball and sealed deep inside their winter burrow, they enter the unyielding torpor of a true hibernator. In this deep sleep, their body temperature drops to about fifty degrees, they breathe once every six minutes, and their heartbeat is about five percent of normal.

In some southern states, groundhogs may arouse in early February, but in the northland, they wait until late March to wake. Upon rising, they are interested in mating and not likely to bother with a shadow or lack of it.

Warmer months are spent in a different burrow, and as ground squirrels, most of their waking hours continue to be lived underground. Time out of the den is used for eating or gathering food.

Notes

February

Pour a cup of water over rock tripe and note the change in texture.

3 On barren volcanic rocks along lake shores, grows a lichen that, in the arid air of February, has the consistency of old leather. This lichen, rock tripe, is sometimes called leather lichen. It flourishes in the northland, large growths covering exposed rocks to the extent that entire shorelines appear brown, gray, or black.

The hardy rock tripe lichen clings to rocks along steep shores and cliffs in much of the northland. In such open areas, the algal component gets needed sunlight, and the fungal member soaks in moisture when available so that the lichen can photosynthesize to survive. In the dry cold of February, it is hard to believe this brown brittle crust is even alive. The five- to ten-inch in diameter flat bodies hold onto rocks with a single central cord which explains the Latin name—*Umbilicaria.*

In rain or melted snow, the lichen absorbs water and becomes flexible, feeling almost slimy. The softened body turns greenish and looks like another kind of plant. In this form, rock tripe has been collected and eaten. Although it is consumed regularly in some countries, most people avoid it until faced with starvation.

Notes

February

4 If such a thing as a generic lichen exists, it is the blue-green lichen so common on trees and rocks. In the genus, *Parmelia,* the many species are widespread across North America and regularly form close-knit mats on available surfaces. The flat thalloid bodies measure about five inches in diameter and grow in an enlarging circle pattern. The outer edges, wrinkled and deeply lobed, surround the center of the thallus, which is folded with a powdery, dark appearance. These lichen growths have been described as looking like dried spilled paint.

Though common on many northland trees and rocks, now, in midwinter, they are easiest to see on trunks of old trees along roads or forest edges. Here lichens are exposed to light and enough moisture to make their own food.

Living on old trees like oaks or maples gives the slow-growing lichens another advantage. Because they grow only about one-eighth inch per year, they need long-lasting substrates such as are provided by these trees. Blue-green lichens use white threadlike growths called holdfasts, or rhizines, to hold onto trees or rocks.

Do blue-green lichens grow more densely on the south side of trees?

Notes

February

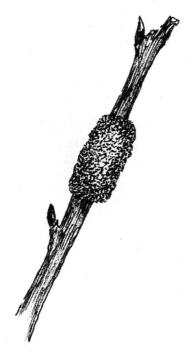

During a walk through the yard, an observant viewer should find many examples of wintering insects in pupal or egg stages.

Notes

5 Insect development, called metamorphosis, can happen by two different routes. During complete metamorphosis, eggs hatch to form active larvae that grow into resting pupae and emerge as adults. During incomplete metamorphosis, eggs become nymphs that grow to adults. The pupal stage is skipped. Both forms of metamorphosis are common in the northland, and we can find insects that winter in any of these stages. These are some examples of wintering immature insects: the grub worms in goldenrod galls are larvae; cocoons and chrysalises are pupae; and dragonfly naiads are nymphs.

Some insects, such as ladybugs, winter as adults, but many adults die in the cold. Most insects that die in late summer or fall deposit eggs, using various ways to protect them from the cold and help them survive winter. Mosquito eggs are laid in water which will be warmer than air; grasshopper eggs are hidden in soil; and those of the walkingstick are buried under leaf litter. Using another method, tent caterpillar moths leave eggs in the open. Attaching the two to three hundred eggs to a twig, they merely coat them with waterproof foam. Apparently this keeps the eggs dry and no ice forms inside though they remain below freezing for months.

February

6 Some cold-blooded animals go into a torpor, or diapause, state in cold weather much deeper than that of warm-blooded animals. Occasionally, we see these critters that seem to be frozen and dead, but to our surprise, they revive. Surviving winter for insects, amphibians, and reptiles means being able to cope with ice. These organisms handle the problem of ice in two ways. Some are able to avoid the formation of ice altogether while others allow it to form but only where they want it.

Those avoiding ice are able to dry themselves or their immediate environment enough to keep moisture out. Without moisture, there can be no ice. Others produce a substance called glycerol that acts like antifreeze, lowering the freezing point of their cells. Gall insects and ground beetle larvae can keep ice from forming in this way.

Others tolerate ice in between the cells, but by using antifreeze, keep it out of cell insides. Some can let more than half of their body water freeze without harm. This happens in wintering adult insects, garter snakes, and baby turtles, but the process is most developed in frogs.

Watch for frostbite during winter walks. Unlike the tissue of these frozen hibernators, human cells are destroyed by freezing.

Notes

February

A scattering of bark flakes on the snow may indicate that a black-backed woodpecker has been searching for food.

7 Wintering woodpeckers are not unusual in the northland. All season we have had downy and hairy woodpeckers visiting the feeder and pileateds in the nearby woods. Two other northern species, the black-backed and the three-toed woodpeckers have stayed with us too, but they remain deeper in the boreal forests.

Each is nine inches long with a black-and-white body. Black-backs have a dark coat while the three-toed has bars on its back. Males of both species have yellow crowns and give a sharp "kik" call. Each has three toes instead of the usual four.

Permanent residents of the boreal forests, they range far north into Canada and south into the Rocky Mountains. Neither is largely migratory, but the black-backs do more winter wandering than do the three-toeds and they may appear in deciduous and coniferous forests. Black-backs flake off bark of dead trees, instead of drilling into wood, as they search for insects. Three-toeds are more at home in burnt-over areas of the conifers. Seeing either of these in February is great winter bird news.

Notes

8 Looking as if they are unable to cope with cold weather, northland ash trees are the first to drop leaves in autumn and the last to grow them in spring. While most northland deciduous trees have leaves for five months, ashes retain their green foliage for only four. Despite this, they live well in the cold and adapt to winter.

Black ash is a common resident of poorly drained swamps, and it dominates some wetlands. Often it shares this home with alder, cedar, spruce, and tamarack. Though common in lowlands, green ash also grows in parks and lawns.

Both kinds of ash trees flower before any leaves are formed; by autumn, they have developed the flat one-winged seeds called samaras. Not the same shape as maple helicopters, these symmetrical seeds are nevertheless designed for the same type of wind dispersal.

However, while black ash seeds fall in autumn, green ash keeps their seeds through most of the winter. Now, in February, it is not unusual to see female trees with clusters of the two-inch-long seeds. At the same time, male trees often hold dead flowers from last summer that resemble fungal growths.

Ash trees, like other trees in your yard, appear lifeless in February, but look closely, the twigs are covered with buds just waiting for spring.

Notes

February

If you are looking for a fast-growing tree, a box elder may suit you. The winged seeds on female trees provide visual interest throughout winter.

9 A medium-size maple with compound leaves, box elder is likely to be forgotten when we look back over the season's maples. We remember sugar maple's sap in spring, silver maple's shade in summer, and red maple's color in fall, but nothing specific about the box elder.

In February, box elder may finally catch our attention. Now, when nearly all maples are devoid of seeds, these small maples still hold theirs and are easy to detect as we travel in the northland. Seeds are produced in fall and the samara twins hang in an upside-down V-shape all winter. A close look shows these winged seeds to be the same helicopter type as seen on other maples.

The leaves of the box elder, which is not as thick or tall as many other maples, grow in groups of three or five. This fast-growing native of flood plains and swamp margins is also planted widely in yards and parks.

Notes

February

10 For much of the winter, these well-known striped members of the weasel family were sleeping in underground dens. Skunks remain dormant during the coldest days of winter, but now in February, with breaks in the cold, they get more active, and we are likely to see or smell these common neighborhood residents. Using old burrows of woodchucks, squirrels, or badgers, which they line with grasses and dead leaves, the critters sleep through much of winter. Often several skunks share a den.

When rising, they forage, almost always at night, for a variety of food items to satisfy their appetite. Winter meals may include frozen fruits and berries, nuts, seeds, mice, shrews, carrion, and garbage. It is the last of these that sometimes brings the night wanderers into our lives. This diet is a big change from the insects that they ate during the warmer months.

A common scene on a February morning is their zigzag track pattern on the yard's frozen snow that tells of a skunk's nocturnal visit. Since they are slow with poor vision, we may be able to approach them undetected.

Follow a skunk's zigzag track across your yard, and you may discover its den—but be careful.

Notes

February

Listen for the mourning dove's call—the first sound of the changing season.

11 Most mourning doves are migratory, but those that choose to spend winter in the northland form flocks and feed on seeds. They will eat various grains, but prefer corn and readily visit sites where it is available.

With longer days now in February, a cold, quiet morning may be graced by the courting song of the male dove. Though it is a mating song, this plaintive call may seem a bit dismal. Indeed, mourning doves get their name from the "coah, cooo, cooo, coo" songs that do not seem to us to be cheerfully amorous.

The twelve-inch-long birds are mostly gray-brown with a long pointed tail. Their head looks too little for the body and the bill is short and small for a seedeater, but they manage by swallowing seeds without breaking them. Mourning doves build platform nests of sticks early in the season, often while snow is still on the ground. Early nesting means early courting as these February songs attest to. Courtship also involves flying a flap-glide display that is so different from their usual flight that it may be mistaken for that of a falcon.

Notes

February

12 Every so often, we hear of wintering critters that seem to waken too early. A chipmunk wanders through the garage in mid-January. To everyone's surprise, a bat flies around the house in February. A gray tree frog is caught hopping in the basement as we put away Christmas ornaments in January. A large brown moth or a yellow-brown butterfly flutters at the windows on clear, mild days in February.

These scenarios make for great conversations, and someone is likely to proclaim them as signs of an early spring, but such is not the case. All the listed animals are hibernators, but although we expect sleeping critters to stay still, most animals said to be in hibernation do not become entirely dormant for the winter. Chipmunks and bats not only wake, they also move around, but too much action depletes stored fats and hurts chances of winter survival. Frogs and insects are dormant in the cold, but they respond when their sleeping site is warmed. This happens when we transfer their sheltered home, which might be under the bark of firewood, into our house. In any case, early rising is not healthy for hibernators.

During a prolonged warm spell in February, watch for early-waking hibernators.

Notes

February

The northern goshawk, like other raptors, disdains the vegetarian fare of bird feeders, remaining in the forest all winter.

13 At two feet long and with wings that span four feet, the northern goshawk is an impressive raptor. Adults are gray above, light below; and have a banded tail and white lines above the eyes. The young are brown with streaked undersides. As is true of many hawks, females are larger than males.

Goshawks go through migratory cycles of approximately ten years, and though good numbers pass through the northland heading south each fall, many remain for the winter. Here these powerful and fast-flying hawks feed on a variety of mammals and birds. Their prey includes hares, squirrels, jays, grouse, and if the hawks are hungry enough, smaller songbirds. Hawks usually pursue prey in flight, but have been known to run after them as well. Goshawks nest in remote coniferous forests, their range extending throughout much of North America. They will aggressively defend their territory.

To see a goshawk fly over a boreal forest on a chilly February and to hear its "kak, kak, kak" call as it surveys the region from a spruce perch is to witness the lord of the forest in its own realm.

Notes

February

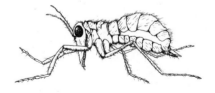

14 A mild spell in mid-February brings changes in winter animals. As temperatures climb to the thirties, we may see insects of several kinds on the surface of the snow. Along with the tiny snow fleas and wingless winter craneflies, the snow scorpionfly, another dark, one-fourth-inch-long insect, also hops on the snows of northland forests. These snow scorpionflies are wingless, having only pads in place of wings, and either walk or jump across the February snow. Long antennae and a large beaklike mouth set them aside from the other winter insects.

They have spent most of the winter beneath the snow, living in mossy clumps. Here they prey on small insects and other animals. Eggs and larvae develop in the moss with the adult scorpionflies emerging in fall about when snowfall begins.

Once on the surface, the snow scorpionflies may encounter some prey, but since they are not in moss, it would be unlikely. They walk and hop freely, and if meeting another, they mate on the snow. Perhaps for these adult insects, the surface functions as a site for mate finding. In any case, evening cold sends them back under the snow.

A small magnifying glass will help you distinguish snow scorpionflies from other tiny snow insects.

Notes

February

Brush away the snow that covers a stand of wintergreen, and you'll find the leaves as fresh and tasty as in midsummer.

15 Within the northland winter woods, several small plants survive the cold by keeping their green leaves. Hidden under the five-month blanket of snow, they are not often seen. Some of these evergreen plants are well-known flowers of hepatica, pipsissewa, pyrola, and twinflower, each well known for their spring and summer flowers. Because its leaves are used for tea or gum, maybe the best known of these plants is snowberry, which is also called teaberry or wintergreen.

Growing on the forest floor, the one-fourth-inch long bell-shaped white flowers of the wintergreen were hardly noticed when they opened last summer. In fall as other deciduous plants lost leaves, wintergreen did not. Not only could we see the shiny, smooth, green leaves, but its red berries added to the forest-floor scene.

The smooth waxy coat keeps leaves from drying and in the warmth beneath the snow, wintergreen withstands winter well. Since these perennial plants grow by underground stems, they may have survived more winters than nearby trees.

Notes

February

16 We watched them in the yard all winter. They outsmarted us at the bird feeder, and they dug up acorn caches on all but the coldest days. Chasing each other, they established their hierarchy. Now, in mid-February, we see another activity going on with the gray squirrels. With a gestation of forty-five days and the first litter due in late March, the time has come for them to mate.

Triggered by hormonal action, the males begin to follow females, and for the first time all winter, they appear to be interested in more than free feeder food. Only dominant males pursue the females. While subordinates may put forth attempts, veterans usually prevail. With much chasing and following, the squirrels mate in the female's territory. Her subsequent pregnancy sends chemical messages that end the amorous followings.

Born in the warmth and safety of a hollow tree, litters are helpless, naked, and blind, but within a month, are fully furred with eyes open. Soon, little heads appear at den openings. By June, they are weaned and by midsummer, on their own. She is ready for a second litter.

The February frolics that you watch from your kitchen window are actually the gray squirrels mating rituals.

Notes

February

On an evening walk, listen for the call of the male great horned owl and the slightly different response of the female.

17 Great horned owls, one of the most widely known owls in North America, are nonmigratory throughout their range. Their twenty-four-inch-long brown bodies boast wings that span four and a half feet, making the great horned owl by far the largest of the tufted owls. Unlike most owls, they have feather tufts growing from the head that look deceptively like horns or ears.

These nocturnal forest birds roost by day, often in the seclusion of conifers deep within the woods. While resting here, they also disgorge the undigested fur and bones of their small mammal prey, and these pellets on the snow tell us of the presence of this night tiger.

Their call for territorial supremacy has been going on all season, but now in late winter, they also begin breeding calls. Most hoot in evening or predawn hours, and both sexes call. The male gives a "hoo, hoo-oo, hoo, hoo," and the female answers with "hoo, hoo-hoo-hoo, hoo-oo, hoo-oo." Great horned owls are among the earliest breeders and in some regions, nests are occupied in February. In the northland, these owls claim empty crow and hawk nests or natural cavities and begin laying eggs in March.

Notes

February

18 Flocks of Bohemian waxwings first arrived in November, and ever since then have stayed in the northland. They wander through trees that still hold frozen berries, and in mountain ash, buckthorn, hawthorn, and crab apple trees, flocks feed and give their high-pitched "zreee" calls. The gregarious birds even crush frozen fruit for each other so that their bodies will be able to digest it. These fruits and berries are lower in nutrition than are either insects or seeds, and waxwings need to eat huge amounts.

At eight inches long, Bohemian waxwings are larger than their cousins, the cedar waxwings. Winter birds are brown with a pointed crest, black over their eyes, and a yellow band on the tail. It is the waxy-looking red and white wing spots that give the birds their name.

Breeding in the boreal forests, wintering birds like the Bohemian waxwing wander far and regularly spend this season with us. Now, in late winter, flocks become more restless and join forces. What was a gathering of thirty to fifty birds in early winter, now may be ten times that in size. Most birds will be heading north within a month.

Even when shriveled and frozen, mountain ash berries provide nourishment for Bohemian waxwings.

Notes

February

Only if you are a real explorer, are you likely to see a shy and elusive timber wolf.

19 The northland is one of the few places in the United States where timber wolves still travel and hunt in packs. In fact, much of their winter was spent in the routine of traveling, hunting, feeding, and resting. Packs of various sizes, usually less than ten, constantly kept watch over their marked territory and made kills, primarily deer, during the entire season. Since the home sites of different wolf packs do not overlap and are separated by a no-man's land, deer that yard between territories survive well.

Now, in late February, mating of the dominant pair occurs. Known as the alpha male and female, they alone produce the pack's offspring. Because the pack as a whole is not involved with the activity of courtship, the members become even more possessive of their territory; trespassing wolves have been known to be killed. During this season, wolves also do a considerable amount of howling.

Our February treks seem wilder when we find wolf tracks or scat at a kill site or hear wolf howls. Though customarily avoiding busy routes, wolves do travel on forest roads and snowmobile and ski trails during times of deep snow.

Notes

February

20 Some of the northland's crows, though largely migratory, remain for the winter. Those that do leave fly only to states just south of us, so it should come as no surprise to us that these dark birds are among the early returnees.

While some migrants pass by quickly, the crows travel in flocks that do much calling and stopping along the way. Feeding on almost anything edible, the gregarious birds fill the early morning quiet with plenty of loud "caw, caw" sounds. In late February, when these noisy birds pause to visit us, the weather is still cold. Daylight has increased, however, and the crows sense the movement of the season.

Migrating flocks on these February days are largely composed of northern birds that keep on going and do not nest in the northland. Many go deep into the forests of Canada. Though wintering and traveling in flocks, crows are solitary nesters and later in the spring will choose high deciduous or coniferous trees for their homes. Nests, built of sticks and bark, are newly constructed each year. Abandoned crows' nests will be used by other early breeding birds such great horned or long-eared owls.

Watch for the returning crows. They may be the first harbinger of spring.

Notes

February

Look now for the bright red branches of red osier dogwood. Later in the season they will again become green.

21 As a shrub less than ten feet tall growing along wet shores and swamps, red osier dogwood gets little attention for most of the year. Oval four-inch-long leaves, simple and smooth-margined, are not impressive. Its blossoms in early summer are tiny and white, not like those of its cousin the flowering dogwood. Even the small white berries are gone when the purple leaves drop in October.

It takes winter days of February for this shrub to get the notice it deserves. In the longer days that have become apparent during this month, the red osier dogwood has responded to sunlight by forming more pigment and developing bright red twigs. The more sunlight they get, the redder the branches become. Plants growing at the base of south-facing hillsides that are drenched in sun develop into bright scarlet plants that early-spring searchers are quick to find. Since these dogwoods spread by lateral shoots, however, they often form thickets, and with less sunlight, the basal branches will not redden.

Notes

22 These large crow-sized woodpeckers wintered with us, but except for our occasionally seeing their oblong chiseled holes in nearby trees, we may not have been aware of their presence all season. Pileated woodpeckers are certainly unique in appearance among the northland species. They carry red crests on their large black bodies with white under the wings, which appears in flight.

Using their powerful bills, they hammer away on aged trees in search of the carpenter ants living within. Woodpeckers may work on the same tree for hours only to return the next day for more. Now, in late winter, we see piles of chips at the bases of these excavated trees. These woodpeckers work with a louder and more consistent pounding than their smaller relatives, and their feeding sites take on an oval or rectangular shape. Nesting excavations, too, will soon be underway in preparation for the impending spring breeding season.

Except for their pounding on trees, these giants are mostly silent, but sometimes they give loud "kik-kik-kik-kik-kik-kik" or "wick-a wuck-a" calls. The sight of a pileated woodpecker is an event to be treasured.

Close your eyes and listen, then follow the pounding noise to find a pileated woodpecker.

Notes

February

Make pencil sketches of the tracks you see in the snow, then try to identify them using a field guide.

23 For about five months of the year, the northland is shrouded with a snow cover. It changes much during this time. Warm November snows are wet and sticky, good for making snow sculptures. The arid cold of January produces dry snow powder, excellent for skiing. The thaw-freeze pattern of late February leads to a thick, hard crust on the snow, poor for sculptures or skiing, but easy for walking.

In the area beneath the snow, no matter how bitter the season, small mammals have had a fairly mild winter. They were less bothered by January snows and cold there than in almost any other location. But now with the warming, thawing, and freezing, the snow becomes harder and tunnels form ice. This crusty snow is hard to live in, and for some shrews and mice, these last weeks of winter are the most difficult.

February is our driest month, and the light, dry snows that fall give a soft cover to the hard, crusty snow. Such a cover makes for great tracking. With mating season beginning, feeding activity in the warmer weather, or the difficulty of tunneling through the snow, lots of animals are out and about, leaving their autographs on the light, crusty snow cover.

Notes

24 Viewing wildlife at fifty-five miles per hour has many drawbacks and certainly is not recommended, but in late February, this is how many of us see the red-tailed hawks that have wintered here or the very early migrants.

These large, well-known hawks are often seen sitting in trees or atop utility poles along the highways. Apparently, the open roads, especially broad interstate highways, give good views of crossing prey. With superb eyesight, the hawks are able to spot the potential food from great distances, quickly fly in for the catch, and still escape the oncoming traffic.

Red-tailed hawks may reach a length of two feet with a four-foot wingspan. The hawks are brown above, light below, and though young and adults are equal size in winter, only mature birds have the reddish tail.

Many red-tailed hawks construct huge platform nests of sticks in tall trees of northland forests. Soon some of these hunting highway hawks will be nesting, but now they look over the bleak scene for tasty rodent meals.

Many birds find food on or along highways. Some look for carrion, but red-tailed hawks seek live prey.

Notes

February

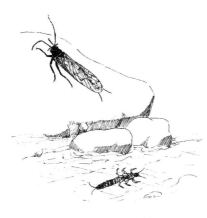

If you see stoneflies along a stream, watch quietly to see if birds also discover them.

25 Stoneflies spent the coldest days of winter as nymphs in the fast-moving, cool waters of streams. Here they crawled among rocks preying on other critters. Now, enjoying some warming and thawing in late February, they crawl to the shore where they are transformed into winged adults.

February stoneflies are dark with long antennae and clear wings that fold over the body, covering the two tail structures called cerci. Though the flies are winged, much of their adult life in spent walking along the edge of a stream feeding on algae. In February, we can see the one-inch-long insects silhouetted against the white snow.

Though seen occasionally in yards, meadows, or woods, stoneflies are never far from open, moving water. Winged adults mate and deposit eggs in the late-winter water. Perhaps by emerging from the stream now, stoneflies avoid the crowd later: mate-finding becomes easier. However, they pay a price for this advantage: winter birds tired of seed diets are quick to spot these dark insects on the crusty February snow.

Notes

February

26 All winter we have seen their hopping tracks, but since both the cottontail rabbit and its cousin the snowshoe hare are nocturnal, we seldom saw the rabbits and hares themselves. Tracks are larger for the hare than for the rabbit, but both show the Y-shaped pattern, with two hindfeet in front of the forefeet. This bounding movement keeps them moving swiftly most of the time. Deep snows of January slowed them, but now crusty cover gives them a solid base on which to travel. Cottontails wintered in brushy areas and woodland edges. Here they survived on a diet of twigs and young buds and avoided predation. Snowshoe hares, too, spent the winter moving between woods, thickets, and coniferous bogs. Wearing their white coats for camouflage from hungry predators, they browsed on twigs of many kinds.

Now, in late February, the crusty snow is littered with their tracks as cottontails and snowshoes actively prepare for the coming mating season. Nights are filled with the battles of males to determine the right to pursue females. Young will be born by early April.

No matter how urban your setting, it's likely that you will see rabbit tracks in the snow.

Notes

February

These early horned larks are usually seen as we drive along country roads.

27 The winds blow hard across open fields. The ground is frozen, and not much food or shelter seems available. This is not the place we would expect to see early migrants, but perhaps the earliest of all migrating songbirds, the horned larks, are here in late February.

Horned larks breed over much of North America and nest in just about any open area. Golf courses, athletic fields, cemeteries, farm fields, prairies, and tundra all have nesting birds. Winter is spent in similar places to the south but although it means coping with wind, snow, and cold, these hardy birds are ready to return early.

Traveling in small flocks, often seen on or near roads, the seven-inch-long brown-gray birds have black face colors and white tail markings. Horned larks get their name from two feathers projecting up from the back of the head. Observing these well-camouflaged birds in fields is difficult, and seeing their horns is even harder.

Flocks walk, not hop, in fields as they feed on weed seeds. They occasionally give the "tsee-titi" call, and a high-pitched, twittering, tinkling song is sung in flight. Often they nest when snow is still on the ground.

Notes

February

28 Many northlanders suffer from acute cabin fever by late February, and so we look for signs of the coming spring. Nature is changing and signs of those changes abound, but the most sought after are the fuzzy buds of a small tree called pussy willow—the true harbinger of spring.

During the rest of the year, we would be hard pressed to even locate these little trees. Growing from fifteen to twenty feet tall in swamps and other wet places, they fail to attract us most of the time—but now we go far out of our way to find these twigs. In late winter, more branches of this tree decorate tables in northland homes than do those of any other plant. Just seeing the stem with buds gets us in the mood for the impending changes.

The gray, fuzzy growths apparently respond to the longer and warmer days. Midwinter thaws can cause them to open early. Most likely these hairy buds are an adaptation for early flowering; cold does not kill them. Within a month, buds open to become the tree flowers called catkins. Male flowers are long and yellow with pollen, while the female's are light green.

Gather pussy willows to cheer up winter-weary family members.

Notes

February

Dead trees in the yard can serve many purposes for wildlife.

29 All winter we watched downy and hairy woodpeckers as they visited bird feeders. Equipped with chisel beaks, these black-and-white birds were able to make use of frozen suet. Now, in late winter, these woodpeckers do more than visit the feeders. Courtship and mating begins in earnest, but instead of using songs, as other birds do, the woodpeckers make use of their powerful bills to send out love notes. Rapidly hammered out on dead and hollow trees, their message—commonly called drumming—resonates loudly.

Both males and females try out several sites until they locate one that gives the desired decibels and pitch. Regularly, for weeks, they will use these signal sites for courtship calls and territorial declarations. Calm early mornings serve as good times for such advertising, and because gutters and siding on houses make great noises, they may be the chosen drums (as many sleepy home owners have discovered). Drumming sites get plenty of drilling, but they are neither excavated nor used for feeding. Apparently they are used only for making noise.

Notes

March

March

Watch the circles of bare ground around tree trunks. Soon you may find green grass—or dandelions.

1 The stormy month has begun. This first week of March may produce some of the greatest weather extremes of the year. Blizzards, ice, and bitter cold or rain and a springlike thaw can open this transitional month. No matter what the weather, one sure sign of the changing season is always present and very welcome.

Earlier sunrises and later sunsets make for longer, lighter days. The sunlight reflects off snow, but not off dark tree bark, which absorbs heat from the lengthening light and gently radiates it back to the surrounding snow. Snow melt may extend out from the trees a few inches to as much as a foot. On tree trunks, plants like mosses get a peek at sunlight for the first time in months, and animals so long beneath the snow have an opportunity to travel to the top.

With the shade from evergreens, snow melt around trees is not as likely in coniferous forests as in deciduous, but the nearby maple woods serves as a good measure of winter's waning. It's still cold and snowy, but the trees tell us of March's commitment to warming and melting.

Notes

March

2 As the days get longer, temperatures reluctantly rise and readings above freezing become more common. With warmer air and sticky, wet snow, critters emerge from beneath the surface cover. If we look carefully, we can see numerous tiny black specks that look like pepper jumping and hopping on snow, especially on clear, warm afternoons. Commonly referred to as snow fleas, they are insects—but not fleas. Less than one-tenth of an inch long, the tiny critters belong to a group of insects called *collembola* or springtails. The thousands scattered on the snow these mild March days do not move with legs or wings as other insects do, but use an abdominal appendage held under the body that springs them up when released.

Springtails live under the snow in leaf litter all winter. Although they may come above ground any time between October and April, they are most abundant in March. Not only is the temperature warm enough (at least twenty degrees) for them to climb up plants to the snow surface and feed on minute decay matter, it is also their mating season. In a forest near wetlands, they may be seen until the snow vanishes in April.

Minuscule snow fleas may only be visible when they jump.

Notes

March

In coniferous forests, look for piles of cone scales that mark a red squirrel's lunch table.

3 All winter the little red squirrels are full of energy and remain active. Though most abundant in coniferous forests, where their feeding on cones creates middens of up to two feet tall, they frequent mixed woods, too, and visits to bird feeders are common. Considerably smaller than gray squirrels, red squirrels are more aggressive and send their larger cousins scampering when the two steal from the same feeder. Unlike gray squirrels, red squirrels often tunnel in deep snow and quickly crisscross our yards with their underground highways.

In early March, the red squirrels turn aggressively on their own kind, and the mating process begins. No doubt, population density and the severity of winter influence them, but—whatever the cause and the degree of intensity—males feud over territory at this time. The common "cherr" scolding call now sounds in the woods more loudly.

Squirrels make their homes in tree cavities or create nests in branches from masses of leaves, twigs, and shredded bark. Here, after a thirty-eight-day gestation, two to five young are born. By May, we may catch glimpses of baby squirrels as they begin their preparation for eventually leaving the nest. A second litter will be raised during the summer.

Notes

4 Most of us who are home owners or renters know raccoons—masked opportunists of the highest order—very well indeed. They seem to devour virtually anything and readily raid human trash and wildlife cache alike. These nocturnal wanderers know the territory completely and take to trees as well as burrows in their quest for food.

During severe winter weather, raccoons enter a partial hibernation. Family groups or single animals curl up in hollow trees or other protected places to sleep until warmer weather arrives. Their winter sleep is not very sound, however, and thaws during the cold months will find them again foraging for food or moving to other denning sites. The small handlike tracks, droppings, and scattered refuse speak of the masked raiders' presence. Recurring cold sends them back to the holed-up life.

Breeding season begins in early March, and raccoons, especially the males, lose interest in sleeping. We see wandering tracks which mark their travel from den to den in search of receptive females. Tracks and sightings that were sporadic all winter now become commonplace. In two months, females will have a litter of four.

Notes

March

Open the window and this house fly will leave. Don't worry about screens. Very few flies are outside trying to get in.

5 All winter we enjoyed a welcome respite from house flies, but now, with milder and longer days, they reappear. These critters are common in human habitations and remain active throughout the warmer months. For many of us, they conjure up unhappy memories of disrupted picnics.

Though most insects die with the coming of cold in fall, a large minority choose to hibernate instead. Hibernation, or diapause, for insects can happen during any of their stages of life. House flies lay eggs in the fall that await spring to hatch, but adults also survive, sleeping through winter. Seeing any adult (an insect with wings) this early in the season, we can be sure that it survived the winter as an adult and did not recently hatch.

Although the flies crawled into house cracks to stay warm for the winter, they now try to get out of windows or doors. If the day is clear and warm, they alight on sunny walls where basking revives them and raises their body temperature. Sufficiently warmed, they resume a life that may take them to dog houses, livestock barns, or trash for food and early-season mating.

Notes

March

6 With his cheeks bulging from his repeated trips to a hidden underground storehouse, the chipmunk remained active well into the cold weather. Now, four months later, the little striped ground squirrel reappears.

Like other small ground squirrels, the chipmunk spends winter in extremely deep hibernation. The dormancy caused by the sleep of true hibernation is almost beyond our comprehension. An active chipmunk's heart beats two hundred times per minute. That rate drops to about twenty per minute and only one breath per minute suffices for respiration. Though some small mammals never rouse all winter, chipmunks do not have enough body fat to keep themselves alive for many months, so they need to wake occasionally. During these times, they relieve themselves of wastes, snack from the food cache they carried in last fall, and may even step outside.

Such a deep sleep may be followed by a slow revival, but soon in the sunlight and warmth of early spring, the chipmunk's chipping call and twitching tail will return. Then, even if more cold returns, the chipmunk will remain active.

Look for frisky chipmunks, small friends that you remember from last summer.

Notes

March

Begin planning how you can control destructive garden insects without the pesticides that can harm beneficial insects like honeybees.

7 With the onslaught of cold weather, most insects hibernate, migrate, or die. Honeybees are among the few insects that remain active all winter. These European immigrants have become so well established in the last three centuries that, secure in the shelter of the hive, they withstand even northland winters.

All the work of last summer's honey-making was not done to sweeten our oatmeal; rather, this high-energy food was produced and concealed in preparation for the hive's cold-weather survival. If other animals do not raid this precious cache, the stored honey will serve as ample food through the five-month ordeal.

During the winter months, the hive is active, and the constant movement of wings and legs combined with the bodies' usual metabolism, generates enough heat to keep the compact clusters of little bodies alive. Bees remain in the hive except during occasional thaws when they fly out to void themselves of feces. Now in March, with longer days, they become restless, cleaning out the hive and flying more often although it will be weeks before flowers are in bloom.

Notes

March

8 The longer days, but still cold temperatures, of March increase our case of cabin fever, and we search frantically for remedies. A day of forty-five degrees and the sight of an early migrant bird offer us some relief, but the pussy willows gathered recently serve as the best medication. Now the quaking aspen, a cousin of the pussy willow, shows its buds too.

Aspen flowering begins as the willow's does, with hairy buds. Perhaps such fuzzy structures absorb sunlight better and allow for stronger survival on this early date.

Not surprisingly, quaking aspen is often confused with the pussy willow. Aspen buds are gray and fuzzy like those of the willow—hence our confusion—but they grow on twigs from the upper branches of a much taller tree. We are able to break off willow stems, but we cannot easily reach aspen buds. Apparently, they get necessary sunlight better on the treetop. While the buds of both willow and aspen grow alternately on twigs, aspen buds are much closer together. The greatest difference, however, is evident later in the spring: when pussy willow buds enlarge to become yellow or green, quaking aspen buds lengthen to look like caterpillars but remain gray.

The aspen branches look different, bumpy, against the blue spring sky.

Notes

March

An indoor-outdoor thermometer with a probe on the end of a cable can make it possible to explore the temperature of air, snow, water, ground—and anthill.

9 Ants are perhaps the most familiar of all insects. Abundant and widespread, they are found in every type of habitat from the arctic to the tropics. These highly successful insects live a social existence in colonies composed of thousands of individuals that are either queens, males, or workers. Many colonies construct mounds or hills that help with winter survival. Deep within these anthills, they stay warm in the heat of the earth, where they are covered by insulating snow.

Ants slow down their activities in winter but never actually stop. With the coming of longer, warmer days in March, they make more trips to the surface, and we may see them in open places such as sidewalks. Though many inches of snow still cover most of the northland, the ant mounds enjoy an earlier melting. Rounded mounds catch more sunlight than do flat surfaces, and the interior of a mound may be up to twenty degrees warmer than the surrounding air. In addition, dark plant debris on the mound tends to absorb sunlight. As if planned by the ants, many huge anthills, up to six feet long and three feet high, are on south-facing hills and therefore in prime position to catch the rays of the spring sun.

Notes

10 By mid-March, we may notice foot-long glossy purple blackbirds in the yard. Grackles are returning from their winter homes in much of the southern midwest, where huge flocks numbering in the hundreds are common. Small flocks of males arrive early in the northland, but larger and louder groups will come later in spring. Grackles get their name from the often repeated "chack" call given by these migrants. When nesting or defending their territory, however, these birds sing a creaky "kagula-leek" song that compares to the sound of an opening squeaky gate.

Larger than other blackbirds, grackles can be distinguished by their long wedge-shaped tail. In bright sunlight, the iridescent head looks purple-green.

Early spring grackles, whom we frequently see walking in open fields and on our lawns, seek meals of seeds, insects, worms, and other small animals. They are not shy about visiting bird feeders, and because they thrive on a diverse diet, they will also raid the nests of smaller birds.

Grackles have adapted well to cities and often live in yards and parks. They prefer evergreen trees for nesting and frequently settle in small colonies there.

Notes

March

Heavy rains and snowmelt flood the earthworm tunnels and deprive them of needed oxygen. They emerge to avoid drowning.

11 Except for those earthworms left squirming on sidewalks and streets after a heavy rain, most of us seldom see these vital soil dwellers. Myriads of them share the yard with us, but although actively feeding, they either stay in their subterranean domain or surface only at night.

These slimy, segmented worms feed on dead plant and animal matter in or on the soil. Swallowing soil debris as they burrow through the ground, earthworms take nutrition from it. Lightly packed soil with sufficient air and water provides the best conditions for both tunneling and feeding: the frozen ground of winter sends these critters wiggling down to soil below the frost line. Here, in deep safety, they survive winter in a slowed-down stage.

Feeling the meltwaters of early spring thaws, the earthworms work their way upward toward the ground's surface, where they again search for decaying material. Deep under they had found a warm winter home, but not much food. During these chilly spring explorations, some worms get trapped in street and parking lot puddles where sunlight and foraging hungry birds catch the first earthworms of the season.

Notes

12 Sunlight both penetrates and reflects off the west-facing walls of buildings, and that heat helps make snow melt faster near the building than in the nearby yard. It's the first place we see green grass in spring and now, in mid-March, the first dandelion blooms here.

This common weed gets its name from the sharp lobes on the leaf. These reminded early naturalists of the teeth of a lion: *dente lion.* Of European origin, it now grows just about everywhere in this country. The perennial and hardy plant survives winter with the help of a long taproot that extends deep below the frozen ground. Leaves remain all winter and that is why this amazing plant quickly responds to the warmth and sunlight of early spring, producing the first blossoms of the season. Indeed, they flower so early that many times dandelions have formed seeds before other early spring flowers have started to bloom. Later in the season, we may battle this prolific plant, but now in March, the yellow flower looks great.

In mid-March, golden dandelion blossoms look more like flowers than weeds.

Notes

March

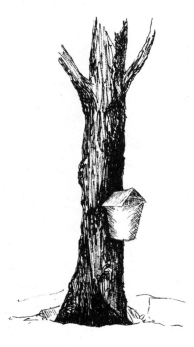

If you have several sugar maples in your yard, you may want to experiment with tapping them, but don't expect to get a full year's supply of syrup.

13 Unlike other trees of the northland that are identified by their leaves, fruit, or bark, the sugar maple is best known by its sap.

Sunny days and freezing nights act as a pump for lifting sucrose made by last year's leaves and stored in the roots of this maple. The sap must be moved to the swelling buds so the tree can leaf out as spring advances. Mid-March days, with lows in the twenties and highs in the forties, stimulate this process. The flow starts intermittently and is at first strongest in the afternoon, but gradually it becomes consistent and remains so for about a month.

For hundreds of years, northlanders have taken advantage of this flow to satisfy their craving for sweetness. Twigs nibbled by winter herbivores or trunk cracks formed by deep freezes now ooze with sap by day and form icicles (sapcicles!) by night.

A sugar content of two or three percent strikes us as incredibly low, but it is higher than that of sap flowing from any other tree. When maple sap is boiled, a delightful maple syrup is created. Sugar bush operators consider thirty to forty gallons of sap for one gallon of syrup the usual ratio.

Notes

March

14 Clear and fifty degrees by midafternoon, a warm March day brings out many winter sleepers. In the sunlight, microclimates exist where even warmer temperatures make critters active. On a bare west-facing brick wall, small black-and-white spiders called jumping spiders claim their hunting grounds.

Less than one-half inch long, the small spiders live up to their name and jump often while moving along the wall. Here, on this vertical battle zone, they seek basking insects. Flies are the preferred prey, and plenty of them sit heedlessly in the sunlight. Jumping spiders, who do not construct webs, use excellent eyesight—the best possessed by any northland spiders—for hunting. Once prey is discovered, a leap that would do credit to an Olympic jumper sends the spider onto the victim to dispatch it quickly with fangs.

As do the flies they search for, jumping spiders spend the winter dormant in tiny cracks and crevices in buildings. While most spiders seek out darkness and sheltered areas to do their hunting, little jumpers get out in the sunlight and open spaces to find their prey.

Critters as interesting as jumping spiders are often subjects for *National Geographic.* **Explore their world with a close-up lens on your camera.**

Notes

March

Even if you don't keep a formal phenology list, you may recall the earliest date you have seen a robin.

15 Well known and well loved, the American robin has traditionally been considered a sign of spring by many. Farther south, these ten-inch-long thrushes, which used to migrate, are helped through winter by bird feeders. In the northland, however, most still leave us for warmer climates, so the first robins seen in March are worth noting.

The male robin with his dark gray back and brick-red breast is the first to arrive at this early date. Males return to familiar grounds and begin to claim their homes; because robins adapt well to humans, nests are often on or near buildings. Soon we see the robins hopping on snow-free parts of the lawn, their heads cocked in search of early earthworms or other available food.

These early migrants do not do much singing, but soon, in the dusk and dawn of backyards and parks, we hear the songs of the flocks that follow. The clear, short phrases rising and falling brighten woods and cities alike. Many listeners remember the "cherrily cheer-up cheerio" call and interpret it as not so much a sign of spring's coming, but of spring's lasting.

Notes

16 In mid to late March, we note changes in the roadside marshes. These wetlands that sat quietly all winter are coming alive with the arrival of red-winged blackbirds. The sight of these first returnees, who readily announce their presence in song, has become a rite of spring for many northlanders. Living up to their descriptive name, males carry red shoulder patches with a border of yellow on their black bodies. Females are brown and streaked with only slight red markings on their wings.

Males are first to arrive in the northland marshes and promptly begin their "konk-la-ree" territorial songs from cattails and nearby trees. Songs continue in the ensuing weeks as more of the eight-inch blackbirds appear, often in large flocks, and within a month, females join the males.

Nests, woven of leaves, grass, and moss, are placed in cattails, reeds, and wetland bushes. Four bluish green eggs, marbled with brown, are deposited there. The highly territorial males become aggressive during nesting and frequently fly at any passersby, including humans.

The red shoulder patches make male red-winged blackbirds extremely easy to identify.

Notes

March

Plant spring bulbs on all four sides of your house and you'll enjoy them for many weeks.

17 With more than a foot of snow covering the frozen ground, it seems a bit premature for a flower to bloom. At this latitude, spring is late, but on sunny south or west-facing hillsides and buildings, spring comes earlier. Indeed, a southwest side of a building, in direct afternoon sunlight may experience spring a month before a shaded snow-covered north side.

The little crocus, only three inches tall, now starts to bloom in these hot spots. A cultivated flower, the crocus hurries its white, yellow, or purple petals and linear basal leaves from the perennial underground bulb. The blooms develop so rapidly that the plant scarcely has a stem.

It will be about a month before the other woodland ephemerals explode with flowers and even longer for most of the garden plants. Crocuses are cultivated in this country but grew wild in their native Europe and Asia Minor. Plants were apparently brought to the northland by those who wanted to speed up spring and now, as the whites, yellows, and purples show on sunny sides of buildings, we thank those who endowed us with this harbinger of spring.

Notes

18 In late March, a strange "peent" call comes from wetlands or woodlands at dusk, and we may see a long-billed bird twittering overhead. The woodcock, an unusual shorebird, has returned. In severe winters, lingering snow delays this bird's arrival a bit, but the woodcock (also known as the timberdoodle) is regularly one of spring's first wetland birds. The stocky brown bird with short legs and wings, long bill, and a banded tail has a special talent: woodcocks are nocturnal and secretive as they feed on earthworms. The long bill is pushed into mud about three inches and with a unique movable tip, opened to grasp the worms—a feat nearly impossible for other birds.

During courtship, this shy bird becomes outgoing. As darkness creeps over the land, the male marches in a squatting pose, bobs the head, and gives a buzzy "peent." This display is followed by his sky dance, in which he spirals up a couple of hundred feet making only twittering wing sounds. At the peak, he sings liquid warbling songs and rapidly descends in a zigzag route, singing all the way. He performs this dance repeatedly many nights until mating.

The best time of year to seek out woodcocks is now, before hatching mosquitoes drive you out of their wetland home.

Notes

March

If your bird feeder persuades a migrant like the junco to remain north for the winter, be sure to keep it well supplied with food.

19 A small gray bird with white undersides, the junco is a type of sparrow. Like other sparrows, it is frequently hard to identify as it feeds in yards and roadsides. But two features make the junco a bit more conspicuous: these ground birds display their white tail feathers boldly as they fly, and they give their ticking call notes regularly as they feed and move in migrating flocks.

Juncos winter farther north than most spring migrants; a few even spend this cold season with us. Most pass to the south, however, and now, in late March and April, their flocks return. They sing frequently during migration, and their loose trill, comparable to that of a sewing machine, blends with the call notes from feeding flocks. Although they frequent open areas during migration, juncos build their nests on the floor of cool northern forests.

Juncos come to feeders regularly and are so associated with the cold that, in some areas, they are known as snowbirds. During spring migration most of us identify them, only as the flocks of little gray birds along roads.

Notes

20 Last summer's garter snakes quietly disappeared into rocky cliffs, tree stumps, and small-mammal burrows, or under buildings for a winter of hibernation. Often this dormant phase is shared with others, and although hibernacula with thousands of snakes like those of the pits of Manitoba are rare, group hibernation is not.

After five months underground, the hardy reptiles are quick to leave: a clear, warm, early spring day calls them to sun themselves in the open air. A temperature of a few degrees above freezing seems sufficient to prod the critters into activity. Indeed, they have even been observed moving over snow and ice. Basking on logs, rocks, or sunning hillsides starts their lethargic systems moving again. Unfortunately for the snakes, roads also offer them a welcome, but dangerous, early-spring warming. Often a snake's dead body crushed on the pavement provides our first snake sighting of the season.

With mating still a month away, this present spurt of activity may soon be followed by recurring inactivity; this second sleep is due to the inevitable chill that precedes the lasting warmth of real spring. Within a few weeks though, all garter snakes will be roused from their hibernation.

Named after the striped garters once used to hold up socks, this reptile is our most common snake. Perhaps because it is often seen in lawns and gardens, it is often incorrectly called a gardener snake.

Notes

March

When you see a kestrel or another raptor looking for prey, test your eyesight and your patience against the bird's.

21 While driving country roads in late March, we may notice a small hawk perched on roadside utility wires. The brightly colored American kestrel, formerly called the sparrow hawk, often rests alone as it surveys the frozen landscape with excellent raptor vision. Prey is usually sighted from these wires or branches, but kestrels frequently hunt from midair. They readily hover to watch a potential meal and perform great aerial dives to capture it. Early in the season, small mammals and birds serve as food, but later in the spring, insects such as grasshoppers are devoured.

Males have blue-gray wings with reddish tails and backs; females are more reddish brown. Both sexes have spotted breasts and black lines extending from the eyes. The long tail and pointed wings of the ten-inch-long kestrel make possible its typically rapid falcon flight. The "klee kill" or "killy killy" calls are part of the feeding-mating display during courtship. Old woodpecker cavities or bird boxes serve as nests.

Notes

March

22 With a foot of snow still covering the frozen ground, we are more than a little surprised to see a butterfly basking on this mild March day. The Compton tortoise shell hibernated as an adult, something out of the ordinary for butterflies. They commonly hibernate beneath bark or in hollow trees but they readily select cabins and outbuildings as well. One Canadian fishing cabin sheltered thirty of these butterflies tucked behind a window shutter. Another hosted an active adult as the cabin warmed on a clear February day.

Spread wings show us an orange-brown pattern scattered with black spots and a dab of white. The three-inch wingspan acts as a solar collector to warm the body on this clear day. When frightened or in danger, the butterflies close their wings, letting their camouflaged undersides blend with the tree bark.

Unrolling its long tongue, the Compton tortoise shell feeds on dripping sap, about the only food available in early spring. Later it will also feed on rotten fruit and animal droppings. Eggs will be placed on aspen, birch, and willow trees where the caterpillars will feed.

A Compton tortoise shell butterfly, carefully captured, may be enjoyed in a jar for a day, then returned to its outdoor home.

Notes

March

23 As long as open water can be found in the northland, mallards will remain north in winter. The ducks flock during the cold and go into the shallows of large bodies of water to feed on whatever they can for the winter. Severe winters with more freezing than usual send them further south. In some cities, these ducks have become semidomestic. They spend the winter in parks where they live on handouts, and some do not even migrate.

With short distances to travel, returning mallards arrive early, and by the end of March, the green-headed drakes and brown hens can be seen dabbling in the open rivers. Bottom feeders, mallards sift edible material from sediment. The absence of ice in lakes, ponds, and swamps bids them to move on and by May, they have begun nesting in wetlands.

In a nest concealed in tall grasses and reeds, the hen deposits up to a dozen eggs and incubates them for about twenty-five days. The drake, so bonded during spring courtship, loses interest, and family rearing is her job alone.

You won't see green-headed mallards heading a parade of ducklings. Only the brown hens provide care.

Notes

24 In late March, snow still covers the northland, but with climbing temperatures, winter's grip has loosened, and we often walk around puddles of meltwater on sidewalks, streets, and parking lots. Ground, frozen for months, thaws and holds water until it is saturated.

We are entering the time between snow cover and green grasses, a period marked by dry lawns, meadows, and fields. Spring fire season will soon begin.

In this short interlude, an opportunistic fungus, snow mold, moves in. Along the edges of waning snow in yards and meadows, we see a network of light threads. This material may remind us of growths commonly seen on compost heaps or on a forgotten sandwich. Like those stringy mildews, snow mold is a fungus, and the numerous threads are tiny branches called hyphae. The mold remains inactive under snow all winter, but now, in melted spots, the warmth and moisture necessary for its existence are temporarily available and momentarily it flourishes. Hyphae grow and produce spores, then, within days, the mold dries and fades for another year.

If you aren't alert, you'll miss the coming and going of plants as ephemeral as snow mold usually is.

Notes

March

You may be startled if a big brown bat flies through your home. Open a few doors and windows. It wants to leave as much as you want it to.

25 The late March sighting of what appears to be a bird with a strange erratic flight could well be our initial glimpse of the season's first bat. This early in the season, the bat may be seeking a meal or just another place to return to sleep. Though bats are normally nocturnal, early spring flights may be in the daytime because few insects are active during cold March nights.

Seven kinds of bats can be found in the northland during warmer weather, but most migrate for the colder months. Our most common hibernating species, the big brown bat, not only stays in the northland during the cold, it may spend winter in our houses. Bats are not true hibernating animals and although they slow down and sleep, they wake and move many times during the winter. A big brown bat that enters the attic in November may emerge from the garage in March.

Their name to the contrary, big brown bats are only four inches long. With a wingspan of a foot or more, however, they look larger when we see them in flight.

Notes

March

26 Spring seems to have actually arrived on a clear day with the temperature in the fifties. The maple woods are bright as plenty of sunlight penetrates and reflects off the snow. Sap flows freely from the tapped trees.

On such a March day, we may glimpse the mourning cloak butterfly emerging from its winter sleep. The mourning cloak gets its name from its dark pattern of purple-black with a yellow margin that reminded early naturalists of the dark clothing worn by people in mourning.

Most butterflies survive winter as eggs, caterpillars, or chrysalises, but the mourning cloak is one of the few adult hibernators. Its winter home, a space behind bark or a crack in a tree, is not warm, but though large parts of the mourning cloak's body do freeze, they thaw in early spring sunlight, and the butterfly may be roused by early March. The large dark wings act as solar panels for excellent basking.

Early rising does have some disadvantages besides the cold. With no flowers in bloom, no nectar is available, and so this hungry critter visits maple trees for a taste of spring sugar just as we do.

The dark wings of the mourning cloak absorb heat as well as the dark jackets we wear that are comfortable now but too warm in midsummer sun.

Notes

March

The stamens and pistil are obvious in showy flowers like tulips. Less obvious but equally interesting, the flowers of trees like the silver maple are worth a second look.

27 Though a native of river floodplains, silver maple has been planted widely in cities, parks, and yards. Neither the biggest nor the most colorful of our maples, it now claims honors as the first to flower in spring.

In late March, buds of silver maples start to look different—bigger and more straggly—from the way they appeared all winter. Looking more closely, we see that the buds have opened to reveal the stamens or pistil. Trees on south-facing hills set the pace, but others quickly follow, and within weeks all silver maples bloom.

Silver maples are usually dioecious (male flowers on one tree, female flowers on another), but occasionally a tree will hold both. Male or staminate flowers are tiny, only about one-half inch long, but when they are ripe with pollen, the whole twig looks yellow. Female or pistillate flowers are the same size and just as numerous, but the branches look red when these are open. Trees hold the ripe flowers for about a month while spring winds carry pollen from male to female, making fertilization complete before the leaves are formed.

Notes

28 By late March, a brown bird, white underneath, with black breast bands, appears on pastures, lawns, and ball fields. The killdeer, shorebird of the type called plover, winters in southern United States and arrives at its breeding range in the northland weeks before ice-out. Here these birds run or walk quickly as they seek early spring meals of elusive worms and insects.

Killdeer are endowed with a strong name, especially for ten-inch-long birds. They get their name from calls of "kill-dee" or "kill-deeah" repeated often on breeding fields. The earliest of these birds arrive in small groups and feed silently. Only with the subsequent return of more killdeer and the inevitable displays of courtship and fights for territory are lawns and fields filled with their calls.

Killdeer take advantage of human habitation: eggs are readily deposited on lawns, cultivated fields, roadsides, parking lots, and driveways. More than one baseball or soccer team has had to deal with this resident. Ideal camouflage usually keeps nesting adults hidden, but if disturbed, they perform broken wing acts with great skill and lure potential danger away.

Examine the sand on a lake-shore or the mud at a river's edge for the footprints of early returning shorebirds like the killdeer.

Notes

March

A tape recording of bird songs will add interest to your bird watching activities. The white-throated sparrow's song should be easy to identify after hearing it a few times.

29 About fifteen kinds of sparrows can be found in the northland, and for many of us, the little brown birds all look alike. However, white-throated sparrows, which show up in the yard in late March, seem to stand out from the others. Brown birds with white throats, they are appropriately named, but they also carry white stripes on the head with yellow near the eyes. Early flocks often accompany other sparrows and juncos.

Spring plumage creates handsome birds, but it is their song that gives these sparrows their identity. Birds appear in no hurry while moving to nesting sites in coniferous and northern deciduous forests and frequently sing while resting and feeding. Their song has been described as two clear notes followed by three quavering notes on a different pitch. Birders remember this as "old sam peabody peabody peabody" or "grand old canada canada canada," and many home owners try a whistling imitation.

White-throated sparrows readily visit bird feeders during their time with us, but they also feed on the ground, where they scratch out seeds among leaves and grasses.

Notes

30 With a length of three feet and a wingspan of five, the large, noisy Canada goose cannot be overlooked. We remember the flocks of last fall, flying in V-shaped formation. Their honking has become associated with cool weather.

For the most part, passing flocks spend winter on the rivers and wetlands of national wildlife refuges in the midwest, but many go south to the Gulf of Mexico. The advancing spring season and breakup of the rivers bring the first Canada geese back to the northland by late March. These small flocks or occasional loners remain quiet as they pause in their travels farther northward.

These large gray-brown geese with black necks and white chin straps hang around the shallows, feeding on whatever they can find until more waters open and they move on. Traditional breeding sites in the northern prairie pothole country are still used, but with hundreds of geese adopting urban and semidomestic lifestyles, many now breed further south. Mated pairs show strong bonding, and ganders become very aggressive in breeding territories while females incubate as many as ten eggs.

Would you enjoy the year-round presence of Canada geese, or would you find them as annoying as people in some communities do?

Notes

March

31 By the end of March, mud and water start to replace snow and ice in the wetlands. Speckled alders, small trees that are extremely common in bogs and marshes, respond to these changes with alterations of their own.

Early spring sees the formation of catkins on many trees, just as they appeared on pussy willows and quaking aspens earlier this month. Alder catkins formed last fall and hung on the tips of branches all winter. Now, with the proper sunlight and temperature, the structures that looked dead all season are bursting into life. Rapidly they enlarge to twice their earlier size and, with maturing pollen, turn yellow. If we merely bump these two-inch staminate flowers, they send forth an aerial pollen cloud. Soon all catkins and the nearby receptive female or pistillate flowers will open.

The male and female flowers of many early spring trees are separate; alders have them on the same tree but at different locations. Long male catkins cling to the branch tips with female cones further back on the same twig. Both grow and enlarge for the new season.

Tap a speckled alder's male catkin over a female cone. Watch the pollen settle. You may be helping create new seeds and new trees.

Notes

April

April

After watching a great blue heron spear a fish, try it yourself. Can you wait as patiently, watch as alertly, and act as quickly?

1 Long before ice-out on area lakes and ponds, the great blue herons arrive along rivers and streams for some preseason fishing. They are the only large wading birds present this early in the spring and with their height of four feet (the reason they are called great), blue-gray body, white neck, and black feathers extending from the head, we are not likely to confuse them with other birds. In flight, herons extend their long legs but fold their head back against their neck.

These big winter birds fish the swamps, shores, and tidelands of the south, but along the Mississippi River they go as far north as open water allows. In the shallows, they wade with such quiet concentration that they do not make even a telltale splash. Prey, now usually fish, but later frogs, is speared with the daggerlike beak in the blink of an eye.

Depending on the final status of summer fishing conditions, heron nests in tree colonies may often be located miles from their present early fishing site.

Notes

2 The turkey vulture, a large black bird with a short head, its wings held in a shallow V, soars north. Turkey vultures that have spent the winter in the southern United States now effortlessly ride the thermals to their northern homes. Though usually migrating in small flocks, they occasionally form huge kettles in the spring. The word kettles describes the appearance of hundreds of birds flying in circular formations, spiraling upward on rising air currents.

This great raptor gets its name from its partial resemblance to a turkey: specifically, because it has a bulky black body and a red head that looks tiny because no feathers cover it. Without feathers, birds do not pick up dangerous parasites and diseases as they scavenge carrion meals. Vultures feed during migration, using their excellent eyesight and exceptional sense of smell to locate available bodies. These connoisseurs of carrion prefer material that has been dead for only about a day over well-rotted decay.

Turkey vultures seek out cliffs, caves, or hollow logs for their nests. Concealment is important for a bird that feeds such smelly food to its young.

Watch for roadkill. How long does it take a turkey vulture or other scavengers to completely clean up a dead animal?

Notes

April

To identify flocks of large, migrating birds, you'll have to notice the birds' color and shape and listen for their call.

3 Most of us assume that V-shaped flocks of large loud birds are Canada geese. Geese are not alone in writing sky V's, however: a closer look and listen tells us of others. Similar flocks of large black birds are cormorants; flocks of noisy, completely white ones are tundra swans.

Tundra swans, formerly called whistling swans, seem immense because of their length of four feet and wingspan of six, but they are actually the smallest of the North American swans. They have earned their name by nesting in the barren regions of northern Canada.

By early April, flocks of these swans move from wintering on the Atlantic coast towards their nesting sites. Eagerly, they push as far north as possible, but if open water is not available further north, they pause in their journey. Resting flocks continue to grow and may reach up to a thousand birds. Soon they become restless and with plenty of calling, flocks rise to continue their travels. By late April the large, loud tundra swan flocks are just an early spring memory.

Notes

April

4 Who are these red-headed sparrows that are now visiting bird feeders? They are purple finches that wintered throughout much of the midwest and are now pausing on their northward spring migration.

In breeding plumage, purple finch males are not purple but rose-red over the head, chest, and rump. Some observers have described this color as that of raspberry juice. Females are heavily streaked and more sparrowlike. Each is about six inches long and bears the characteristic seed-eating beak.

Migrating flocks call often with a "pit" or "tick" sound and occasionally sing the fast and lively warble song. Like many moving birds, they feed constantly and remain restless while with us.

Breeding takes place in the boreal coniferous forests but finches also seek out Christmas tree plantations. Here, in concealed nests, purple finches raise four young.

You'll need to check your bird feeder every day if you want to see all the spring migrants. Many, such as the purple finches, are here today and gone tomorrow.

Notes

April

Most plants form seeds in late summer or fall. The hazel, however, begins seed development before it leafs out. Look for the tiny purple female flowers now open on branches.

5 Small hazel trees have been hanging out over trails all winter and we may find it difficult to walk along them without hitting the branches. Long catkins suspended at the end of the branches since last fall look different today. The developing pollen in these male flowers, called catkins, turns them even more yellow in color. Our bumping the twigs sends a puff of golden dust into the air. Hazel flowering has begun.

Many trees have these male structures called catkins: similar formations are on alder, birch, willow, and aspen. Here the male cells (pollen) grow to maturity; then, because this pollen is located on the ends of branches, it blows off in the wind. In order for sexual reproduction to occur, the cells need to contact female cells formed in female flowers. In many instances, this means pollen must blow from catkins on one tree to female flowers on another tree. Trees with male and female flowers are dioecious. Hazels, however, are monoecious; along the same twigs where catkins grow are tiny purple female flowers. Only one-fourth of an inch wide, the little flowers put forth several thin colorful sepals that add a diminutive beauty to the spring scene. Hazels, which have no leaves until mid-May, begin their seeds in April.

Notes

April

6 April is a time of change in preparation for the coming seasons. Despite the appearance of spontaneity, nature has actually been getting ready for months. Among the many examples of April's growth are the rabbits and hares. After a late-winter mating season, rabbit and hare babies are adding their presence to the newness of spring.

Cottontail rabbits are the first to be born, and the immature young, naked and blind, are placed in a fur-lined depression under a shrub. At this early date, the young need to cope with cold nights, but they grow so fast that they are weaned, furred, and able to disperse within a month. This rapid maturing allows the mother to expand her family by bearing another three litters during the year.

Because of their slightly longer gestation, snowshoe hares give birth a bit later in the month. The relatively mature young are born in a secluded forest nest, already furred and with their eyes open. Like young rabbits, juveniles leave home quickly enough for the hare to have three more broods.

If you're fortunate enough to discover a rabbit or hare nest, don't disturb it, but look closely: hares are born with hair, rabbits are not.

Notes

April

Some nests can be removed from roof overhangs after the young have fledged, but not phoebe nests as a second clutch of eggs will soon be laid.

7 Despite the fact that early April, with only a few insects visible, seems too soon for this insect-eating bird to return from migration, the phoebe does, in fact, return now. It is the first flycatcher to come back from wintering elsewhere. Having spent the cold months in southern United States, the gray-brown bird with white underneath is quick to return to claim hunting and housing sites in the northland.

Phoebes have adapted well to human habitation and shortly after the birds' return, "fee-be" calls proclaim their ownership of the yard. Within weeks, this early migrant takes advantage of the porch, garage, or outbuildings as available sites on which to place its mud and grass nest lined with moss. The shelter of a roof or overhang proves highly beneficial for this April nester.

Besides providing space and food, nesting in April allows the phoebe to raise two broods, which is unusual at this latitude: white eggs fill the nest in spring, but after these firstborns fledge, a second brood is raised. We will hear the plaintive "fee-be" call repeated for the next two months; nearer the nest, chipping notes are audible.

Notes

April

8 At one time perhaps the most abundant bird in the United States, eastern bluebird numbers dropped drastically with the introduction of house sparrows and starlings. Fortunately, the recent success of well-designed bluebird houses and trails have been helping populations make a comeback. This thrush with a dark blue back and red breast winters in southern states as far north as Missouri. By late March small flocks make their way to breeding sites, and soon we can hear warbles of "chur chur-lee chur-lee" again. It is not unusual at this time to see bluebirds frequenting the same birdhouses they used last year.

At seven inches in length, the eastern bluebird is one of the smaller thrushes, but it is well known and much loved. Bird-watchers look for early spring arrivals along roadsides, in open woods, and around shortgrass pastures. Here the bluebirds seek meals of field insects such as grasshoppers, crickets, and beetles. They search, as well, for natural nesting cavities like old woodpecker holes if no birdhouses are available. The grass-lined hollows hold the clutch of three to six light blue eggs later in spring.

You can make a difference. Add one or more houses to an eastern bluebird trail. Then commit yourself to caring for it.

Notes

April

When chorus frogs are singing together, it can be hard to locate a
single frog. But listen carefully and
look closely. Perhaps you'll find a
tiny frog hidden in the grass.

9 A shallow pond, now filled with meltwater and early
spring rain, may disappear by midsummer. With the
evaporation typical of summer, the shallow pond will lose
the water it now contains, but at this time it is the temporary
home of a few critters. Among them, chorus frogs abound.
Their one-inch-long striped bodies make them stand out
from other frogs, but they blend in with the grassy ponds
where they breed.

Chorus frogs get their name from their practice of
singing in groups, as they do through much of April. The
males' song is often compared to running a thumb over
teeth of a comb. Not as loud or rambunctious as some frog
calls, it is still very persistent. While most frogs call in the
evening or night, chorus frogs often sing much earlier in
the day with only the advent of the cool early morning
stopping them.

The successful male entices a female into his realm, and
together they produce a small mass of fast-developing eggs
that they attach to pond grasses. When, in May, males lose
interest, chorus frogs leave the ponds to pursue a life on land.
Mysteriously, they are seldom seen for the rest of the year.

Notes

April

10 Just a week ago this pond was frozen and quiet, now it is open and noisy. Wood frogs, recently awakened from the long sleep of winter, explode in the excitement of a new breeding season: the evening jubilation of courting and calling will continue all night.

The two- to three-inch-long wood frogs are various shades of brown with a black patch behind the eye; some also have a light line down the back. Various explanations are given for their name. The best, perhaps, is that during most of summer these frogs hunt in the forest, avoiding wetlands.

Wood frogs breed quickly and gregariously. Males float in a supine position on the surface and sing amorous "gluck-glucks" that have been compared to ducks' quacking or horses on cobblestone. The male declares a territory and when the female joins him, they produce masses containing hundreds of eggs. Indeed, the eggs appear to be too many to come from bodies this size. These eggs will be tadpoles by early May, and the new batch of wood frogs will hop onto the forest floor during July. The pond, now so filled with their activity, will have no wood frogs by the month's end.

A simple hand lens will magnify wood frog eggs and the tadpoles that will soon hatch from them.

Notes

April

A nearby pond can be a never-ending source of interest and pleasure. Even an underwater leaf may bear new life—an egg of a spring peeper.

11 Ice still covers much of the pond and there may be more snows in the next few weeks, but spring is making its move. Changes in temperature and daylight bring responses: today the first spring peeper calls. The weak "peep" lasts only a few seconds, but within days, sounds will be more powerful and constant as others join this pioneer.

The spring peeper is a small brown tree frog about one inch long with only an X-shape on the back breaking the color pattern. The Latin name of *Pseudacris (Hyla) crucifer* refers to the cross it carries, and the common name, peeper, denotes the call these small amphibians emit. With the use of his powerful vocal cords and an inflated singing sac, the male pierces spring evenings with a deafening sound that can be heard a mile away.

After sleeping through the winter under pondside leaves, the males have awakened to forces of propagation. Peeping calls serve two purposes: they interest females and also proclaim a section of pond as claimed territory. After the mating process is completed, eggs are deposited singly on plants under the pond water. April nights will still freeze and eggs need to be deep to survive the ice.

Notes

12 In early April we can still see ice on many northland lakes, but with rivers and small ponds open, some eager waterfowl are arriving. Wood ducks are among those quick to return, and the brightly colored birds now appear in the cool waters.

These medium-sized ducks may be the most colorful in North America. The male, now in full plumage, displays green head feathers in a crest, with whites, purples, and blues over the rest of his body. In a good example of sexual dimorphism, females are gray with white eye markings that give them a spectacled appearance. Undersides of both sexes are light colored.

After wintering in the southern United States, wood ducks return early to their breeding sites on woodland ponds. Nests are in tree cavities, a characteristic which gives rise to their name. These ducks also readily use nesting boxes.

The pairs or small flocks that appear in April often stay in shallows and are difficult to approach. Swift flight, accompanied by squeaking calls, alerts the entire group. As a result, we may find it difficult to observe wood ducks from the distance they demand of us.

Are you finding it difficult to approach shy creatures like wood ducks? Binoculars will bring them close without disturbing them.

Notes

April

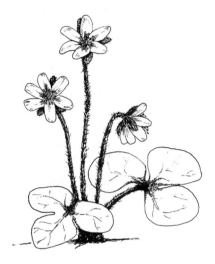

If you want to see all the spring wildflowers, including hepatica, in bloom, you'll have to plan a weekly walk in the woods.

13 The first forest wildflower, a welcome sight each April, will soon bloom. Soon the woods will be filled with these spring ephemerals, but the first is usually hepatica. With no leaves on trees, spring flowers grow in a bright forest, and the south-facing hillsides provide the sunniest of conditions for them.

Hepatica, or liver-leaf, gets its name from the three-lobed leaf that reminded early naturalists (who were often also physicians) of the lobes of human livers. These plants are perennial, and when leaves of many ephemerals fade, these persist even through the winter. As a result, hepatica gains a head start in spring. Its flowers vary from white to a deep purple and though six is the usual number of sepals (it has no petals), twice that number can be found on some plants.

The early blooming flowers, which close at night and on cloudy days, last into May, taking advantage of the early bees and flies for pollination. Their dependence on insects does not end here: the seeds are collected and stored by ants who consequently disperse hepaticas.

Notes

April

14 By mid-April, rivers may still retain some ice along the edges, but for the most part, their waters are open. Ponds and small lakes are already clear, and even the large lakes are near breakup. Waterfowl of many kinds now appear swimming in lakes and rivers; on any day we will see at least ten varieties. Some breed here and will be around for the whole summer, but most are resting and will soon resume their journey farther north.

Myriads of ducks flock here. Those we can see in the open waters include mallards, black ducks, both green- and blue-winged teal, northern shovelers, wood ducks, ring-necked ducks, lesser scaup, buffleheads, and goldeneyes. Crowds increase with the presence of other waterfowl: Canada geese, cormorants, mergansers (common, red-breasted, and hooded), white pelicans, tundra swans, pied-billed grebes, coots, and loons. Along lakeshores, early shorebirds such as yellowlegs wade near great blue herons and bitterns. Gulls and bald eagles clean up the winter fish kill, and osprey try spring fishing. Though crammed with birds now, the waters will soon empty of all but the local breeding birds.

Practice your waterfowl identification skills this week. There will be no better time.

Notes

April

Dog and cat owners should check their pets carefully for ticks from mid-April through June.

15 As a result of April's melting snow and increasing daylight, meadows become very dry. Indeed, April is often called the fire month because of the frequency of grass fires. Wood ticks are among the little critters that survived winter and now emerge in these dry ecosystems for their next phase of life.

Waking from hibernation, they quickly mate and both male and female look for a meal of blood. Only the female takes huge amounts, enough to expand her size by about ten times as she produces eggs.

Living mostly in the open fields, they are erroneously called "wood" ticks. Particularly abundant in the tall grasses of dry meadows, they climb up and with outstretched legs wait to grab a passing animal. Once on the host, they locate a secure spot and use mouthparts, not legs, to hold on and feed for several days.

Ticks are cousins of the spiders and have eight legs attached to their flat oval body. Though some species carry disease, wood ticks seldom cause anything more than an irritation and an itch. These ticks will remain active in our meadows for the next two months.

Notes

16 Days have been warming, and temperatures reach above the fifties regularly now. Most of the snow is gone and the dry meadow is even devoid of the mold that quickly grows in the wake of the departing snow. With greens just starting to appear, the meadow pauses between snow and grass.

Meadows insects, however, are already active as critters wake to the spring. The queen bumblebee, the fertile female that survived the winter, now seeks a site for a new colony. Last fall, she mated, then hibernated alone under a log; now the one-inch-long black-and-yellow hairy bee alone begins her family. She flies near the ground in a search for a burrow or mouse nest to claim for her home. Once a spot is chosen, she collects grasses, mosses, and leaves into a soft ball inside the nest. To this is added pollen gathered from early blooming flowers or trees. Her eggs are deposited on the pollen. Within four or five days the eggs hatch and eventually develop into sterile females that will take care of the broods of summer. It is not until late summer that the fertile males and females develop that lead to the breakup of the hive.

It's unlikely that you'll ever see a bumblebee nest. Their social life takes place underground.

Notes

April

Take time to examine closely the forest floor. Natural treasures such as the nest of the hermit thrush may be hidden near your feet.

17 During a typical spring, a variety of thrushes—Swainson's, gray-cheeked, wood, and hermit thrushes, as well as the veery—pass by as part of spring migration. Of these five thrushes, only the hermit thrush winters in southern United States; the others travel to Central or South America. It comes as no surprise, therefore, that the hermit thrush is the first to arrive in the April woods. Residents of northern conifer and mixed forests, most hermit thrushes are just passing through, but the brevity of their stay does not stop these shy birds from singing. Spring evenings are enlivened by the music of these woodland flutists.

Its brown coloring with many dark breast spots suits this dweller of the forest floor well. Only the reddish tail that the bird habitually lifts and slowly drops serves as an easy field mark for identification.

The name hermit refers to the bird's shyness and to its habitat of dark forest thickets, where on or near the ground, it hides a nest composed of twigs, bark fibers, grasses, and moss and lined with conifer needles. Three or four light blue eggs are laid in this well-secluded nest.

Notes

April

18 Few places in North America have the spring warbler migration of which the northland can boast: each year, area birders can see at least twenty-five species. Though most of these warblers move through May woods, the first arrive now, in mid-April.

After a winter in the southern United States, sometimes as far north as the southern Great Lakes, yellow-rumped warblers have a shorter distance to fly than other warblers that wintered in Central America. Yellow-rumped warblers, formerly called myrtle warblers, get their name from a yellow patch on their rump, but they carry yellow on their belly sides and head, as well. Their Latin name means tree dweller with a crown. In the spring males' body feathers are blue-gray with black on their chest and face; females are brown. Both are highly streaked.

Early arrivals, often in flocks, give the checking call note regularly. Only with the subsequent arrival of more warblers do they sing the slow trilling warble we recognize. Warblers, breeding birds of coniferous and mixed forests, place their nests in spruce, tamarack, or birch trees.

It may be difficult to differentiate between the calls of various birds, but it's easy to know that you are hearing some type of warbler. In mid-April, it will probably be the yellow-rumped warbler.

Notes

April

A variety of birdhouses placed around your yard may attract a corresponding variety of birds, including tree swallows, who aren't terribly fussy about their home.

19 By late spring, we will have tree swallows, rough-winged swallows, bank swallows, cliff swallows, barn swallows, and purple martins, which are also swallows, all residing in the northland. Of these six swallows, the tree swallow seems to be the pacesetter. Not only does it arrive in early April as the first spring migrant, it also starts the autumn migration.

Dark and glossy, blue-green above with white below, the slightly brighter males are hard to tell from females. In true swallow fashion, they are strong fliers and perform aerial acrobatics while catching insects.

Though tree swallows winter from southern United States to Central America, they remain further north than other swallows and return to breeding territory before them. Once returned, tree swallows quickly move into wooded swamps and open woods, often near fields, for nesting. Here they live up to their name and take over old woodpecker holes, fence posts, and other hollow sites that they line with feathers. These birds readily use man-made sites as well, nesting in purple martin apartments, wood duck boxes, bluebird houses, and even mailboxes.

Notes

April

20 Woodpeckers—downy, hairy, and pileated—have been with us all winter, but now another family member, the yellow-bellied sapsucker, appears on the scene. Females have black-and-white patterns that on the male are supplemented with a red throat and forecrown. The yellow belly is light and not easily seen.

After wintering in southern United States, yellow-bellied sapsuckers are regular migrants of mid-April. By the end of the month, we frequently hear their nasal, mewing "cheerrrr" calls from the woods. There they seek a tree as a nesting site; their preference is for aspen. A fungus-affected aspen proves to be a good home with its soft inner wood, which is easy to chisel and tough outer wood, which offers formidable protection from predators such as raccoons. Though the sapsucker may choose the same tree as it did last year, it chisels out a new cavity, rarely using the old ones.

Sapsuckers drill orderly rows of small holes in living trees. Here they feed on insects or, as their name tells us, the spring sap. The line of holes is readily visible and affords us a good sign of the sapsucker's presence.

Look for little holes lined up in rows on living trees. That signals that a yellow-bellied sapsucker has been feeding on sap or insects.

Notes

April

Pull a few wild onions and use them to flavor a meal. When picking wild plants, be sure to take only a few from a stand, leaving many to reproduce.

21 Bathed in bright sunlight and soaked with moisture from the recently melted snows, the leaf-rich forest floor of April is an excellent site for the growing spring plants. When most plants now appear, both leaves and flowers are present. The wild onion, or wild leek, however, fills the woods of late April with greens and fragrance, but though leaves abound, flowers are absent.

Like tame onions, the wild leeks have large white bulbs underground. Here they survive winter, and here, too, they store food made on these sunny spring days. The bulbs are actually layered leaf and are very tasty. Many a wild-foods fancier has used these bulbs to add a taste of the April woods to a backyard cookout.

The bulbs give plants energy to grow and open flowers in midsummer. While the leaves grow to maturity during a few weeks in April and make plenty of food, the flowers develop in the shade of June and July. If we had no previous knowledge of the wild onion, its lack of leaves in summer might lead us to believe it was an entirely different plant.

Notes

22 This woodland pond is temporary, created by snowmelt. By midsummer, evaporation will have claimed its contents and only a low spot in the forest will recall the pond of April. Aquatic critters common in other ponds tend to avoid this ephemeral home. Fish and turtles need permanent water, and only a few frogs have attempted families in this pond. Even most aquatic insects grow up elsewhere. It takes a specialized organism to live in a spring pond that will be dry or frozen the rest of the year. Such a critter, the fairy shrimp, flourishes in this pond each April.

About one inch long and orange in color, the small crustacean seems content as it lies on its back and swims with its eleven pairs of legs. Undulation proceeds from tail to head as the fairy shrimp moves. With gills on its legs, it continues this movement even when not swimming.

Fairy shrimp not only do well in the short-lived ponds of spring, they live nowhere else. The female-only population produces eggs that fall to the bottom and dry up before being revitalized in the meltwater of another spring. This type of reproduction is rare among animals.

Carry a few small plastic containers when you walk in the woods. Scoop up water from small ponds for further investigation with a hand lens or microscope. If you collect a fairy shrimp, you can see it without magnification.

Notes

April

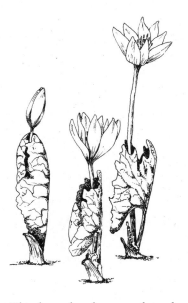

Bloodroot has been used to dye fiber. You won't want to dig up enough to color a sweater, but you could cut a single root to see the bright red juice.

23 Hepatica usually marks the beginning of the wildflowers' blooming on the spring forest floor. Now in the maple woods, bloodroot opens to become the second plant to flower.

Bloodroot gets its name from the bright red-orange pigment in the plant's roots. The perennial stores food in these roots, and in the sun of the April woods, grows huge leaves and flowers within days of awakening. Eight large white petals make it stand out, but the huge deeply grooved leaves also clarify its identity. The plants grow in groups, and a lone bloodroot is rare—perhaps a sign of a new colony or the last of an old one.

A true spring ephemeral, bloodroot snatches the sunlight while it can. Quickly it blooms in the April woods and just as quickly drops its petals and fades. By mid-May, when many of the spring flowers are just beginning, bloodroot is history. The second of the woodland flowers to bloom in spring becomes the first to wane with the passing season. Only wilting leaves and ripe fruit with seeds mark this spot by midsummer.

Notes

April

24 Spring arrivals that are heard before being seen are not unusual. Often the call of the loon or the song of the robin is our first announcement of their return. When you hear a sound at night, however, from a seemingly empty sky, it becomes a bit more mysterious. What you may be hearing is the breeding flight display of the snipe.

The common snipe, formerly called Wilson's snipe, has the wading legs and the long probing bill of a shorebird. This brown bird carries streaks and patterns of white on most of its body; its tail is orange banded. Feeding alone in wetlands, it is hard to approach. Often, we become aware of the snipe's presence only when it gives a sharp "scaip" sound and flies off with a zigzag motion.

In April, shortly after returning from winter in the southern states, snipes fly an erratic pattern in a breeding display. With vibrating tail and wing feathers, they make eerie fluttering sounds known as winnowing. The display continues at night and in the early mornings above the birds' wetland habitat until breeding has been completed. This long-billed shorebird then blends into the marshes and remains quiet for the rest of the season.

New campers are sometimes initiated by sending them on a snipe hunt. Since the common snipe is quite elusive, their hunt is not likely to be successful.

Notes

April

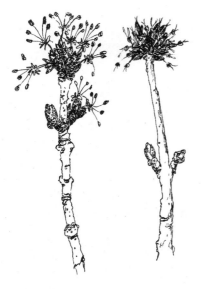

25 Trees have been flowering for the last few weeks. We first saw catkins hanging from branches, exposing pollen to the wind. Later in the spring other trees blossom with larger, more typical flowers. Red maples now blooming in yards, parks, and woods are not as showy as some trees, but they do bear tiny flowers with miniature petals and sepals. The trees are dioecious—male and female flowers are on separate trees. This explains why some trees never produce seeds. Female flower parts are called pistils and male parts are known as stamen. In dioecious trees, females produce pistillate flowers and males, staminate flowers.

Red maple gets its name from the bright crimson leaves of autumn, but its pistillate flowers are just as red on these spring days. The orange staminate flowers are not as bright.

Wind scatters large amounts of pollen from staminate flowers to fertilize pistillate flowers resulting in the winged seeds often called helicopters that form on female trees later in the spring.

Observe the entire flower to seed cycle in several species of trees, including red maples. At what point can you begin to recognize the developing seed's shape?

Notes

April

26 Though many trees are flowering with catkins, leaves are still weeks away. The open forest canopy lets sunlight in, and the forest floor becomes colorful with spring wildflowers. Hepatica and bloodroot began the display, and now a little plant called spring beauty adds its delicate flowers.

Grasslike leaves surround the five small pink petals. Colors vary from pink to lavender, but all spring beauty petals contain lines called nectar guides. These darker lines extending the length of the petals are thought to be the plant's way of directing bees and butterflies towards the nectar site in the center of the flower, thereby ensuring pollination. With flowers that stay open only about three days, closing at night and in cloudy weather, this aid is essential. Male and female parts mature separately, lessening the possibility of self-fertilization.

Like many spring ephemerals, perennial spring beauty survives winter in underground, bulblike corms. Its spreading roots create vast growths that carpet sections of the woods in May. As trees leaf out, shade eventually stops the plants' growth and they fade into the summer woods with only the explosive fruit capsules remaining.

Delicate wildflowers like spring beauty should not be picked. The fragile blossoms would fade rapidly, so it's better to enjoy them in the forest.

Notes

April

Does the ruby-crowned kinglet sing during lake ice breakup in your area? Do other natural events always occur in pairs?

27 A quiet afternoon's walk in late April will confirm that several kinds of warblers and thrushes have arrived. Among those causing movement in the trees are tiny gray birds that sing long high-pitched songs. The ruby-crowned kinglets have returned.

Only four inches long, ruby-crowned kinglets are one of our smallest birds. They are gray with white wing markings, called bars, and white eye rings. Males carry a scarlet crown that gives them their name kinglet, but this adornment is usually hard to see. These diminutive bundles of energy constantly flick their wings as they flit through branches, eating insects and singing.

Winter is spent in southern United States. In April they are passing through en route to breeding grounds in the boreal forests. Unlike many migrants, traveling flocks readily sing during migration. Their long song has been described as three or four high notes, several low notes, and a variable chant of "tee tee tee, tew tew tew tew, ti-dadee, ti-dadee, ti-dadee." This lengthy phrase uttered in late April has become associated with lake-ice breakup for many northlanders.

Notes

April

28 Well-known and beloved residents of our northland lakes, common loons winter in the coastal waters of the Atlantic Ocean or the Gulf of Mexico. The birds return north early in spring, and although ice still prevails on many large bodies of water, loons appear wherever they can find open water. Soon loon calls, reminding us of last summer, echo in the northland.

Up to three feet long and weighing eight pounds, the loon is one of the heaviest birds. Its solid bones (most birds have hollow ones) account for much of this weight. A master of diving and underwater swimming, the loon feeds on fish swallowed headfirst. Even the name comes from a Scandinavian word for diving bird.

The loon pays a price for being heavy and well-adapted to swimming. Legs situated far back near the tail enable the loon to swim well, but compel it to walk poorly; and it must nest near the water's edge. The heavy body that helps in diving becomes difficult to lift in flight, and the loon demands a long water runway or large lake for its takeoff.

In April, it may be during flight that we see or hear them as they yodel their way to the north.

Close your eyes and listen to a recorded loon call. Magically, you'll be transported to a summer evening on a northwoods lake.

Notes

April

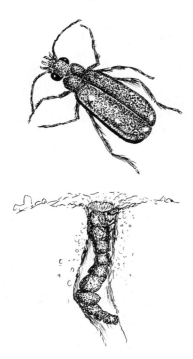

Tiger beetles are wary. Observing one is a true test of your patience and stalking skill.

29 Walking down a sandy road on a sunny day in late April gives us a chance to see active spring critters before the coming foliage hides them. Spiders, ground-nesting wasps, and ladybugs all scurry about, but hardest to approach are the tiger beetles. With a three-fourth-inch-long body and long legs, tiger beetles carry a variety of patterns colored from green to yellow-black on their backs. All possess large jaws and good eyesight. So sensitive are they to our presence that we need to look about ten feet ahead just to see them. Typically, they quickly fly or run off, not allowing us a close look.

Their name refers to the predaceous habits of the adult beetles. With quick movements, they seize their prey and hit it against the ground until it is dead. Body fluids are sucked out and parts chewed with powerful jaws. Larvae in soil burrows hunt in a more sedentary way, content to snatch passing prey.

Adults waking from the winter feed in the open road-sides. Also common on beaches and sandy fields, they are highly influenced by clear skies; even passing clouds slow their activity.

Notes

30 A snoring sound comes from the swamp. A bit deceiving, this sound usually associated with boredom or sleep is the excited call of mating male leopard frogs. Periodically, the frogs add a few grunts to the monotonous snore on this late April evening.

These frogs get their name from the black spots that cover their green bodies. Adults are about three inches long and, because they often leave water to hunt and hop in meadows and yards, they are also called grass frogs.

Leopard frogs avoid the temporary ponds that may be frequented by others. Instead they snore from the larger wetlands of swamps, lakes, or permanent ponds. Calls of wood frogs, chorus frogs, and spring peepers fill the swamp air, and the leopard snores may be hard to decipher. Females, however, hear the lackadaisical male calls, and soon jellied masses of eggs float in the marsh. Hundreds of tadpoles will soon become part of the swamp's fauna.

Within a month, breeding ceases. Adults then carry on a terrestrial existence hunting for insects, spiders, worms, or other frogs all summer.

The floating, jellied eggs of the leopard frog are relatively easy to see. Collect a few and watch them hatch and become tadpoles. Then return them to the pond so they can eat and finally become frogs.

Notes

May

May

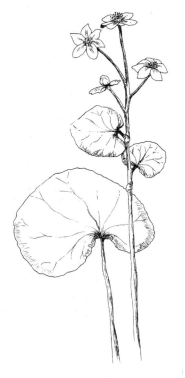

1 Its yellow-gold flowers and wet habitats make the marsh marigold deserving of its name. Our wetlands are colorful now as these flowers bloom. In the unblocked sunlight of early spring days, they grow to be up to eighteen inches tall with huge heart-shaped leaves.

Like many of the spring wildflowers, marsh marigolds are perennial, surviving winter in underground stems called rhizomes. Flowers may be one and a half inches across and usually have five petals. With variations, however, some plants have as many as ten. When in full bloom, yellow marsh marigold patches are easy to see even by speeding motorists glancing at roadside swamps.

Marsh marigolds are often called cowslips. This name refers to the odor of the swampy areas where they grow: the swamps smell like cow dung or cow slop. The name cowslip is also applied to a plant that in the northland is called bluebell.

A child's first bouquet, clutched in their loving hands, may be a dripping bunch of marsh marigolds.

Notes

2 Early in the spring wildflower season, an unusual-looking but attractive flower blooms on the forest floor. Dutchman's breeches grow best in the bare maple woods where sunlight reaches the ground before being obstructed by a leafy canopy.

Carrotlike leaves are evident, but it is the flower that makes this plant so unique. Hanging from a drooping stem, the white blossoms are composed of two parts. Depending on our point of view, they look like either extracted molars, complete with roots, or miniature pairs of pants. The latter image leads to their common name, dutchman's breeches.

Two spurs filled with nectar project from each flower. Spurs are formed by the fusion of petals. Nectar attracts the attention of early spring bumblebees, who subsequently pollinate the flower.

The leaves of the plant produce plenty of food but die in the shady forests of summer. Underground tubers, however, assure the survival of dutchman's breeches during winter.

Imagine discovering dutchman's breeches and not knowing its name. What would you call it? Give some plants that you don't recognize names that are easy to recall.

Notes

May

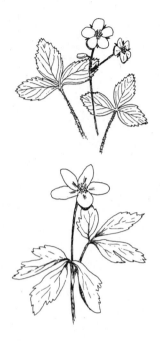

When you find clusters of wild strawberries, take note of their location. You'll want to find the strawberries again when the berries are ripe.

3 Wild strawberry and wood anemone are two wildflowers of May which may often be confused with one another: both are small with five white petals and three leaves. If we take a closer look, however, we'll notice some ways to tell the two apart. The leaves of the wood anemone are more deeply cut—so much so, that a single leaf may appear to be five. Wild strawberry has, clearly, three rough-toothed leaves with no deep cuts. The flowers are also different. Though both plants have many stamens in the center of the flower, the wild strawberry's are yellow; the wood anemone's are white.

Perhaps the easiest way to tell the two flowers apart is by their different habitats. Wood anemone lives up to its name and can be found on the forest floor. Wild strawberry is a plant of meadows.

Another big difference: wild strawberry produces a sweet red berry that ripens in early summer. The berries are eaten by many critters (including humans). Few eat the green spiny fruit of wood anemone.

Notes

4 Trees can be slow in responding to warm weather, appearing reluctant to trust that spring has arrived. Though many have had their catkins for weeks, their leaves are still wrapped in winter buds. The woods will be green by the latter part of this month, but now each tree seems to be waiting for the others to open first.

A small tree makes this first plunge. Despite the danger of late frosts, elders pioneer the greening of the woods. Like many plants of the forest floor, the elder needs time in sunlight before shade dims the landscape.

Large compound leaves pour from the huge buds that have held them all winter, and long green leafy fingers emerge holding the broccolilike buds of the flowers in their grasp. Later these flower buds will give the tree white flowers and red berries that contribute to the common name of elderberry.

As though on cue, other trees soon follow the example of the elder, and within two weeks, the woods will explode in foliage.

The red berries that grow on northland elderberry trees are seldom eaten by humans.

Notes

May

The brief life of the spring azure butterfly reminds us that we must take an observant walk through our yard and neighborhood often, or we'll surely miss something—and it may be beautiful.

5 Sunlight and warmth quicken the pace of spring. In early May, both bees and butterflies appear in the yard. The spring azure, or common blue, is one of the smallest and earliest butterflies of spring. Blue above and white below, the tiny butterfly can stretch its wings only about one inch.

The spring azure is not the first butterfly to appear in the spring. This honor belongs to other butterflies that hibernate as adults. However, it is the first butterfly to emerge from its chrysalis.

Mating and laying eggs are about all that can happen in the short life of this little blue butterfly. The adult stage lasts only a week or two, and then the spring azure will exit before most butterflies enter for the season. After the adults die and the eggs hatch, the caterpillars feed on leaves of dogwood, cherry, and viburnum. Here these larvae are discovered by ants, and in one of nature's symbiotic relationships, are cared for by the ants until they form a chrysalis.

Notes

6 While most spring wildflowers advertise their colorful blossoms, the wild ginger, known in some regions as heartleaf, keeps its flower on the ground. Two large heart-shaped leaves cover it as if embarrassed about its purple flower. Three sepals fuse to form an inch-long flower that does not get seen or pollinated by butterflies or bees. The wild ginger relies on a ground-roving beetle for this task.

The name ginger refers to the gingerlike odor of the roots. Formerly it was used as a flavoring or tea.

The rootstock allows the wild ginger to survive the winter and is shared by the whole group of gingers that grow together along the edge of the woods. Each clone sprouts leaves and flowers quickly in the spring while sunlight is available but wanes in the summer. This process is typical of many of the fast-growing spring wildflowers called ephemerals.

If you come upon a large patch of wild ginger, take a small piece of root, dry it, pulverize it, and steep it for a teatime drink.

Notes

May

When caterpillars attack your garden, you'll be delighted to find that the chipping sparrow makes tasty meals out of them.

7 When a repetitious chipping sound comes from shrubs and bushes in the yard, the chipping sparrow has arrived. This small brown bird with a light underside and a reddish brown crown gets its name from its continuous song.

Our yards and gardens provide the chipping sparrow with plenty of insects for food. When bug hunting is bad, the hungry sparrows eat seeds.

The five-inch-long bird seeks both space and privacy, hiding its cup-sized nest constructed of grass, hair, and string in the fork of an evergreen shrub.

With ample food and shelter, the chipping sparrow is right at home with us. From spring arrival until fall departure, this little sparrow may well spend more time in our yards than we do. Rejoicing in its favorite feeding, nesting, and singing sites, it proclaims ownership many times each day. It is no surprise that these chipping sparrows are reluctant to leave us when cold weather moves in.

Notes

8 Longer days and spring rains change the forest floor. Wildflowers and fiddleheads now grow among the dead leaves. Fiddleheads get their name from the coiled shape of fern fronds as they unroll in the spring. The small unrolling plants look like the scroll at the end of a violin or fiddle.

Nearly every kind of fern survives the winter by allowing the frond above ground to die while the rhizome survives underground. Now in May, rhizome buds unroll into the new fronds for this year.

Located, as they are, on the forest floor, fiddleheads use scales and hairs to protect against grazing animals. The new plant tissue beneath, however, is soft and tender. For this reason they are often eaten by human gatherers. Use caution, though: not all are equally tasty, and some kinds are very bitter. Considered just an interesting food for us, fiddleheads are celebrated in some communities of eastern Canada, where they are eaten in great amounts.

Fiddleheads can be steamed lightly and served with butter, using the same cooking technique you would use with asparagus.

Notes

May

People who contend with Canada thistles know how tenacious they are. It's difficult to imagine how a creature as fragile as the painted-lady butterfly could help control them.

9 A common orange-and-black butterfly of spring is the painted lady. Glancing at it casually, we could mistake it for a monarch, but a closer look shows many differences. The color on the top of the wings is offset by brown and gray patterns beneath. Large circles called eyespots are on the hind wings, but it's the pink spot on the front wing that gives the painted lady its name.

The name thistle butterfly may be more accurate since the larvae feed on the leaves of the Canada thistle. Many of these black spiny caterpillars will strip the thistle bare.

Painted ladies are both cyclic and migratory. Being cyclic, they have years of population highs and lows. Being migratory, they winter in the southern United States and return early in the spring. Upon arrival, the adults lay eggs and die by the end of the month.

By late summer, the next generation of painted ladies will feed on soil minerals and garden flowers.

Notes

10

Each year around the tenth of May, we can hear a loud clear "teacher, teacher, teacher" song fill the woods. Announcing its return, the ovenbird claims forest territory for the coming season.

The ovenbird's name comes from its nesting habits. The birds make a covered nest of leaves on the ground and deposit eggs inside. This structure reminded early naturalists of an oven. Another name, the teacherbird, comes from the bird's loud song.

With brown on its back and spots on its belly, it appears to be a sparrow or thrush as it hops on the forest floor. However, an orange crown distinguishes the ovenbird from those birds.

For the next two months, as this bird raises its family, its song will continue to dominate the songs of other forest birds. There will probably not be a day on which it does not sing. It seems ironic that such an inconspicuous bird with a hidden nest would issue such loud proclamations.

Because they face predators, many birds hide their nests very successfully. Train yourself to really look, not just casually scan, when you're on a hike. You'll be surprised at how much more you will see.

Notes

May

11 Fast-growing wildflowers in the spring woods are common, but bellwort is the speediest, growing up to a foot tall in two weeks. Although large leaves make the six petals of the flower hard to see, it is now in full bloom, its yellow blossoms drooping as if exhausted. The yellow petals hanging down reminded early naturalists of a bell, and wort means plant: thus, the bellwort.

A smaller cousin, wild oats, is in bloom too. Wild oats, which gets its name from the oatlike leaves, has a pale bell-shaped flower which looks even more like a bell than bellwort. This plant is sometimes called pale bellwort.

Bellworts of both kinds grow in deciduous woods and may have many other ephemerals nearby. Like many spring wildflowers, bellworts quickly fade as spring grows into summer.

The Latin name for bellworts, *Uvularia*, is interesting. The uvula is the flap of material that hangs down from the roof of our mouth near the throat. This reference to the human body is one of many in wildflower names.

Challenge family members to look around your yard and give names to plants that associate them with body parts. Bleeding heart is obvious; bellwort or *Uvularia* is less so. Activities like this help us pay attention to what we are seeing.

Notes

12 Several kinds of violets bloom in and near our backyards. Although we may expect them all to be purple, many are not. About ten kinds of violets are found in colors of white, yellow, or purple. Each has five petals arranged with a middle petal hanging down like a lip. This petal is usually marked with purple nectar lines which seem to direct bees to nectar. When they collect the nectar, they also pollinate the flowers.

Violets are all perennial, and to know them we must notice not only their color, but whether they are stemmed or stemless. Purple violets range in color from blue to red. Nearly all are short and stemless. Except for one large-stemmed type, white violets are stemless and short. The stemmed, yellow violets may grow nearly one foot tall and are probably our largest violets. Though many violets grow only in woods, some grow in yards.

The heart-shaped leaves persist throughout the season, and violets have second flowers in the summer. These small and unopened flowers stay near the ground, but both flowers produce seeds.

A recurring dilemma for gardeners, whether to ruthlessly eliminate the little violets that are so lovely—and so invasive. What is your decision?

Notes

May

Large-flowered trilliums are easy to spot, but other wildflowers, like the nodding trilliums, hide under large leaves. You'll discover more if you gently explore with your hands as well as your eyes.

13 By the middle of May, hundreds of large-flowered trilliums cover the hillside, turning it white. As these flowers fade by the end of the month, the petals change their color to pink and purple, but now they are still snow-white. Standing a foot tall and boasting a flower three or four inches across, the large-flowered trilliums are hard not to notice. With three leaves, three petals, and three sepals, the plant is well-named, and like us, bees and butterflies find it irresistible.

The large-flowered trilliums are not the only ones blooming in the woods now. Not as abundant nor as showy, the nodding trillium is common too. Nodding trilliums also grow about a foot tall and have three large leaves. The flower, however, is bent over and tucked under the three leaves; a casual passerby would probably not even notice it, but bees find and pollinate it. The bending flower gives the nodding trillium its name.

Whether the flower is large and showy or small and inconspicuous, trilliums grow rapidly in the sunlight. Shade quickly turns these trilliums into memories.

Notes

The large heart-shaped pattern on the grosbeak's breast has given this bird the nickname of bleeding heart.

14 A sparrowlike bird with a large beak who visits the bird feeder about the middle of May often sends feeder watchers to the bird book for its identification. This mystery bird, the female rose-breasted grosbeak, has none of the features of the male. He is a showy bird who blends his white belly and rose-pink bib with a black head and back. She is streaked and spotted.

The grosbeaks live up to their name, using their large powerful beaks for breaking seeds. This explains their visits to the bird feeder as soon as they return from migration. They also eat insects and berries.

Among most songbirds, only the males sing, but both the male and female grosbeaks sing loudly and frequently, using their songs to claim a section of woods as home.

Once their territory has been established, the pair of grosbeaks will build a loose nest of sticks in shrubs or low trees. This pretty bird with a loud and beautiful song makes poorly constructed nests, which have been known to fall apart before the young have fledged.

Notes

May

Enjoy the wild plum and juneberry flowers now. Later, the juneberries will be edible without further preparation, but the plums are only good for jelly.

15 Our local roadsides come alive in early May as small trees—wild plum and juneberry—bloom and delicately scent the air. White blossoms decorate these fragile trees scattered throughout the understory of a forest that, in the northland, is still bare of leaves.

Blooming for only one week, wild plums display their abundance with gusto. One-inch flowers with five rounded petals cover every branch, and the entire tree buzzes as bees gather nectar. Loosely attached petals easily dislodge, creating white showers that accompany rain and wind. In late summer, small, bitter plums develop.

Growing on spikes, juneberry flowers have five long narrow petals that continue blooming into late May. The juneberry gets its name from the time the berries are said to be ripe. Though true some years, in the northland berries are more likely to ripen in July.

Another name for this tree, serviceberry, comes from the old name, sarvis. Still another name, shadbush, tell us that the tree blooms when shad swim upstream.

Notes

16 Finding mushrooms in May is unusual, but now morels grow on leafy forest floors. Most mushrooms emerge in the late summer or fall, but the morel is so likely to be seen at this time that it is sometimes called the May mushroom.

Although the morel is also known as the sponge mushroom, it does not form its spores (seeds) as true mushrooms do. Morel spores are formed within a porous cap, not on the underside of an umbrella-shaped top. This porous cap is shaped something like a pine cone and, like the stem, is hollow.

Morel is a very distinctive-looking fungus but it can be confused with another called false morel. False morels are more likely to grow in the fall, and they have their cap attached to the stem at the top and not at the base as does the morel.

Morels are not only edible, they are delicious when sauteed in butter. Many a collector has kept the location of a good growth of these mushrooms a secret. With the underground growth preserved, they return each year.

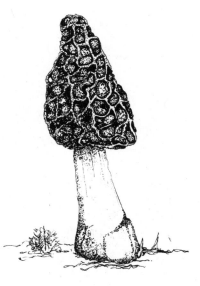

Unlike other woodland plants, morels and other mushrooms may be picked freely. The edible portion of mushrooms is just the fruiting body. As long as the underground fungus remains, when conditions are right, mushrooms will emerge again.

Notes

_____

_____

_____

May

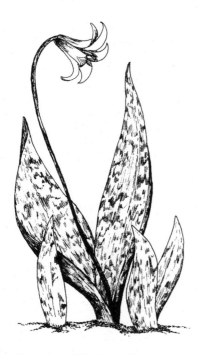

17 In damp maple woods, we can discover many yellow and white trout lilies blooming. The six petals of the single flower curl back when mature, revealing the red stamen. The two leaves are pointed and blotched.

The name trout lily relates to spring phenology. An early naturalist observed that they bloom at about the time trout swim upstream to spawn. Other names given to this plant include fawn lily, because the leaves look somewhat like the two ears of a deer, and dogtooth violet, although the origin of that name is unknown.

A typical growth of trout lilies has many plants, but only a few (almost always less than 10 percent) have flowers. The sterile nonflowering plants are making food that will be stored in the roots for another year when they will bloom. These many plants are connected underground and are all clones of a single trout lily plant. Many plants indicate that a colony is old. A trout lily colony may, in fact, be older than nearby trees in the forest.

Since trout lilies don't bloom every year, the flowers should not be picked. The seeds formed in those flowers provide the only method for starting new colonies.

Notes

18 Perhaps one of the strangest looking plants in the spring woods, jack-in-the-pulpit has a flower with no petals. The leafy mass (the spathe) resembles a pulpit complete with a canopy. In the midst of this purple-green growth, a floral spike (the spadix) stands like a preacher. At the base of the spadix are tiny flowers, either male or female. The plant is dioecious: male and female flowers grow in separate plants. Though hard to observe, the flowers are pollinated by flies that investigate the interiors of the flowers.

Jack-in-the-pulpit grows to be two feet tall. The two large leaves are in pairs, each divided into three leaflets, thus giving the plant the appearance of having six leaves. The flower grows from a stalk at the base of the leaves.

Jack-in-the-pulpit is also called Indian-turnip. This name refers to the Indians' use of the root to make flour. Most of the plant above the ground is toxic and should not be eaten. This includes the stalk of bright red berries that replace the flowers in the fall.

Native Americans and settlers used many plants for food. That does not mean that it's wise or ecologically sound for us to do so. Be thoughtful and cautious when gathering wild food.

Notes

May

Some wonders of the natural world seem inexplicable. Great crested flycatchers, for instance, often bring a shed snakeskin into their nest.

19 If we listen carefully in the early morning, we may hear the "greep" of the great crested flycatcher added to the early morning serenade of robins and phoebes. This crested nine-inch-long bird is the largest flycatcher in this part of the country. Greenish feathers cover its body, which is marked by a yellow belly, cinnamon wings, and a tail mark.

As its name implies, the great crested flycatcher feeds entirely on insects and, in the fashion of a true flycatcher, snatches many in midair. It appears to have a special fondness for dragonflies.

Ever since he arrived back from migration in mid-May, the male has loudly proclaimed his nesting territory. The "greeping" song carries far on clear, calm mornings.

This flycatcher is a cavity nester and readily nests in hollow trees and birdhouses. Nests are made of twigs, leaves, hair, feathers, and fibers.

Notes

20 On this warm spring evening, spring peepers, chorus frogs, and leopard frogs are calling. Suddenly we hear a long, high-pitched trill that announces the addition of the American toad to the night chorus.

The toad holds its elevated note from ten to thirty seconds. From a rough and warty looking critter, we don't expect such a high-pitched sound.

Like the wood frogs, toads are explosive breeders—all breed at the same time. After a few days and nights of trills, the toads are quiet again until next spring.

Though they are relatives of frogs, toads are land animals. Living and feeding on land, most of the time they avoid contact with water. It is only now in May that they return to their origins and string their eggs along the edge of the pond.

Soon the toads will be back in our yards and gardens, but we will not hear their trills again until next May.

Toad eggs can be distinguished from frog eggs because they are laid in long double strands that cling to rocks and weeds along pond edges. They'll hatch into tadpoles within two weeks of being laid.

Notes

May

The human voice is quite flexible. Try mimicking various birds, either by singing or by whistling. When you think you're pretty good, try calling a bird, using your new skill.

21 The redstart, a common but not well-known warbler, lives in yards and along the edge of woods. The five-inch-long bird is mostly black with red spots on its chest, wings, and tail. The female looks similar but wears gray instead of black.

Redstarts sing frequently as they move through our trees and shrubs. Before sunrise, they proclaim territorial boundaries, then simply continue singing for much of the rest of the day. Sung by both male and female, the song is a repetitive, but sometimes varied, series of four or five notes.

Redstarts use fibers, grasses, hair, and feathers to construct their three-inch wide nests in the fork of a tree or shrub ten to twenty feet above the ground. Here they raise their young.

Redstarts will be with us for about another two months as their family grows. Like many of the migrating warblers, redstarts feed on insects and caterpillars that are abundant in our summers.

Notes

22 Baneberry, one of the largest of the spring wildflowers, grows to be more than two feet tall. Large branching leaves, similar to those of the elderberry, surround clusters of white flowers. Each of the many blossoms in this round arrangement has four to ten thin petals. Long stamens make these tiny flowers appear fuzzier than they really are.

Later in the summer, baneberry will have red or white berries. The name baneberry tells us that the berries are bad or poisonous. Indeed, the entire plant is toxic.

Baneberry is a midspring wildflower. Instead of blooming quickly while trees are bare as the early spring wildflowers do, it flowers when the trees are leafing out. Unlike the ephemerals, baneberry stays with us during the summer. When the red and white berries are ripe, the rest of the plant will still be here in the shade of the maple woods.

When you take children into the woods, they should be cautioned to not eat anything without asking permission, and young children must be watched. A few plants, such as baneberry, are poisonous.

Notes

May

Pin cherries and chokecherries will both provide fruit for jellies in late summer, but the pin cherries will be too tart and the chokecherries, too astringent, to eat right off the tree.

23 Our roadsides and forest edges have two kinds of cherry trees in bloom: the pin cherry and the chokecherry. Both trees are small, seldom reaching twenty feet in height.

The pin cherry is the first to bloom; the white flowers appear with the leaves in the middle of May. One-half inch in diameter, the five-petalled flowers grow in flattened whorls of four or five blossoms.

Chokecherry trees are already fully leafed out when their white flowers appear. These flowers are even smaller than those of pin cherries, but because so many grow on a four-inch spike, they are easy to see.

Like many of the tree blossoms, these cherry flowers do not last long. Spring rains and wind scatter the petals, but not before the insects pollinate them. By mid to late summer, we will see the results of this pollination in the red berries of the pin cherry and the purple-red berries of the chokecherry. But now, at the end of May, it is blossom time.

Notes

24 Although the swamps and marshes have been alive with animals all spring, the flowering plants native to the swamp are slower to appear. Unlike the flowers of the woods, they encounter little competition for sunlight and moisture and thus can wait to bloom.

The possibility of lingering ice delays the flowering of the first swamp plants. But now, in late May, the water calla sends up a large white flower and huge leaf from its creeping underground rhizomes. The heart-shaped leaf wraps around the white flower as it grows up to a foot tall. The flower consists of a big white petal (spathe) holding the short golden center (spadix). This spadix is actually composed of many tiny flowers. Water calla is definitely the center of attention in spring swamps and marshes.

The flower persists for a month, during which time it is pollinated. By late summer, the berries are formed. The heart-shaped leaves remain in the wetlands all summer, and besides making food for the perennial plant, they serve as home for many critters of the swamp.

Bogs and swamps provide a fascinating look at a world very different from our backyards. Put on your boots and take plenty of insect repellant. It's worth slogging through stagnant water and braving mosquitoes to see plants like the water calla.

Notes

May

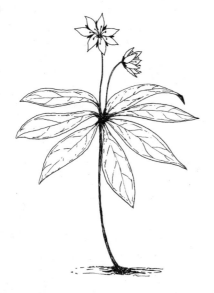

Although this plant is called star-flower, it is not the only wildflower named for stars. Can you name another one?

25 Although many kinds of wildflowers are blooming in the May woods, only the starflower has seven petals. Occasionally, we must admit, the starflower will have six or eight petals, but seven is its usual number. This fact makes the plant one of nature's oddities: seven-sided figures are rare anywhere in the natural world.

Standing about six inches tall, the starflower has pointed white petals of equal size and a whorl of leaves that extend in every direction below the flower. They provide a green background for the white flower. Typically, the flowers grow singly but two on a plant are not uncommon.

This low-growing perennial is common in the maple woods where it grows with other late spring wildflowers. The leaves of the plant emerge before the woods get shady, but by the time the flower blooms, the tree leaves overhead have made their appearance. In this woods, the starflower persists, often blooming for much of June.

Notes

26 Columbines are now in bloom along the south-facing rocky cliffs; they delight us with their large red-and-yellow flowers hanging in a bell-like fashion. With plenty of sunlight, the plants themselves grow quickly and will stand nearly two feet tall.

Their five hollow petals have long spurs that extend beyond the base. Including the spurs, flowers may be two inches long. Spurs and petal exteriors are red; the interiors are yellow.

It is the spurs that give columbine its name. The word means dove, and the five spurs remind some observers of a group of doves in a circle. The Latin name, *Aquilegia*, tells us that others have seen these spurs as talons of an eagle. The spurs contain nectar, and this flower, named after two kinds of birds, is often visited by another—the hummingbird. Bees also visit and do the bulk of the pollinating.

Besides growing along rocky hillsides, columbines grow along trails and open woods. Given enough sunlight, plants stay in bloom into July.

To further your botanical education, explore the Latin names of plants. *Aquilegia*, **the Latin name for columbine, might require a dictionary, but other Latin words can easily be deciphered.**

Notes

May

Is it any wonder that people have been fascinated by the mystery of flight. Creatures as different as daring dragonflies, droning bumblebees, hovering hummingbirds, and soaring eagles all fly.

27 During the night, more critters have emerged at the edge of the pond. Under cover of darkness, the dragonflies have grown into adulthood. With longer days and warmer temperatures, late May seems to be a good time for them to grow up.

Immature dragonflies have lived in the water as nymphs since hatching last summer. These nymphs reached a length of about one inch and were voracious feeders on other critters of the pond. After surviving the darkness of the winter, nymphs now proceed to their next stage.

In true insect fashion, this maturation seems magical. Nymphs climb out on a stem, entering the world beyond the water. Docks and piers do just fine for this coming-of-age ritual. In the light of dawn, nymphs split their shell (exoskeleton) down the back, and adult dragonflies escape. Their wings unfold and dry in the early morning light, and the new dragonflies dart off with the grace of veterans. Now they will feed (eating many mosquitoes), mate, and lay eggs in the same pond that served as their childhood home.

Notes

28 The northern red oak, one of the biggest trees in the woods, gets its name from its leaves, which in the fall will turn beautiful shades of red. In the fall, too, it will produce a crop of acorns, but in late May, the oak tree flowers.

The northern red oak is monoecious (male and female flowers grow on the same tree), but the flowers are separated from each other. Male flowers (catkins) are as long as the emerging leaves and hang at the end of the branches. Female flowers also develop now, but are so small that they can hardly be seen as they bloom at the base of the leaves. Most trees that form catkins do so before the leaves are on the tree, but oak leaves grow with the catkins.

Pollen from these long catkins is transferred by the wind; a good deal of that pollen is needed to ensure formation of acorns. After producing pollen, the catkins fall and will cover the yard during the next few weeks.

At this latitude, summer does not last long, so acorns mature in the second year.

If you plant a red oak and are patient, you and many generations to come will find pleasure in the wildlife drawn to your yard by the red oak's nutritious acorns.

Notes

May

Repeatedly, we find that wildflowers are pollinated by bees. If insecticides are used carelessly, the result could be fewer bees—and fewer flowers.

29 We can find bluebells easily: they flourish in wet open sites at the edges of forests or on roadsides. There, with plenty of moisture and sunlight, they grow up to two feet tall.

Bell-shaped flowers hanging from the ends of the stem give bluebells their name. The one-half-inch-long flower is actually pink before it opens and becomes more purple as it matures. With large oval leaves and many five-petaled bells, the bluebell (*Mertensia*) is an attractive late spring wildflower.

Blooming now in late May, the flowers persist into June. Slowly they fade after pollination, and small seeds called nutlets form on the branching stems. Again, it is the bees that are the pollinators.

A larger bluebell flower that grows in the south is sometimes called cowslip but in the northland, cowslip is a name applied to marsh marigolds, not to bluebells. Interestingly both bluebells are called lungworts, another example of a wildflower named after a body part. Probably the bluebell served as a folk medicine.

Notes

May

30 We should have no trouble in finding the blue-bead lily: it is common in our northern forests. In fact, it is found only in the cool conditions of the northwoods.

The plant, which grows to approximately a foot tall, holds its three to eight flowers bent gracefully in the characteristic lily pose. Three yellow sepals join three yellow petals to form each flower. The two or three basal leaves are long and wide, much like corn leaves in appearance—hence the plant's additional name, corn lily. The name blue-bead lily refers to the dark blue berries that appear on the top of the stem in the late summer. Leaves of the blue-bead lily grow in the early spring and may be confused with the leaves of wild onion.

Huge patches of closely bound plants are common: all these blue-bead lilies are connected by underground stems and are essentially one plant. Flowers begin to bloom in late May but last only a few weeks in the shady forests. The basal leaves, however, remain for the summer. Insects, abundant in these woods, provide pollination.

The blue-bead lily's genus name *Clintonia* is a tribute to DeWitt Clinton, naturalist and governor of New York. No matter what your occupation, you can also be a naturalist.

Notes

May

Split a lima bean; you can see within it a tiny plant surrounded by the nourishment that will support the plant's early growth. It's harder to believe, however, that in a minuscule aspen seed resides the beginnings of a tall tree.

31 Seventy degrees and clear skies are not conditions that bring snow, but that phenomenon appears to be taking place in our yard. White fluffy material floats in the breeze of this late May day.

The source of this storm, however, is not a cloud—but quaking aspen trees.

Tiny seeds, each attached to a bit of fluff, are dispersed by the wind. Since quaking aspen are dioecious (male and female flowers on separate trees), the seeds were formed earlier this spring when the wind carried pollen from the male to the female trees. Now, on the currents of this windy day, seeds are blowing from the female trees and will scatter widely.

As often happens in nature's dispersals, many of the seeds fall on inhospitable places. Fluff coats the streets, sidewalks, houses, ponds, rivers, and even spider webs. Still, the problem is not a major one for the aspen trees: by making a great multitude of seeds, quaking aspen can afford to lose many.

Willow and cottonwood also make warm-weather "snow," but unlike the cold-weather snow, it does not last long.

Notes

June

June

The fragrance of lilacs, appealing outside, is so intense that many people find it overwhelming indoors.

1 Lilac time signals that spring has truly arrived. This small tree (or shrub) grows in dense clumps and is seldom more than twenty feet tall. Stems not more than a few inches in diameter are covered with heart-shaped leaves about three inches long. During most of the year, the lilac appears to be just another small tree.

But in spring, the beautiful flowers that come in shades from purple to blue to white, emitting an unforgettable fragrance, make the lilac unique. These one-half-inch-long tubular four-petaled flowers grow in long clusters. They begin to bloom individually, but at the peak of lilac time, each flower is open.

We are not the only ones to notice the color and fragrance of this flower: many other critters do as well. Butterflies, moths, bees, wasps, flies, and hummingbirds all stop by to check out the lilac. Lilacs begin to bloom in late May, but it is typical for lilac time to be at its peak in early June.

Notes

June

2 In the southern part of the United States, the flowering dogwood, a small but well-known tree, grows. Each spring it bears blossoms bigger than the leaves. In the northland, we enjoy the large-flowering dogwood, a plant that is only six inches tall. Bunchberry, or Canada dogwood, has a large white flower that is essentially a copy of the flowering dogwood.

Bunchberry gets its name from the red berries that grow from a single white flower. Six leaves arranged in a whorl provide a green background for this blossom. The structures that appear to be four petals, are actually leaves and are correctly called bracts. The bracts surround the numerous true flowers. The tiny flowers are complete with male and female parts.

Large expanses of bunchberries, all connected to an underground stem, are clones of a single plant. Although nonflowering bunchberry plants have four leaves, those bearing flowers have six leaves that supply the additional nourishment needed to develop flowers and seeds. By fall, all the leaves add a purple color to the forest floor, blending with the red berries to offer us a lovely autumn scene.

Canadensis is a species name that is part of many northland plants' Latin names—including bunchberry. The connection to Canada is obvious. If a plant species name is *canadensis* or *groenlandicum*, you can guess that it tolerates cold weather.

Notes

June

Human children are most certainly altricial, totally or partially dependent on their parents for many years. Consider how quickly white-tailed deer fawns or red fox kits or baby robins must learn to care for themselves.

3 Since last fall, for about two hundred days, the doe has been carrying her baby. Now, in the shelter of the shady woods of late May or early June, she gives birth to her fawn.

Baby mammals are either altricial or precocious. Altricial babies are born helpless and depend on parents for all their needs; precocious young are quite capable at birth and can walk quickly thereafter. Hoofed mammals tend to be precocious, and this is true of the fawn: it is born covered with hair and able to walk.

Wearing a brown coat with large white spots, the fawn spends the month of June sleeping and feeding. When resting, the fawn remains curled up in a protected spot on the ground, and the white spots on brown look like sunlight penetrating the trees and dappling the forest floor. Such camouflage is important, for at these resting times the fawn is in danger from a coyote or fox that is not likely to bring down an adult deer but will prey on the young. Soon the fawn will travel short distances with the mother—we may glimpse them together during these brief excursions. It will nurse often and grow quickly. Frequently the fawn is an only child, but as does mature, they often have twins.

Notes

June

4 Black flies, only one-quarter inch long, bearing two wings on their hunchbacked bodies, look quite insignificant. We would not be likely to take note of a small insect like this were it not for the fact that the female flies, abundant during late May and early June, use us as a source of the blood protein that they need to help them form eggs.

Black flies slash us with sharp mouth parts, add an anticoagulant, then lap up the blood that seeps into the wound. Because of the hordes of flies, it is not unusual to get many bites at one time. Attracted by body heat, more and more attack. We get itchy, bloody scabs as a remembrance of our visit to their territory. Black flies are active in the daytime, and the direct sun does not deter them. The young develop in fast streamwater, and though they do travel as adults, they are never far from some moving water. Fortunately for us, adult black flies live only a few weeks.

Both males and females also feed on plant nectar, often visiting flowers. One such flower is the blueberry. No doubt, they pollinate the flowers and make it possible for berries to form in the midsummer.

While you viciously slap at the voracious black flies swarming around you on a portage, try (it won't be easy) to think of the delicious late-summer blueberry pies that will result from their work as pollinators.

Notes

June

5 Most of the plants in pasture meadows are eaten by the cows that wander there, but one tall yellow plant is left alone. Cows avoid the tall buttercup because of its disagreeable taste; not being consumed, it spreads throughout pastures.

The plant is about two feet tall, much taller than other buttercups. Five-petaled flowers are borne on several branches extending from the main stem. Each petal is a shiny yellow, giving the plant its common name.

Leaves are more numerous near the base of the plant than on the stem; all are deeply cut. Such a leaf pattern may resemble the footprint of a bird, this explains the name crowfoot, which is given to the entire buttercup family.

The tall buttercup is one of the first meadow flowers to bloom in the spring. Before the month is over it will be joined by others that will paint pastures yellow, orange, and white. Many of these wildflowers, including the tall buttercup, are aliens brought here from Europe. They look beautiful to casual observers, but farmers think of them as weeds.

Any plant or animal can, when moved to another environment, one with favorable conditions and without predators, become a weed. Many yard plants are aliens.

Notes

6 These are the days when we can see the largest butterfly of the summer flitting among roadside plants. Nearly five inches across, the tiger swallowtail's yellow wings striped in black provide the tiger part of its name. Swallowtail describes the hind wing extensions that look like tails of swallows.

Being large and colorful can be dangerous as well as beautiful, and many adult tiger swallowtails have scars from an attack which they survived. In butterflies this usually means that a section of a wing is missing. A close call with a bird results in a gouge the shape of a bird's beak.

Tiger swallowtails sip nectar from a variety of flowers, but they also visit trees to lay their eggs. One researcher has said that tiger swallowtails can be found anywhere there are trees.

After the adults lay eggs and die in late summer, the caterpillars hatch and feed at night on leaves of lilac, aspen, birch, and cherry. In the fall they form a chrysalis that protects them throughout the winter.

The tiger swallowtail butterfly derives its name from resemblances to a mammal and to a bird. How many plants or animals can you think of that are named for other plants and animals?

Notes

June

Mammal, bird, reptile, and fish babies vary from adults mainly in size. Amphibians and insects, however, have several distinct stages. The white grubs that are June bug larvae look nothing like the adult insects. How many larvae can you match with their adult form?

7 The large beetles that visit during warm nights of early June are the June bugs (or May beetles). About one inch long and stout, their thick reddish brown exoskeleton is characteristic of beetles. Beetles belong to the order *Coleoptera*, which means sheath-wing.

We usually see them after we've heard them: these are the large bugs that fly into window screens. The beetles, which feed on leaves of several kinds of trees in the yard, are distracted by house lights as they fly by. Confused by the light, they keep trying to get in until, exhausted, they fall to the ground. We hear the buzzing sound of their wings in this futile attempt to get inside.

Their larvae are the white grubs that many a gardener has turned up in the garden. Here the beetles live three years feeding on living and dead organic material. Given the mild days and short nights in June, we are likely to spend evenings outside where we will see these residents that share the yard with us.

Notes

June

8 We all know that trees grow, but at this time of year we can actually see it happening. Unlike us and many other animals, trees continue to grow during every year of their long lives.

Trees grow in three ways. They grow down and out at the tips of their roots. Obviously, we cannot see this process. Trees become wider in the trunk or stem, and we can see this, but only by counting the annual rings when a tree is cut. Trees grow taller and spread out wider at the tip of each twig; this increase is visible in the new growth that appears at this time each year.

Growth tissue is called meristem; it is located in the soft new material near the end of the twig. In the sunlight and rains of spring, a fast-growing new shoot may extend two feet in one season. Because of its slightly different green, we can detect this new growth, which is especially visible on pines, where it is called candles. This spurt of energy fades, and the tree waits a year before it again grows taller.

When a tree is cut, you can read the trials and tribulations of its life in the growth rings. During years of stress from drought or insect infestation, little growth occurs, so rings are close together.

Notes

June

Environmentalists have helped protect baby sea turtles on their journey to water. Could you give a safe journey to painted turtles, or is there another critter that needs a helping hand?

9 In late spring, an animal that we expect to see in water wanders up on land. The female painted turtle sometimes drags her shell long distances to find an appropriate spot for her eggs. This walk is undoubtedly dangerous for her, and many turtles do not live to get back to the waters they left. Sandy soil seems to be best for digging, but painted turtles also lay eggs in lawns, golf courses, and rocky soil and even in roads and driveways.

Digging with her hind legs, she makes a depression and deposits the eggs. Then, without ever seeing them, she covers the eggs with soil. The warmth of the sun will serve as an incubator for the next three months. Usually eggs hatch in fall, but some do not hatch until next spring, and some never hatch. They may have been packed too tightly in the soil, or they may have been unearthed and eaten by animals such as skunks or raccoons which smell them underground.

When they do hatch, the inch-long baby turtles head for the safety of the nearest water. This walk is slow and dangerous, but they rely on their sixth sense of where the water is, enabling some to survive.

Notes

June

10 On warm June evenings, ponds, marshes, and shallow lakes echo with the sound of breeding gray tree frogs. Their call, similar to a loud wailing buzzer, declares mating and defines territory.

For a frog that spends much of its life in trees, gray tree frog seems an appropriate name. This simple name is often inaccurate, however, since the frog can also be green. These three- to four-inch-long frogs may be the northland's best example of critters that can change color. They tend to be grayer when they are on bark and greener when they are on leaves. It appears that the frog's skin cells are highly sensitive to the temperature of the material the frog is on and respond with changes in color. The benefit these changes provide is quite obvious: excellent camouflage.

Frogs deposit their eggs on these noisy nights, but soon they go back to arboreal living. By the end of the month, the ponds and marshes are silent. Even the tadpoles leave the water as they mature, joining the adults by late summer. We may see gray tree frogs in the next few months, but only during June will we see and hear them in ponds and marshes.

It seems incongruous—frogs in trees—but that's where the gray tree frog lives. Can you think of any other critters that live in unexpected places?

Notes

June

Forest tent caterpillars are actually quite pretty if you can get past the fact that they are devouring the leaves on your trees. Some critters can be appreciated individually but are tough to take in bunches.

11 A tent caterpillar is the larval form of an inconspicuous brown hairy moth about one inch long. It is these larvae, not the moths, that are well known. We have two kinds in the northland. As they feed, eastern tent caterpillars form tents of silk at the base of branches on cherry and apple trees. Forest tent caterpillars lay down silken mats and trails as they travel. These larvae feed voraciously on leaves of alder, poplar, oak, willow, birch, ash, aspen, and maple—with the last two of these reputed to be their favorites. During peak population years, they defoliate entire forests, and we call them army worms.

Populations vary widely, with a population explosion occurring about every ten years. Dangerous population levels would occur more often if were it not for a striped fly, the sergeant fly, that lays eggs in the cocoon, stopping the development of the forest tent caterpillar.

These caterpillars have hairy blue-black bodies about one inch long. Eastern tent caterpillars have a light line the length of the body, whereas the forest tent caterpillars display a series of diamond markings instead.

Notes

June

12 In the acid soil of swamps and forests, grow three kinds of lady's slipper orchids: pink, yellow, and showy. They have several things in common. The flowers of each are composed of two types of petals. Those that stick out sideways are colored differently from the large lower petals. The lower petals join to form an inflated ball-like lip.

These lips are the pink and yellow shoe of lady's slippers, which are also know as moccasin flowers, and they facilitate one of the dependent relationships of the plant. Their large size and bright colors attract bees and encourage them to investigate. The bees enter near the middle of the lip, but because of obstacles, they can exit only at another opening near the center of the flower. Here the bees collect pollen as they leave, which they then carry to the next flower.

Yellow and showy lady's slippers have stem leaves; the pink lady's slipper's leaves are basal. All lady's slippers have a fungus growing on their roots that allows them to absorb nutrients. So dependent are the orchids on this fungus that the roots cannot function without it, and the tiny seeds need it to germinate.

Wetland preservation and restoration focuses on wildlife, particularly ducks and geese. But many plants also require a marshy habitat. Drain the marshes and we will lose the lady slipper's orchids.

Notes

June

13 A small bird that feeds on bugs and has a loud, energetic, and beautiful song is destined to be a favorite with the home owner. No surprise, then, that many of us put up birdhouses to attract the house wren.

The house wren is a small brown bird, usually less than five inches long, with few distinguishing marks. Its wings and tail are the easiest places on which to see the many dark bars that stripe the body. Wrens are light brown underneath with a stripe above the eye. House wrens do not carry their tail erect or cocked as frequently as other wrens do.

House wrens appear to be full of energy when we see them in the bushes and shrubs of yards, gardens, and parks. Their exuberant song has been described by listeners as a cascade of bubbling whistle notes. Wrens are cavity nesters, and if not able to find natural sites, they improvise well. They have been known to nest in many substitute cavities including a cow skull, the leg of work pants hanging on a clothesline, the pocket of a scarecrow, flowerpots, and even boots.

If you're hoping to attract a house wren or any other specific bird to your yard, don't just build a birdhouse, build the right birdhouse—the right size, the right material, the right size hole—and then put it in the right place.

Notes

June

14 Although we live with mosquitoes from spring thaw until fall freeze, they are probably most abundant in June. It is of little consolation that only twenty-eight of the fifty kinds of mosquitoes found in Minnesota bite humans.

Both male and female mosquitoes have a long mouth part called a proboscis. He feeds on plant sap, and she would do the same were it not that her developing eggs need blood protein. Although this blood can come from a variety of animals, she usually chooses the blood of warm-blooded animals, including humans. Such animals give off carbon dioxide and warmth that attract mosquitoes. Once the mosquito locates a host and lands, she feels for a soft spot and makes a slight cut. To keep blood from clotting, she injects an anticoagulant, then sucks enough blood to double her body weight. After digesting this transfusion, she lays her eggs in water, and she is then ready for another family.

Mosquitoes are by nature most active at dusk and dawn. Unfortunately, in shady forests, long June days may give mosquitoes the impression of a perpetual dawn and dusk.

Although mosquitoes can fly long distances, they may be breeding in small water containers and puddles in your yard.

Notes

June

Consider one similarity between plant and animal reproduction. Most female reproductive cells are created sparingly—one cell for each potential new individual. Male cells are produced in profligate numbers—thousands, even millions, at a time.

15 The main reason a plant produces flowers is to have a device for sexual reproduction, and for that purpose, it produces both male and female cells. Nonflowering plants also get variation and diversity from sexual reproduction, but lacking flowers, these plants use other means often mistakenly called flowers.

Pine trees do not flower, but each year in June they form male and female parts for sexual reproduction. Our three native pine trees—white, jack, and red (Norway)—all produce a large amount of yellow dusty pollen (male cells) from the male cones on the ends of their branches. These cones are only a half-inch long and grow in large clumps. Pollen blows from the male cones to the larger female or seed cones nearby, where new seeds are formed.

Using wind to hit a target is not highly effective, so more than 99 percent of the pollen blows elsewhere, missing the seed cones. Pollen falls everywhere, but we notice it most when it dusts a pond or lake, turning clear water the color of lemonade.

Notes

June

16 The nights of June are alive with fireflies. At the end of long June days these living lights appear. Fireflies, or lightning bugs, are named inaccurately since they are actually a type of beetle. They produce a cold light by combining a chemical called luciferin with luciferase (an enzyme) and oxygen. This controlled bioluminescence takes place in the fireflies' abdomen.

Though the how of firefly lighting is understood, there is still some question regarding the why, although it appears to be part of the mating ritual. Typically, the male flies and flashes his light for a specific duration and in a specific color while the female glows her response from the ground. These lights in the night can bring male and female together. Time, season, and variations in the flight distinguish the different species.

A deceptive light is used by the female of a type of predatory firefly; she mimics flashes of males of other species, enticing interested males who then become her next meal.

When the evening air seems filled with fireflies, watch them. Notice when, where, and for what duration they flash their lights.

Notes

June

Lupine leaves are described as palmate; the leaves radiate from a common point. Other plants have pinnate leaves; those leaves appear on alternate sides of a stem. This distinction is important if you want to use a plant identification guide effectively.

17 During June, large expanses of our local roadsides display blooming lupines which grow up to two feet tall in these poor soils. Lupines are members of the pea (legume) family. Late summer seed pods verify this relationship.

Although blue is the typical color of the lupine flower, purple, pink, white, and yellow appear as well on the spikelike cluster that extends above the leaves. Seven to eleven leaflets compose the large palmately compound leaves. These leaves, about five inches in diameter, follow the path of the sun from dawn to dusk, folding up at night.

The name lupine is old and appears to have originated with shepherds. *Lupus* is the Latin word for wolf. Shepherds, observing that lupines grew in poor wasteland, thought that the plant robbed the soil of nutrients, causing the soil to be poor. So they named this plant after something that robbed them of their sheep—the wolf. Actually, lupines have nodules of nitrogen-fixing bacteria on their roots that put nitrogen into the soil and so improve it. With a complex network of roots, once lupines are established they will persist.

Notes

18 A porch light left on all night in early summer may attract the large green luna moth. Its palm-sized wings are light green, outlined with purplish brown. Clear eye spots mark each wing and the hind wings are drawn out into long sweeping curved tails. The thick white body has large feathery antennae.

Luna moths are named after the moon for what appears to be two reasons: the green camouflage that allows them to sit still all day and fly at night makes them rare in the daytime; and the curves at the edges of the extended hind wings remind some observers of waxing and waning moon phases.

Large and beautiful, the luna moth is also well designed by nature. Its body contains stored food from last summer which not only helped it survive the winter in the cocoon but sustains it now. Having no mouth, adults do not live long. After mating, the female uses the last of her energy to deposit her eggs. Caterpillars hatch and feast on the leaves of alder, aspen, willow, and birch before forming a leafy cocoon that is concealed all winter by ground leaf litter.

A human spends nine months as a fetus, twenty years or so as a child, and perhaps sixty or eighty years as an adult. How different life is for insects. Adult insects often lead brief lives. The beautiful luna moth, the climax of the species' life cycle, lives only one week.

Notes

June

Garden iris demonstrate the results of hybridization. The flowers are much larger than those of wild iris, and they are available in many colors. Some hybrids are less hardy than their wild cousins, but others have been bred for hardiness as well as beauty.

19 One of the most attractive wildflowers is found in one of the least accessible places. The iris displays its colors in often impassable wetlands, where it adds blue to the mundane marsh. We, unfortunately, are limited to distant roadside visits unless we prepare ourselves with wading boots.

Yellow-white centered sepals fill in the otherwise blue flowers. It is no surprise that these plants are also called blue flag. It must have been the rainbow pattern in the sepals that suggested the name iris. Leaves of the iris are grasslike, similar in appearance to small cattails; they grow to be only two feet tall.

Because iris grow from underground tubers and rhizomes, they can survive the winter, flourishing in large interconnected patches. Laterally, the rhizomes claim more of the marsh for their own each year.

After displaying their presence in the marsh for a month, irises fade. Pollinated flowers give way to the podded fruits and seeds of late summer.

Notes

20 The daisy, a familiar summer flower with a yellow center surrounded by white rays, now blooms in the fields and meadows. A composite, the daisy is not a single flower, but a combination of two different types of flowers. The ball-like yellow center is actually composed of many tiny, but complete, flowers. These are called disk flowers and contain male and female parts. Often called petals, the fifteen to thirty white ray flowers are female only. Each has a small Y-shaped structure, the pistil, at the base of each ray.

The word daisy is derived from an early name, day's eye. The yellow center represents the sun; because the flower closes at night, the flower is said to possess the day's eye. Another name, oxeye, suggests that the yellow center looks like the eye of an ox, although most oxen have brown eyes.

Introduced from Europe, the daisy has been extremely successful in this country and grows in nearly every field, meadow, and roadside during June. It is a center of attention for bees, wasps, butterflies, moths, flies, and spiders, all of whom visit regularly.

"He loves me, he loves me not." Perhaps it is because plants surround us that they are part of our folklore. Daisies tell us about love; four-leaved clovers predict good luck. Do you know any other sayings or rituals that refer to plants?

Notes

June

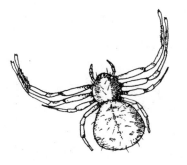

Join the insects visiting a sunny meadow full of wildflowers. Sit right on the ground. Watch quietly and listen. You'll be amazed at the many insects you will see.

21 Daisies at the edge of the meadow are constantly visited by butterflies, bees, and flies. At one daisy, a hapless bee has been immobilized by the local predator— a crab spider. Crab spiders are so named because they hold their legs laterally.

Many kinds of crab spiders exist, but a white one is most common on a daisy in June. These spiders do not make webs but depend on deception to catch insects. They remain still on the flower and wait until an insect visits for nectar, then grab it and inject venom from their fangs. Venom not only subdues the victim but also liquefies its insides so the spider can then dine by sucking it dry. The hollow insect skin (exoskeleton) is cast off.

If found sitting on a black-eyed Susan, the white crab spider will be yellow. This color change helps with deception, but no matter what the spider's color, two pink stripes are always on the abdomen. The female is twice the size of the male, and she is more likely to be seen hunting on flowers. She even chooses to lay her eggs there.

Notes

22 Sunrise arrives very early on these long days of June. In anticipation of the new day, many songbirds begin to sing in the predawn light. As early as a quarter past four, the wood peewee welcomes the day with its plaintive call.

The wood peewee is a well-named bird. This little flycatcher lives in mature forests and sings a clear and slow "pee-wee" or "pee-a-wee." During the calm of these early mornings, it is easy to hear the wood peewee's call. That call may be the only sign of the little bird's presence; we are not likely to see such a small, plain bird in the big forest. The peewee is about six inches long, and nearly all its plumage is dull gray-brown except for a light throat and belly.

After its early morning performance, the peewee is quiet for much of the day until it offers a musical encore at dusk.

The wood peewee nests in large trees. A small nest belonging to a small bird in a tall tree is even harder to find than the bird itself.

The wood peewee is named for its song as is the chickadee. If you were to name the critters around your home for the sounds they make, what would those names be?

Notes

June

Do you have a favorite flavor of honey? Because the nectar bees collect depends on the locale and the season, the honey they make varies in taste and color. Basswood, alfalfa, raspberry, and more—choose the taste that you like best.

23

Raspberries and blackberries will not ripen until later in the summer, but now they are in full bloom as they prepare for this event.

They are both members of the rose family, and each has flowers of five white petals.

Blackberry flowers are large, more than one inch across, while raspberry flowers are so small that we easily miss them. However, bumblebees and a host of other insects do not overlook these blossoms. The flowers, which possess many long stamens, are readily pollinated and usually produce large numbers of berries.

If conditions are not good and the plants that bloom so well now do not make berries, they will reproduce anyway. Both the raspberry and the blackberry have perennial underground stems that send up branches called canes. These canes grow during the first year of their two-year life span and in the second year produce flowers and berries. At the end of the second season, the branches die, but they are quickly replaced. These growing, fruiting, and dead canes form a network of arching, prickly brambles that make it difficult to walk through berry patches.

Notes

June

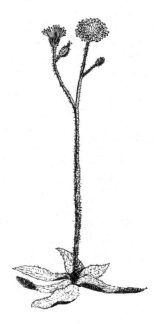

24 Because the forest is now shady, June wildflowers grow best in open meadows and fields. A drive down side roads takes us through scenes tinted yellow, white, and orange, all blended with green.

Many different wildflowers contribute to this landscape. Daisies bloom white and buttercups yellow, but orange hawkweed dominates in June. Most of the flowers that make up this colorful meadow are aliens and are considered weeds. This realization reminds us that a weed is a wildflower that is not appreciated.

Orange hawkweed may have been brought here from Europe by herbal doctors who used it as a cure for eye diseases. The belief that orange plants were good for eyesight and that birds with good sight, such as hawks, drank the juice led to both the name and the medicinal use of orange hawkweed. It is also called Indian paintbrush or devil's paintbrush. While the former name belongs to another plant, the latter name describes ranchers' disdain for this composite that, because it is avoided by cows, spreads like dandelions, taking over the pasture.

Summer wildflowers are as hardy as spring wildflowers are fragile. Pick daisies, buttercups, and orange hawkweed by the armful and bring summer sunshine inside.

Notes

June

How many times have you seen the frothy spit of a spittlebug and not investigated? Let your curiosity run free and you'll learn a lot about the natural world.

25 When we look among the meadow wildflowers during June, it is not unusual to see what appears to be a mass of frothy spit. The foamy suds appear on the stem of nearly any meadow plant and also on bushes and trees. Though there are folk stories regarding its source, the froth is not made by the plant but is formed by a small insect living on the stem—the spittlebug or froghopper.

Gray-brown oval adult spittlebugs are one-fourth inch long. Last fall, the females deposited their eggs on the stems of plants, near the ground. A small green nymph developed in each egg.

The nymph gets plenty of food from the sap of the stem but needs more protection. So, in one of nature's more creative ways, it makes its own house. Excreted sap is mixed with an intestinal enzyme to produce a soapy liquid. Using its abdomen, the nymph blows air into this mixture, covering itself with foamy bubbles that provide a protective shelter. Many a would-be predator is deterred by this spitlike covering.

By midsummer, nymphs have matured, and the spit is gone.

Notes

26 Thrushes are well-known songbirds that often sing loud, melodious songs from deep in the woods. Several kinds familiar in the northland include the wood thrush, Swainson's thrush, hermit thrush, and veery. Since all are about seven inches long, wear brown or red-brown on their backs with spots on their undersides, and sing variations of flutelike songs, they can be hard to tell from each other.

The veery stands out as being the most different. It is more red-brown, not as spotted, and less of a flute player. Instead, the song of the veery is usually described as being a rolling series of descending "veer" notes; thus the name.

Although the veery is one of the early morning songsters, it is best known from its song at dusk. Often it sings for more than half an hour after sunset as though trying to revive a dying day. Since the veery is a resident of shady forests, it is more likely to be heard than seen. It is, however, the most common of the four kinds of thrushes in the northland, and many of us enjoy the veery as a regular June evening guest.

It's pretty obvious that you're more likely to hear a veery if you live near a forest preserve than if you live in a newly developed area that was planted with saplings. For most of us, however, fields and forest are just a short walk or brief drive from our home. It's worth the walk or drive to hear a veery.

Notes

June

Although caterpillars gobble up leaves, butterflies don't have jaws or teeth, so they live on a liquid diet. You may try to attract white admiral butterflies with half a peach. You might, of course, get ants instead of butterflies.

27 White admiral butterflies are common along the roadside during late June. Here they spread their wings and bask in the warmth of the sunlight or feed on the minerals available. Unfortunately, passing cars take a heavy toll.

The white admiral (also known as banded purple) is a black butterfly with a large white band across each of its four wings. This pattern is similar whether seen from above or below. Like other purple butterflies, it has a row of red spots on the hind wings.

Although we often see the white admiral along the roadside, it is mostly a butterfly of the woods. It basks on the trunks of trees and feeds on light-colored forest flowers but has some other options for food as well. These include sap, rotting fruit, dung, and even the honeydew from aphids. These butterflies are also attracted to sweat and visit clothes hanging outside.

Adult white admirals are not with us long: within a month, they lay their eggs and die. The larvae (caterpillars) eat leaves of poplar, hawthorn, basswood, or juneberry.

Notes

June

28 Most of us recognize that song sparrows and savannah sparrows are common in the northland. Each of these brown birds has a streaked breast with a large central spot that makes the birds hard to distinguish from each other. The savannah sparrow, however, has a shorter notched tail, streaks on the head, and a small yellow mark above the eye.

The biggest differences may not be in their bodily features but in their lifestyles. Their choice of habitat and their songs make it possible for us to distinguish one from the other. The song sparrow nests in small trees in yards while the savannah sparrow nests in fields and meadows. The song sparrows' nests are built a few feet off the ground while savannah sparrows' nests are on the ground.

The song sparrow's melody starts off with a series of short, clear, repetitive notes followed by a buzzy "towee" and ending with a trill; the savannah sparrow has just a buzzy trill. Each bird sings often during the breeding season and even sings at midday.

The song sparrow is well named; the savannah sparrow is not. An early ornithologist collected a specimen in Savannah, Georgia, where the birds winter but do not breed.

If birds all built their nests six feet off the ground, the trees would be filled at that level and empty elsewhere. Instead, birds like the savannah sparrow nest on the ground. Others like the song sparrow nest in low tree branches, and still others live at many other level throughout the forest canopy, making the most of available territory and food.

Notes

June

Where do you stand on a controversy that has been around since pioneer days—what should be done with wild strawberries? Do you eat 'em in the fields, still warm with summer sunshine, or do you capture that sunshine in strawberry preserves and serve it up on snowy winter days?

29 Only a few weeks ago, we saw the five white petals of blooming wild strawberries. They blossomed in the meadow when most of the early spring wildflowers were blossoming in the woods. Now in late June, we find ripe wild strawberries in these same meadows. Strawberry plants spread by lateral branches called runners and, therefore, grow in large groups or patches. In these meadow patches, strawberries take advantage of warm June rains and long hours of daylight to produce berries.

The first ripe strawberry, discovered and sampled, marks the beginning of the berry season. Many local residents (human and otherwise) will continue to search avidly for berries during the next several weeks.

Wild strawberries have a red pulpy texture with seeds on the outside, much like their tame cousins, but with two noticeable differences. Wild berries tend to be sweeter in taste. Wild strawberries are also small, often about the size of a fingertip. It's more work to pick a quart of them—but well worth it.

Notes

June

30 Ponds, swamps, and shallow lakes get plenty of sunlight during this month and, like the fields and meadows, respond with prolific plant life. In many ponds, white and yellow water lilies bloom in late June. Actually, despite their names, neither kind is a lily.

The white water lily's circular leaves are about a foot in diameter with a deep cut from base to edge. Its large white flowers are composed of many sepals and petals that, like the leaves, float on the surface. Until they have been pollinated, open flowers close in the midafternoon

The yellow water lily (also known as pond or bullhead lily) has only five or six sepals with many small fleshy petals in its flower. The long heart-shaped leaves float, but the flower extends above the water's surface.

Once pollinated, both water lilies pull their flowers underwater where the seeds are formed. Seeds are dispersed by the water, and the plants survive the winter under the ice.

Visit a pond at various times during the day. You'll find that some flowers, such as the white water lily, are open only in the morning; others open under the midday sun; still others remain closed until dusk.

Notes

July

July

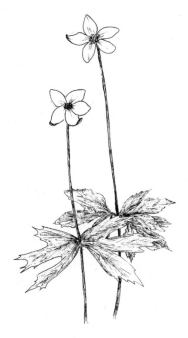

When we think of flowers, we often focus on their showy petals. The anemones remind us that flowers are parts of plants modified for reproduction. Petals are not essential to this process.

1 Early spring wood anemones are long gone, but anemones are still with us. In early July, damp roadsides and meadows sport a lovely white flower that stands one to two feet tall. Five sepals, no petals, and big deeply cut leaves clasping the stem are characteristic of the Canada anemone.

Also known as the Canada windflower, it fills large sections of roadside meadows with one-inch blossoms that persist for a month. With all the other flowers blooming in such meadows, this one can get overlooked by us.

An even less noticeable cousin, the thimbleweed, is another anemone that blooms along the roadsides now. Unlike the Canada anemone, thimbleweed grows up to three feet tall, but because it has greenish sepals and no petals and grows as solitary plants, it blends in with the rest of the foliage.

Thimbleweed remains inconspicuous until its one-inch-long thimble-shaped fruits announce its presence. These fruits become hairy as they mature in late summer.

Notes

July

2 By the time July arrives, the hectic pace of caring for the young and continuing to sing has slowed in the bird life around us. The young of most birds have fledged, and although they still demand some care, they are getting more independent.

When the young mature, birds' activities change: they no longer need territories as before. Having less need to declare their home base, birds sing less, and songs that have been with us for nearly two months slowly fade.

Some, of course, do persist: the yellowthroat continues to shout its "witchity, witchity, witchity" from the marshes and tall grasses. Even after its family has been raised, this bird remains to feed, proclaiming its presence long after most birds have stopped. Its habitat is unusual for a warbler since most warblers are forest residents.

As might be expected, the yellowthroat is bright yellow underneath. The males alone hide their eyes with a large black mask.

Those beautiful bird songs that seem meant to entertain us are basically just a mating call. We're just lucky to listen in. We're fortunate that a few birds, like the yellowthroat, continue to sing through this part of summer.

Notes

July

Many flowers are apparently without fragrance, at least to human noses. A single specimen of the tiny twinflower might also seem to be unscented, but when drifts cover the forest floor, the lovely fragrance permeates the woods.

3 The boreal forest floor is not a place where we expect to find wildflowers blooming during the summer, but one that does do well here is the tiny flower known as twinflower.

Twinflower gets its name from the flowers that are borne in pairs on a short stalk a few inches above a creeping stem. Nodding, bell-shaped flowers about a half-inch long are white with tinges of pink. The slightly larger elliptical leaves are evergreen, as are those of several other summer boreal flowers.

A perennial with a creeping stem, twinflowers form mats that cover a significant area of the forest floor and may be many years old. In early July, their many tiny flowers give color and fragrance to coniferous forests.

Linnaea, the genus name for this plant, refers to Carolus Linnaeus of Sweden who developed the modern system of plant classification. Of the thousands of plants that he described and classified, it is said that this little flower was his favorite.

Notes

July

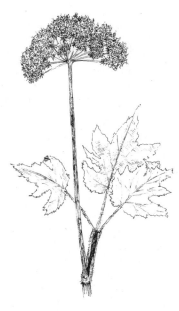

4 Other roadside plants may be as tall as the cow parsnip, but when it comes to sheer bulk, none equals it. This gigantic plant grows up to ten feet tall with a hollow stem approaching two inches thick at the base. Its colossal dimensions are consistent: the foot-long, maple-like leaves attach to the stem in an inflated point. It's hard to believe that a plant of such mass grows to this size during one season. Bears are one of the few animals able to eat such a large plant.

Cow parsnip is a member of the mustard family (as are carrots and cabbage). Its flowers are borne in umbrellalike clusters nearly a foot across called umbels. Looking at these flowers, more than one casual observer has mistaken cow parsnip for Queen Anne's lace, which is related but does not grow in most of the northland. After flowering from June to August, the umbels hold small seeds on big stems that stand through much of the winter.

How many mistakes do we make? We misidentify a plant, learn the wrong name, and use it forever. Do you call this roadside plant cow parsnip or did you think it was Queen Anne's lace?

Notes

July

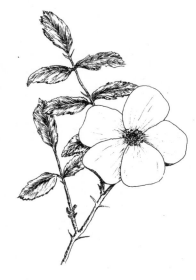

Wild roses have them, so do raspberries and blackberries. Yet, strawberries and blueberries do not. What are they? Thorns, of course. Although the flowers lure insects for pollination, the thorns discourage browsing mammals.

5 Roses are so well-known as a flower of cultivated gardens that we tend to forget their wild cousin, but each July we are reminded of its presence by the big pink flowers that bloom on prickly shrubs along roadsides. The three-foot tall bushes dismay solitary flowers among the compound leaves and woody stems. Unlike many garden roses, the wild variety has only five petals on the two-inch wide flowers.

These long-blooming flowers offer us an excellent opportunity to watch pollination by insects. The fragrant showy petals attract their attention, and the flower provides ample space for the critters to alight and collect nectar. Many well-developed pistils in the center are surrounded by numerous stamens coated with pollen. It is difficult for a visiting insect not to get pollen on its body, but since the stamens are bent away from the pistils, the insects are likely to carry pollen to another flower. The pollinator, most likely a bumblebee, therefore assures cross-pollination and not self-pollination; the former process promises us roses with more variety and stronger offspring.

Notes

July

6 By the time July arrives, frog songs exist only as memories of spring. The ear-splitting calls and trills that emanated from crowded ponds are now long gone, but one frog that began calling in late spring still calls. The green frog plucks out its call, often compared to the twang of a loose banjo string, well into the midsummer nights.

The green frog gets its name from the green color that usually appears on the head or face. The body colors vary, and many times, despite their name, these frogs are not green. Even the green on the face can be nearly absent.

The bullfrog is usually not found in the northland, but the green frog—about the same color—is often called by that name. With a three-inch-long body it is much smaller than the huge bullfrog but is the northland's largest specimen.

Highly aquatic, our green frog is not likely to be seen far from large bodies of water. It plucks its banjo on the shores of lakes, rivers, and wet swamps where it breeds.

Green frog tadpoles spend a full year in the tadpole stage before becoming frogs. No doubt many of those tadpoles become meals for other critters and don't make it to adulthood.

Notes

July

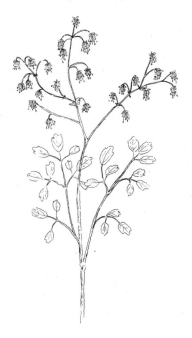

Male birds are often larger and brighter than females of the same species. In meadow rue, we find a similar situation in the plant world. Only the male meadow rue plant has showy blossoms.

7 When we meet a member of the buttercup family, we expect to see a flower with colorful petals, but the tall meadow rue is completely bereft of petals.

Not only does this strange family member flower without petals, it also bears the male and female flowers on separate plants. Dioecious trees are common, but it is unusual for herbaceous plants of the buttercup group to be dioecious. Both male and female plants grow to be nearly six feet tall; each is covered with many small three-lobed leaves. The male plant's flowers have purplish sepals filled with numerous white threadlike stamens; the effect is that of a plant covered with fuzzy balls. The female plant, which has pistil flowers that are almost the color of the foliage, is seen much less often.

Tall meadow rue adds its unconventional flowers to the roadside botanical scene that is so rich in midsummer. Its flowers last until August, and even without petals, they buzz with insect activity.

Notes

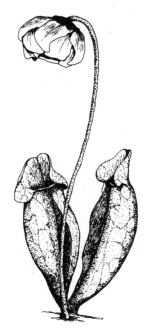

8 Most wildflowers are better known by their blossoms than by their leaves, but, even though the pitcher plant has large flowers, it is the leaves that give this plant its fame. Nearly a foot long and formed like a hollow pitcher, the leaves are heavily veined with red or purple and are often half full of water. Nodding three-inch flowers with large purple petals and a huge flat pistil grow at the top of a two-foot stalk. These flowers and leaves make the plant impressive enough, but it is what the plant does—it eats insects—that makes us take note.

Flower and leaf odors entice insects to enter the hollow leaves, where slippery walls with downward-pointing bristles keep them trapped. Eventually, the unfortunate prey fall into liquids and are quickly digested by powerful enzymes that make needed nutrients available to the plant. Growing in a bog as it does, the pitcher plant apparently does not get enough nutrients from the acidic soil, so it supplements its diet with these snacks.

A powerful flashlight will enable you to peer into the pitcher plant as well as into other dark recesses like burrows in the ground and holes in trees.

Notes

July

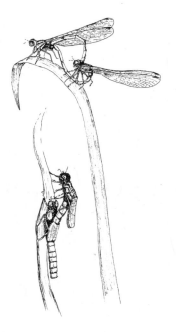

Next time you visit a stream, notice the dragonflies and damselflies. Identify each species by how they hold their wings.

9 Midsummer heat in meadows and marshes may slow us down, but it has not lessened the activity of insects, including bees, butterflies, dragonflies, and their cousins—the damselflies.

Half the size of dragonflies and narrow bodied, damselflies appear to be dainty and weak fliers; hence the name. Dragonflies hold their wings out sideways, perpendicular to their bodies when they are at rest; damselflies hold theirs parallel to their bodies. The thin abdomens of damselflies are often brightly colored with blues and reds.

Damselflies are never far from the water of their youth. Nymphs survive winter in ponds or lakes and emerge as adults in early summer. The predaceous life of the nymph continues when it becomes an adult and feeds on small insects near the water. Often, as it patrols its domain, a damselfly will land on a boat, dock, or angler.

Male damselflies use a tail clasper to grasp the female behind her head. Copulation takes place in the air, and they may fly in tandem for days before dropping eggs in water.

Notes

July

10 With a tiny green body, a long bill, and a red bib on the males, the ruby-throated hummingbird is a showy bird. But we are not likely to see it, and because it has such a little song, we do not hear it sing either. Rather, the tiny hummer is heard beating its wings more that a hundred times per second and thus earning its name. The tiny bird has powerful wings but such weak legs that, even though it can perch, it cannot walk.

Its incredible wing beat allows for amazing aerial maneuvers: the hummingbird is able to fly forward or backward, up or down, and even hover. All these movements are needed as it uses its long bill to feed on the nectar of flowers. Many flowers are visited, but now, in July, jewelweed and day lilies are hummingbird favorites.

Hummingbird females place their two-inch nest on a branch about fifteen feet from the ground. To us, the nest looks like a small knot on the tree. In this lichen-covered home, she raises her young on a nectar-rich diet. The male does nothing to help with family duties.

If you want to attract hummingbirds to your yard, plant flowers that they find appealing. If you choose to place a feeder near your window, consider supplying a commercial food that offers more than simple sugars.

Notes

July

Spiders make good subjects for observation. They also model patient waiting. Do you have the patience to watch them until their next meal arrives? They must wait. Can you?

11 In the marsh, on a dew-covered early morning, the plants droop and drip with sunlit sparkles. Attached to the foliage, a large circular spiderweb sags with clinging night water.

These circular webs are called orbs, and though usually constructed vertically to the ground, this one is at an angle between vertical and horizontal. A spider called the long-jawed spider made this web at dusk last night and kept vigil until dew settled in. The big web is two feet in diameter; fifteen spokes reach to the hub where the owner usually sits. The spider now, however, stretches its long legs and body on a nearby plant, and we can easily see why it is also called stilt spider. A half-inch-long body appears three times longer with these legs.

Technically, spiders have no jaws, but they have fangs on structures called chelicera. Long-jawed spiders use big chelicera with fangs to subdue prey.

Dew-covered webs make for good pictures but are not effective for hunting. At dusk, the long-jawed spider will disassemble the old web and assemble a new one for more hunting and waiting.

Notes

12 Among the most common roadside plants of midsummer are the sweet clovers. Sweet clovers are biennials and grow to be four feet tall during their second year. In the northland, yellow and white sweet clovers bloom from June until September.

The tiny flowers are formed on long clusters at the top of the stem. This is different from the ball-shaped arrangement seen on many other clovers. However, similar to many clovers, the leaves grow in groups of three. Sweet clovers are members of the pea family (legumes), and like other members of this family, they have nitrogen-fixing bacteria on the roots that add nitrogen to the soil and thus enrich it.

At one time, sweet clovers were widely used on dairy farms for pasturage and for hay. They have now been largely replaced by alfalfa. One critter, though, that definitely does not ignore the sweet clovers is the honeybee. When sweet clovers were extensively grown, beekeepers could get two hundred pounds of honey per colony. The name sweet clover refers to this property and even the Latin name, *Melilotus*, means honey plant.

Apparently alfalfa is more prolific or more nutritious for cattle, but a hayloft filled with sweet clover hay is a symbol of summer that one might feel nostalgic about.

Notes

July

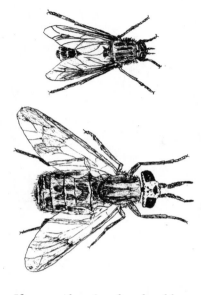

If you can bear it, take a hand lens along on a summer hike and watch a horsefly take a bite out of your leg.

13 A couple of lesser-loved critters of midsummer are the deerflies and their larger cousins, the horseflies. We identify these insects as flies because they have only two wings; most insects have four.

Horseflies are large and may reach a length of one inch; deerflies are about half that size. Each has huge colorful eyes and mostly clear wings. A close look shows us that the wings are quite beautiful.

While the males are content to feed on nectar and the pollen of flowers, the females use their sharp mouth parts to cut skin and suck the blood oozing from the wound. To form eggs, these females need more protein than is found in flowers. Many mammals, including humans, serve as blood donors, and these flies are named for common victims. We know as deerflies the bugs that fly around our heads and even get caught in our hair as they try to bite. Horseflies are more direct in their flight and bite ankles and legs rather than heads.

Both flies winter as aquatic predatory larvae, pupate in the spring, and emerge in June to spend the midsummer in wet areas. Strong fliers, they range widely.

Notes

July

14 Skippers—small butterflies that get their name from their rather erratic, jumping type of flight—may be the most common butterflies of midsummer. Many people believe that skippers are not true butterflies because they have a type of antennae different from that of other butterflies, as well as a resting pose that differs. Most butterflies bask with their wings out flat, but skippers bask with hindwings flat and forewings perpendicular.

Skippers are abundant with approximately two hundred and fifty kinds found in the United States. Three of the most common ones are the northern golden, the long dash, and the European. All are less than an inch in length with patterns of yellow-gold on the wings. The northern gold and long dash are butterflies of the woods edge. Each has a gold-and-brown pattern, but the northern gold displays more yellow. The European is common in grassy fields and sports wings of only yellow-gold.

The European skipper was brought to this country early this century. It has been very successful and may be our most common butterfly. Basking or puddling sites may host hundreds of skippers on hot days.

When a new plant or animal is found, naming it can be a problem. Is it different enough from similar critters to call for a new species name? Could it even be part of a newly discovered family? Or are the differences merely superficial? Those questions have been asked about the skipper butterflies.

Notes

July

15 On farms, July days are often filled with hay-making. Two well-known plants, red clover and alfalfa, are often grown for hay. Though initially planted in farmers' fields, each escaped long ago and now grows along roadsides and in yards.

Red clover blooms earlier than does alfalfa; the red ball-shaped flowers that can be found almost any day from May to October are clusters of tiny red or purple florets. The plant grows to be two feet tall and has leaves grouped in threes.

Alfalfa, which does not bloom until June, offers more variety in its floral colors. Most are a deep purple, but flowers of pink, white, and yellow all exist in alfalfa fields. As tall as red clover, alfalfa has longer flower heads and leaves that are also grouped in threes.

Both red clover and alfalfa are imports and have been widely planted as hay crops. Each is a perennial that, when established in fields, will last for many years. Both plants contribute more than hay: they are good honey crops and, as legumes, add nitrogen to the soil.

Farmers don't find it efficient to grow alfalfa, soybeans, and corn in the same field at the same time. So they rotate crops, alternating hungry crops like corn with legumes. Unlike farmers, nature opts for the variety you'll see in a field of wildflowers.

Notes

July

16 Most trees blossom in spring so that by mid-July the fruiting season is far advanced, but one that waits until now to bloom is a large resident of the mature deciduous forest, the basswood.

Large heart-shaped leaves make the tree easy to identify but make the flowers harder to see. The umbel flower clusters hang from ribbonlike bracts that allow the fragrant creamy yellow blossoms to be easily discovered by bees— even if not to be so easily seen by us. Each small flower drips with nectar, and a basswood tree in mid-July draws hordes of bees and other insects who create a humming tree audible from many yards away. Most of the bees are honeybees; gourmets regard basswood honey to be the finest. July, with its warm days, is the best month for bee activity and so it is not a surprise that a tree depending on bees would wait until July to bloom.

Two common names of the tree, basswood and linden, both refer to the trees' wood. Basswood from bast wood, tells of the tree's fibrous nature. Linden indicates that the wood is light.

Several times each season beekeepers remove frames filled with honey from hives. That's how they can separate basswood honey from other flowers.

Notes

July

Next time you hear a red-eyed vireo's call, begin counting. How many times is it repeated in fifteen minutes or an hour? Who gives up first— you or the bird?

17 A common resident of forest and parks, the red-eyed vireo has been with us since the middle of May. From then until now, its song has been heard from the treetops each day, even in hot July when most songbirds stop singing.

The song is a short, often repeated phrase that has been compared to the bird's saying, "See me, hear me," with pauses between. It appears to get carried away with the song, restating this monotonous message for hours each day; the vireo has been known to repeat it more than twenty thousand times. Such repetition has led to the bird's nickname—the preacher bird. Though the sermon that began in spring and continued through the cool and hot days is still being preached, it is slowing down. Birds sing with less intensity now than earlier in the summer. By mid-July, the young have fledged, but adults will preach a few more weeks.

Red-eyed vireo is a name that combines two colors and two languages. The eye of the adult is red; the body, green. *Vireo* is Latin for green. Both sexes wear a gray cap over a white line above the eye.

Notes

July

18 In mid-July, the first mushrooms appear in woods and yards. Some of the earliest and most colorful are the small waxy caps: red, orange, and yellow mushrooms that grow in groups straight from the ground, not on dead wood. Waxy caps are a varied group of mushrooms, and though often brightly colored, they are also seen in drab browns and grays. Cap shapes vary from flat to conelike with surfaces that may be wet, sticky, or dry. The caps are less than three inches across. Gills, colored the same as the cap, are attached to its underside and connected to the top of the stalk.

Mushroom spores (seeds) form under the cap on tiny growths between the gills and fall off when ripe. If the cap is removed and placed, gills down, on a paper, spores fall on the paper and make what is called a spore print. Spore prints show us the color of the spores and are helpful in identifying mushrooms.

Because the spores of waxy caps are white, place the caps on dark paper when you make a spore print. If you don't know the color of a mushroom's spores, pick two and place one on dark and one on light paper.

Notes

July

Fritillaries deposit their eggs on only one plant species—violets. Other critters are equally specialized in their feeding, housing, or breeding requirements. Doesn't this kind of specialization make reproduction more difficult instead of easier?

19 On a summer day, the meadow is filled with myriads of insects. Joining the grasshoppers, bees, and flies are the less numerous, but more obvious, butterflies. Fritillaries, large orange-brown butterflies, are sure to get our attention. Their wings are orange with a black-brown pattern of lines that include arcs, zigzags, and checkerspots. The name fritillary refers to these checkerspots. The underwing pattern of numerous silver-white spots and lines is unique.

Three large fritillaries—the aphrodite, atlantis, and great-spangled—are quite common in the northland. Smaller ones, the silver-bordered, meadow and little crescent, live here too.

Although adult fritillaries feed in the meadow, in the late summer, shortly before they die, they go to the woods to deposit eggs on violets. The eggs hatch in the fall, and dormant caterpillars survive the winter. They begin feeding in spring with the growth of new violets, and adults emerge in summer and return to the meadow.

Notes

_____

_____

_____

_____

July

20 In late May, ponds and swamps resonated to the trills of toads. They claimed a territory and, with an invited mate, proceeded to string eggs in the shallows. Now in July, we can see the next chapter in this continuing story.

Within a week after the eggs were laid, they hatched, and the tiny dark tadpoles blended in with the fauna of the pond. They grew quickly on a diet of algae and in July are ready to begin metamorphosis. Externally, they gain four legs while, internally, they lose their gills and algal appetite. From the swimming, algae-eating tadpole of June emerges the hopping, insect-eating toad of July.

At first, they continue to live at the edge of their home ponds. The young toads get used to breathing and eating new food. During this adjustment time, they absorb nutrients from their now useless tails. Since hunting is difficult in the wetlands, they move to better grounds, so at this time we may see many fingernail-sized toads making their exodus from the pond. As veterans of life in the pond, the toads have survived many dangers there, but now they must face the perils of life on land as they hunt and continue to grow until fall.

Set your mind at rest: toads do not cause warts. But wash your hands after handling a toad as a poisonous substance on its skin could be irritating. This material comes from a gland behind their eyes.

Notes

_____

_____

_____

_____

July

21 Last month, buttercups and hawkweeds painted roadsides and meadows yellow and orange. Now in July, it is the black-eyed Susans that add color to the country scene.

Unlike many other meadow flowers, the black-eyed Susan is a native of North America. It is not really black: a close look shows its center to be more of a purple-brown, and it is often called the brown-eyed Susan.

With widespread roots, the plant does well in dry sandy soil and grows to be two feet tall with three-inch wide flowers. A composite, the dark disk flowers in the center of each blossom are surrounded by yellow ray flowers. While the disk flowers are true flowers and are both male and female, the ray flowers are neither. These ten to twenty sterile rays only attract pollinators, but they do that task well. The flowers experience a constant flow of traffic from bees, wasps, flies, butterflies, and moths. Though needing flying insects, the plant apparently does not appreciate crawling ones, and the stiff hairs on its stem discourage them.

When you find a plant with an unusual characteristic, such as the black-eyed Susan with its hairy stem, don't walk by without asking yourself why. Then check your reasoning in a reference book.

Notes

July

22 Wolf spiders that matured this spring now reproduce in midsummer. After surviving winter as subadults, they grew and molted. Now they are ready to mate and produce eggs.

Like many nocturnal spiders, they mate at night, and like many other spiders, they produce their eggs in a sac; but unlike most spiders, who hide their sacs in webs, the wolf spider carries hers.

The body of the wolf spider is black or brown, and the sac is gray or white. We can see it easily when she attaches it to her spinnerets (tail end). Carrying the sac for two to three weeks, she does most of her traveling and hunting at night, although we may occasionally see her in the daytime as she runs across a flat surface.

When the eggs hatch, she bites open the sac, and the twenty to thirty young emerge to climb on her abdomen and hang on for about a week. Because she stays in hiding, we rarely witness this stage. With the next molt, the young leave to lead a life of their own.

Most spiders deposit their eggs, then leave them. Many die before the next generation is born. Wolf spiders seem more like humans. They carry the developing eggs and even the infant spiders.

Notes

July

Watch what becomes of the milk-weed plant later in the summer and fall. The pink blossoms will change dramatically.

23 Milkweed, a summer flower, begins blooming in June, continues until August, but peaks in July. It gets its name from the white, sticky, bitter liquid that protects the plant from animals, but many insects have adapted to living on it.

Milkweeds grow to a stout two or three feet tall, becoming common in roadsides and meadows because of the large complex underground rhizome that connects many plants growing from a single rootstock. The average milkweed has eight ball-like clusters of flowers with seventy-five florets in each cluster. The fragrant pink flowers are hard to pollinate, so on most plants only four or five seed-filled pods will form.

In order to become pollinated, milkweeds attract and catch insects. A fragrant flower with plenty of nectar, the milkweed has many visitors, but some insects lose their footing in the slippery feeding site near the nectar and get stuck in nearby cracks. Only strong insects are able to get free by jerking out a tiny saddlebag of pollen.

Notes

July

24 In the heat of midsummer, the surface of ponds teems with activity. Whirligig beetles frantically spiral across the water searching for food, and dragonflies hunt along the edge. The fisher spider hunts here, too; its legs touch the surface, alerting the spider to movements and possible prey.

Though called fisher or fishing spider, it seldom lives up to these names by catching fish. Its swimming prey are more likely to be aquatic insects, which it may have to run after to catch. This spider is one of the largest found in the northland, but by spreading out its weight, it can run across the pond surface, often for long distances.

This large striped spider, is often confused with the wolf spider, which bears spots on its abdomen. Though most of its hunting is done on or near water, many a cabin owner has been surprised to find this large visitor on a wall. Deadly to insects, the spider is harmless to us.

In summer, the fisher spider produces an egg sac that is half her size. She uses her jaws to hold it under her until the eggs are ready to hatch.

Many creatures that live in lakes and streams have water repellant body coverings. Ducks, for instance, have oily feathers that protect them from cold water. Fisher spiders are covered with nonabsorbent hairs that trap bubbles and make the spiders buoyant.

Notes

July

Pollination can easily be demon-
strated to children on large flowers
like the wood lily. Gather pollen
on your finger from the stamens,
then wipe it across the pistil. Tie a
bright ribbon on the lily so you
can find it again, and observe it as
the seeds develop.

25 Most of us know this red-orange roadside flower as wood lily but others may call it Michigan lily, Turk's cap lily, or tiger lily. In July, the tall bright plants are easy to see along roadsides, and the flowers last longer than those of their domestic cousins, the day lilies.

Many flowers are mistakenly labeled as lilies, but these roadside plants, characterized by three colorful petals and three sepals, are true lilies. On the wood lily, the flowers all are a brilliant red-orange. When fully open, they fold completely back to the base, looking a bit like Turk's caps.

Roadsides provide ample sunlight for these lilies to grow well, but they also thrive at the edge of wetlands and woods. Large, brightly colored flowers get plenty of attention, and hummingbirds join the myriad of insects that frequent them. The perennial wood lilies are well equipped for pollination with huge stamens and pistils that extend far beyond the petals. Apparently, wind can pollinate these summer flowers if insects don't manage the task.

Notes

July

26 In late July, we begin to see signs of the changing season. As we drive along country roads, we notice a sure sign of the shorter days: flocks of swallows perched on roadside wires, high above the robust summer growth. Made up, for the most part, of tree swallow family units, they are the first of the impending migration.

After breakfast, the ever-increasing flocks gather until hundreds fill the gaps between poles. After feeding and resting, the families and extended families grow eager, and soon the huge flocks move on.

Tree swallows, light underneath with a blue-green back, may be joined by the brown rough-winged swallows and the colorful cliff swallows. Of the several kinds of swallows summering in the northland, tree swallows arrive first in the spring. Their early return guarantees a home and feeding site before the vernal rush. Now, in late July, they again find it advantageous to depart before the autumnal crowds of a month from now.

Just as birds make the most of available territory by living at various heights in trees, their staggered migration, begun by the tree swallows, makes it more likely that all species will migrate successfully.

Notes

_____

_____

_____

_____

July

Forest fires are feared and often fought, but they are essential if mature forests are to be renewed. The blackened ground soon abounds with new life, and the cycle begins again.

Notes

27 Forest fires create open spaces that allow plants to colonize quickly and reach for the sunlight that freely penetrates the forest floor. Fireweed gains its name because it is an early resident in these burned-over sites, but fire is not necessary in order for this five-foot tall purple-flowered plant to invade. Any open space will do, so throughout the northland, fireweed patches fill gaps along the margins of woods and meadows.

A long tapering cluster of rose-purple blossoms sits atop the erect leafy stem of this plant. Numerous four-petaled flowers make up the foot-long cluster. They bloom profusely, but the one-inch flowers don't all open at the same time. Flowering proceeds from low in the cluster to high, and thus fireweed flowers tell of the season's progression. By late July, the climb has neared the middle. With their rich purple blossoms, fireweed patches in full bloom demand attention from all passersby. Hummingbirds and insects, especially bumblebees, do not simply pass by: they are constant fireweed visitors.

By fall, even the top flowers will fade into long pods of fluffy seeds that will be dispersed by the autumn winds to open sites.

July

28 Blueberry time is a favorite season for many northlanders and provides an annual ritual celebrated by berry pickers young and old. Low bushes that held urn-shaped white flowers two months ago gave way a few weeks later to small green berries and now advertise blue-black sweets.

The fleshy berries are actually fruits filled with as many as a hundred seeds, but the seeds do not harm their taste, and they are devoured by many animals, including humans. Though songbirds and small mammals gobble with gusto, it is the black bear who reigns over the patches. Bruins sit among the plants and, in their haste, consume mouthfuls of leaves and twigs along with the desired berries. As they travel throughout the forest, the bears and other critters pass on the seeds in their droppings and help create new berrying sites.

Low woodland blueberries grow best in dry, sandy soil. Moderately tolerant of shade, they grow profusely in the acid soil of jack pine forests.

Though it is not needed for the survival of the blueberry bushes, a fire can effectively revive an aging patch by ridding it of old and dead vegetation.

Combine the different but equally delicious flavors of fresh and cooked blueberries in a single pie. Pour half of the fresh berries into the baked pie shell. Simmer the other half with cornstarch and sugar. Cool, then pour the cooked berries over the fresh ones. Perfection!

Notes

July

If you've been making mushroom spore prints, be sure to try it with the boletes. The prints should look very different from those made with gill-bearing mushrooms.

29

Although most mushrooms appear later in summer, some grow in July. Typically, mushrooms are umbrella shaped with spore-producing gills under the cap. But now, on our lawns under pine, aspen, or birch trees, a different type of mushroom appears. Although boletes are the same size and shape as other mushrooms, they differ in one respect: boletes have no gills under their caps. Instead they have an underside surface full of tiny holes called pores.

Pores are the openings of tubes that serve as the spore-producing sites in these mushrooms. The pore arrangement varies with the many kinds of boletes or pore mushrooms but the caps are typically brown and bun-shaped, and they may be dry, slimy, or scaly. The pore surface may be a different color than the cap; often it and the stalk will bruise with colors of blue-green, black, or red when handled or cut.

Boletes grow in association with many trees and sometimes form the circles called fairy rings. Most common around red or white pines, they are also found around birch and aspen; the rings grow larger with each passing year.

Notes

July

30 A loud buzzing trill from high in a tree is often heard in midsummer. Cicadas, the noisemakers, are robust insects with one-inch-long black bodies fitted between two-inch-long clear wings. While most insects use wings or legs to produce sounds, cicadas have their own devices. Drumlike organs in the almost totally hollow abdomen vibrate, and the resonance provides buzzes, scratches, or trills unique to each of the seventy-five North American species. On hot days, males court silent females with these arboreal sounds.

In many areas, cicadas are called harvest flies because they appear during harvest season. They are also, incorrectly, called locusts, but are not related to the grasshopper family.

Both young and adult cicadas have piercing mouthparts for feeding on tree sap. While the adults feed on branches, the subterranean nymphs feed on roots. Though cicadas usually live one to three years underground as nymphs, some southern species spend either thirteen or seventeen years as nymphs before a mass emergence of adults.

Notice the different methods insects use to make sounds. Many rub their legs or wings together, but none do as the cicada does.

Notes

July

If you are trying to interest children in nature study, introduce them to plants like jewelweed that *do* something. What child can resist exploding seeds. After the action is over, encourage the child to offer an explanation of the plant's behavior.

31 Dew droplets forming on the leaves of this orange flowering plant are responsible for the name jewelweed. Early-morning sparkles in late July confirm this choice.

This light green plant grows up to four feet tall on succulent stems, the juice of which, according to herbal medicine, is a treatment for poison ivy. It grows thickly and rapidly in wet areas with moderate shade. Orange flowers hang from the main stem on stalks of their own. These spotted horn-shaped flowers have a long blooming season, lasting most of the summer. Bright colors, a long season, and plenty of nectar make the jewelweed popular with bumblebees and hummingbirds.

This common annual is widely known as touch-me-not. Though this name implies that the plant is dangerous to contact, it is the seed pods that suggested this name. When ripe, the inch-long pods explode on impact, scattering seeds in every direction. This type of plant self-dispersal is rare in the northland, but it's effective for the jewelweed, whose seeds fall in nearby wet places.

Notes

August

August

Consider taking a video camera into the woods, or set it on your back porch and focus it on a flower garden. The camera will give you the ability to watch the activity of plants and animals repeatedly. Perhaps you'll even capture bladderwort in action.

1 The bladderwort now joins the waterlilies, loosestrifes, cattails, and arrowheads that are blooming in swamps. The one-half-inch-long yellow flower of the bladderwort grows alone on a plant that has its carrotlike leaves on or just below the surface. Among the leaves' many branches are numerous small green sacks called bladders.

At first glance, the bladders appear to keep the plant floating in this aquatic ecosystem. A closer look tells a different and more dynamic story: bladders on the water's surface are light in color and have a small opening into the hollow center. Unfortunate insects that are attracted into these openings are trapped and drowned as the plant responds quickly and sinks underwater. Not only does this innocent-looking aquatic plant catch and eat insects, it does so with a speed unequalled in the world of plants. Bladderworts pull the insect prey underwater too fast to be seen by the human eye. Only with the help of a stop-action camera can the deed be recorded. Digestion takes place later within the bladders, which, when filled with prey, turn a darker green.

Notes

August

2 By August, we expect the birds' breeding season to be completed and the fall migration to be beginning. August is not the time to look for active nesting, but goldfinches surprise us; they begin building nests when other birds are done.

While most birds are busy with nesting and raising young, goldfinches feed and fly over fields with the carefree spirit of singles. Their late nesting coincides with the maturity of bull and Canada thistle flowers. Thistles bloom in midsummer and after pollination form the fluffy material called down. Down is produced to disperse seeds by wind, but it is used by goldfinches as a lining for their nests. Down is so essential that the birds do not nest until it is available in late summer. Then they produce four to six eggs.

Late nesting does present some problems, but the down helps the young deal with the chill of late summer. Fortunately, goldfinches are late migrants and do not travel far to their winter home. They seem to be in no hurry to leave, and some even winter in the northland.

Thistledown insulation may be helpful, but it's still hard to believe that tiny, naked, baby birds can survive cold wet nights that would cause hypothermia in humans. Nests filled with thistledown must be amazingly efficient sleeping bags.

Notes

August

Creeping bellflowers escaped from gardens to inhabit roadsides. If you have a suitable location in your yard, you may want to dig up some bellflowers and other meadow wild-flowers and reestablish them on your property.

3 Many late summer flowers are white-, yellow-, or purple-petalled composites. We do not see many bell-shaped blue flowers in bloom now, but the creeping bellflower, an introduced plant and garden escapee, flowers in August.

These plants live up to their name, forming runners that creep along the ground in relatively straight lines. Groups of plants from a common rootstock become established along roadsides and forest edges where they grow up to three feet tall.

The blue flowers are borne on only one side of the stem and appear to be turning away from other growth. The cluster of flowers, called a spike, forms at the top of the leafy stem. It blooms first at the bottom, then proceeds upward: the last flowers to open are those at the top. Such a flowering scheme is common among plants with floral spikes. By September all the flowers have opened, and this summer flower is complete.

Blue bell-shaped flowers are likely to get few pollinators. Only bumblebees and moths visit the bellflowers.

Notes

4 Several plants are named for the time of day in which they bloom. We are familiar with morning glories, four o'clocks, and also the evening primrose, a wildflower that blooms along roadsides and wasteplaces in early August. The two-inch-long yellow flowers open their four petals any time from four to ten in the evening. The twilight-blooming flowers release a strong fragrance that attracts the attention of the only available pollinators, the moths. The petals are so large that one of the moths even sleeps in the partially opened flower during the daytime. Not willing to miss any opportunity for pollination, the evening primrose remains partially open all day for any bees that care to visit.

Many of our summer flowers are aliens of European origin, but the evening primrose is an example of a North American native that has become established in Europe.

The evening primrose is a biennial. A first-year plant forms a rosette of reddish green leaves on the ground. In its second year of life, it grows to be about four feet tall with large flowers clustered only at the top.

You can experiment to find out what aspect of light plants such as the evening primrose respond to. Is it length of day, brightness of light, or heat? Record sunrise, sunset, and light and weather conditions over several days or weeks. Make parallel notes on when the flowers open and close.

Notes

August

Examine closely a rough, ridged tree trunk. Could a northern pearly eye butterfly be hiding in full view but well camouflaged? Perhaps you'll find another critter the same color and texture as the bark.

5 In midsummer, butterflies are common in meadows but uncommon in forests. A large brown butterfly known as the northern pearly eye does, however, inhabit deciduous woods—often near streams or marshes.

The northern pearly eye gets its name from the twenty eyespots that mark the otherwise brown wings. A pearl appears in the center of each eyespot on the underside of the hindwing.

Living in the forests, adults forego nectar, feeding instead on sap from various trees, including willow, poplar, and birch. Eggs hatch in the fall; caterpillars overwinter and in spring feed on nearby grasses.

Adults live for two months of the summer. With their cryptic brown camouflage, they are able to bask on bark with safety despite their two-inch-wide wings. Their eyespots, best seen from the underside, intimidate other critters by making the northern pearly eyes appear aggressive as they fly out in pursuit of passing butterflies and other insects.

Notes

August

6 By early August, roadside and meadow plants have reached maturity, and many of them exceed many of us in height. Smaller plants are shaded out and cannot compete here. Along the edge of swamps and ponds, however, small bog plants continue to flourish. Arrowhead, one of these plants, now blooms in swamps.

Arrowhead gets its name from its large pointed leaves, which grow to be about a foot long. The leaves are not only pointed at the end, they also sport two long extending flutes or spurs near the base. The large rounded white flowers are composed of only three petals and grow in small clusters above the leaves. The flowers may persist through August but not into the fall. The leaves and flowers grow on a plant that extends two feet above the water.

As many of the swamp plants do, arrowheads survive the winter in underground tubers. These starch-filled growths contain the plant's nutrients and allow it to live for many years. Arrowhead tubers are edible, and if anyone is willing to go to the bother of digging them out, after processing, they serve as a starchy potato substitute.

Many wildflowers reproduce by seeds and also clone themselves vegetatively. Seeds will start new plants even if muskrats, ducks, and geese gobble up tubers. Or if the water is too deep for seeds to germinate, the tubers will continue to multiply.

Notes

August

7 Few wildflowers grow in the deep shade of midsummer woods, but shade-tolerant ferns do well there. Ostrich fern, lady fern, interrupted fern, and bracken all flourish in the rich soil of deciduous forests. Perhaps the best-known fern, the maidenhair, is also one of the most attractive.

In shady woods, often at the edge of swamps or on rocky hillsides, the maidenhair fern thrives. Its single stem branches into two fronds of circular or semicircular blades. This branching growth pattern, which gives the fern its common name, makes it grow out more than up, and even under ideal conditions, it does not grow more than twenty inches tall.

Numerous fan-shaped small pinnae (leaflets), notched on one side and smooth on the other, are less than an inch long. Only one to five sori (spore containers) are borne on the underside of these fertile pinnae. Extensive rootstocks creep underground. Like most ferns, maidenhair is a perennial, surviving the winter in its roots. An established growth of this fern lasts many years.

Notes

August

8 August lawns do not need mowing as often as they did in early summer, but growth still continues. Mushrooms of many kinds appear as though formed by magic, growing today where nothing grew yesterday. The russula is one of the most common and most varied mushrooms. *Russula*, which is both the common and Latin name, refers to its often reddish color, but russula are also green, white, yellow, and purple. A mold grows on some russula making the whole mushroom look orange. They vary greatly in size, ranging from the diameter of a quarter to that of a plate. Though differing from each other in many ways, russula mushrooms also share some traits: spores dropped from gills under the cap are white; gills and stem are white; and the entire mushroom breaks easily like chalk.

Russula grow on organic material in the soil. Though common in the northland, they do not grow in the huge numbers that many other mushrooms do. August lawns often host some russula, and these mushrooms appear in the woods as well.

Not usually eaten by people, russula provide food for deer, squirrels, insects, and slugs.

Appearances sometimes deceive. The most obvious characteristics of russula mushrooms vary greatly. If you want to identify them, you need to ignore the size and color so you can check the truly distinguishing characteristics.

Notes

August

Humans are omnivorous, and so are cedar waxwings. It's advantageous for a species to be able to survive, at least for a time, on either plant or animal food.

9 August is the time of early harvest, and berries from many plants are ripe now. Juicy red pin cherries grab the attention of many mammals and birds. One of these birds, the cedar waxwing, never misses an opportunity to gobble up pin cherries.

Cedar waxwings are gray-brown, seven inches long, and crested. They bear a yellow band on the tip of their tail and red spots on their wings. These red spots, which reminded early naturalists of sealing wax used on envelopes, gave the bird its name: the waxwing.

Since returning in the spring from its winter home, the cedar waxwings have dwelt among us, raising young in trees and shrubs. Now, they gather ripe berries and gorge themselves, sometimes swallowing so many berries that they can hardly fly. Flocks feed until full; their high-pitched "zeee" sound comes from trees for hours. The birds remain together for migration later in the fall, and when the berries are depleted, they show the talents of flycatchers and feed on insects in midair. When neither berries nor insects are available, wintering flocks return to the southern United States.

Notes

10 Of all the wildflowers in North America, it may be the yarrow that is most widespread. The flat-topped white flowers above carrotlike leaves may be found growing from ocean beaches to mountain meadows. Though never the dominant plant in any site, it grows in all types of regions, avoiding only shade. This Eurasian import is now well established in North America. Plants grow up to three feet tall, and we can find them in bloom from May to September.

Clusters of composite five-rayed flowers form the flat floral arrangement on top of each plant. Rays, which like the flowers are white, surround the tiny disk flowers. The finely divided leaves are often mistaken for those of carrots or ferns.

Tradition has it that yarrow was used to help stop the flow of blood; Achilles is said to have carried it with him to treat wounded soldiers during the Trojan wars. This explains yarrow's Latin name, *Achillea*. This useful plant was brought to North America by herbal doctors.

Next time you read a classic, take note of the plants and animals mentioned in the book. Can you find them in your area? Do they now have different names? One reason for Latin names like *Achillea* is so plants can be identified no matter what their common name.

Notes

August

If tomato worms (sphinx moth larvae) invade your garden, they can be controlled by picking them off. It's not much fun, but it's completely safe for the environment.

11 We know most adult butterflies better than we do their larvae (caterpillars), but the converse is true of moths: the larvae are better known. Though sphinx moths are large and easily seen as they feed on flowers, their caterpillars have given them their name. The large, fat, green worms, often called tomato or hornworms, are young sphinx moths. Typically, they have a horn or spine on the rear end, and though it is harmless, many expect it to sting. When in danger, the caterpillar raises up its head and arches its body in a sphinxlike pose. The large horned larvae are usually left alone as they feed on leaves.

About a hundred species of sphinx moths live in North America. One of the northland's most common, the great ash or pen-marked sphinx, feeds on green ash or lilac in its larval stage. We may encounter this large green worm in yards or parks where these trees abound.

Adult sphinx moths have gray bodies with narrow wings, black wavy streaks on the larger forewing, and a color pattern on the smaller hindwing. Adults may be called hawk or hummingbird moths because they use their long coiled tongue to sip flower nectar in evenings.

Notes

12 The forest floor is still littered with leaves from last year's trees, and were it not for the shade, it would look rich enough to support a growth of flowers. Instead of many flowers growing here, however, only the strange Indian pipe grows.

Indian pipe is named for its single flower, which grows on a curved stem; together, the flower and stem are said to resemble a peace pipe. With its unusual properties—no chlorophyll and no need for sunlight to produce food—Indian pipe grows well in shade. This plant with its white stem, leaves, and flower acts as an epiparasite, feeding indirectly on roots of green plants. Its nourishment comes from contact with mycorrhyzae (fungal threadlike growths) that interconnect with roots of surrounding trees. Once established, Indian pipe comes back each summer.

Usually growing in small groups, Indian pipes reach six to ten inches in height. The nodding flower straightens up after blooming and, turning brown, remains in this position all winter. Vestigial leaves with no chlorophyll are useless, and the entire white plant is often believed to be a fungus instead of a flowering plant.

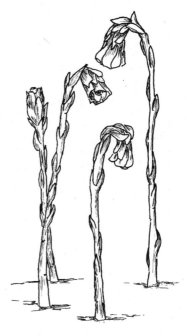

Surrounded by green leaves, we may still forget the importance of chlorophyll. Only when we marvel at plants like Indian pipe that appear to exist without it, do we recall that chlorophyll, directly or indirectly, is essential for plants.

Notes

August

Try to capture a spider web. Spray a piece of black construction paper with hair spray. Quickly place it on an orb web. With luck, the strands will cling to the paper.

13 Dew-drenched meadows are calm on late summer mornings, and in early sunlight, webs of the night hunters can be seen. Spiders create webs of many shapes and sizes, but probably best known are the large circular ones called orb webs. Up to three feet in diameter, most are vertical and are attached to branches or buildings. Fences and signs seem to have a special appeal too.

Orb webs, constructed as a snare to catch flying insects, are made of two types of threads. The spokes or rays that pass through the center are not sticky; therefore, the spider is able to walk on them. Insects are caught in the spiral threads. They quickly tire as they struggle, becoming easy prey for the web owner who waits patiently in the hub. Webs are constructed at night, and hunting is over by dawn; then we can see the webs, but not the spiders, who hides in their retreats.

One maker of large orb webs is called the shamrock spider because of the markings on its large round abdomen. The one-inch-long spider is mostly brown with striped, hairy legs.

Notes

August

14 A light purple flower growing up to six feet tall is now calling our attention to the wetlands. Joe-pye weed lifts its fuzzy dome-shaped clusters above other swamp plants while its leaves, in whorls of four or five, surround the dark stem.

The unusual name of joe-pye weed is believed to have come from an American Indian of colonial times. Joe Pye, a highly skilled herbal doctor, used plants to treat many illnesses and valued the root of his namesake plant for treating the symptoms of typhus.

The many light purple flowers of joe-pye weed appear in branching floral arrangements. Composite flowers are typically composed of ray and disk flowers, but the joe-pye clusters consist of ray flowers only. Standing much taller than other marsh plants, joe-pye weed catches the attention of human passersby with the butterflies it attracts and the bees that keeping buzzing around it on these late summer days. Like many plants of the wetlands, joe-pye weed is perennial, and after the flowers fade and the seeds disperse in autumn winds, it survives underground to return next year.

We may wonder how herbal doctors knew or guessed that joe-pye weed reduced fevers. Perhaps they were using the plant to cure another symptom and discovered a desirable side effect. Serendipity still happens for medical researchers.

Notes

August

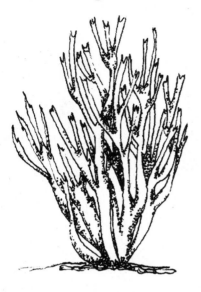

15 In late summer, a rotting log often appears to come alive as small light brown "trees" grow from its sides. Coral fungi, commonly seen on logs but also found on soil, branches repeatedly as though it were a small tree or bush. The name coral refers to its superficial resemblance to oceanic corals.

Summer rains cause vegetation to decay in the forests, and so, like many of the fungi, corals flourish now. Not making its own food, a fungus gets nutrients from decaying logs or organic material in the soil. The parts seen above the surface are dwarfed by the hyphae (threadlike roots) below the surface, where the nutrients are absorbed.

A closer scrutiny of the coral fungus shows two traits of interest. Spores similar to mushroom spores are borne on branches from tiny stalks called basidia, making coral a cousin of mushrooms. In many species, tips of branching stems open to reveal a crown shape.

Coral fungus is typically three to five inches tall, and though usually light brown, it is highly variable in color.

To study nature carefully, you may need to magnify it. Start your nature study kit with a 5- or 10-power hand lens. It's easy to carry and weighs only a few ounces. Keep it in your jacket pocket and it will be available next time you come upon interesting plants such as coral fungi.

Notes

August

16 They have been active since spring, but now, in August, bats become more energetic. Of the several species of bats in the northland, little brown bats and big brown bats are the most common. Both regularly roost in buildings, leaving at dusk to feed—often over lakes and rivers—and returning by dawn.

In late summer, little brown bats go through mating rituals. Their nightly flights take them to caves, mines, or buildings where they gather in large flocks for mating before migration scatters the population. Though mating occurs in late summer, fertilization does not happen until next spring, and the gestation of fifty to sixty days brings birth in late June. Female little brown bats store viable sperm until spring from the mating that takes place on these August nights.

Most of the little brown bats will soon be migrating. Further south in a cave or other suitable retreat, they go into a torpid state similar to, but not identical with, hibernation.

Construct a home for little and big brown bats and you'll help solve your summer insect problems. They eat tremendous quantities of mosquitoes and other flying insects.

Notes

August

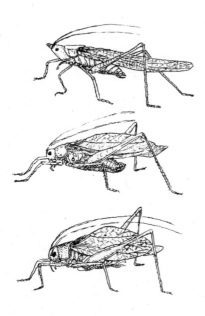

Add katydids to the critters you can easily identify. Their long green antennae are an easy-to-remember feature. Pause in the evenings and listen to their songs.

17 August days are strangely silent. With the nesting season over, songbirds no longer declare their territories, and treetop songs cease. But when trees become silent, meadows come alive. Buzzes and clicks from grasses and wildflowers tell us that late summer is breeding time for katydids, a kind of grasshopper. Although their song is not as melodious as the songs produced by avian vocal cords, katydids sing for the same reasons that birds do, and as is the case with birds, the male of the species is the songster.

Katydids, who do most of their calling on warm afternoons and evenings, rub rasping organs near their legs and wings to produce sounds, a method called stridulation. Bush or meadow katydids tirelessly click and buzz nearly all day; angle-wing katydids creak in the evenings; while cone-head katydids "chi-chi-chi" through the afternoons and evenings.

While other grasshoppers have short antennae, katydids have long ones—often as long as their body. Most are green and blend in with meadow grasses and leaves.

Notes

August

18 August is still summer and often quite warm, but because of the later sunrises and earlier sunsets, some birds are migrating. One of the early travelers, the sharp-shinned hawk, begins its long migration period now but continues late into the fall.

The sharp-shinned hawk is a small hawk, only about one foot in length, with short rounded wings and a long tail. Adults sport a gray back, red bars on the underside, and black-and-white bands under the tail. The young are brown with brown stripes on a lighter breast. Only the adults have red eyes. The sharp-shinned hawk gets its name from its long pointed feet. It feeds on small mammals and songbirds in its forest habitat.

Sharp-shinned hawks nest in much of Canada, and now, after nesting, they slowly migrate to wintering grounds in southern United States. Unlike many raptors, they do not migrate in flocks, but appear alone or in pairs as they drift by. Their low flight allows them to find places to feed and rest. For many more weeks these little raptors will pass by as they work their way south.

We don't think of hawks as backyard birds, but during migration, they may stop in your yard to eat or rest.

Notes

August

Notice the soft texture of this large tough plant that stands tall all winter.

19 Mullein, one of the biggest and thickest of the late summer wildflowers, now stands along the roadsides. Mullein grows up to eight feet tall, and with its thick stem and huge, flat, soft leaves, it is an impressive sight. Surprisingly, the blossoming spike is composed of small flowers, each with five yellow petals.

Mullein, a plant introduced from Europe, is a biennial. In the plant world, this means that it has a life of two years—from spring of one year to the fall of the following year—and needs to survive a winter. During the first year, mullein grows only slightly above the ground and forms a flat circular leaf arrangement called a rosette. Food is made and stored in the roots so that it will survive and grow the second year. Large, soft, flat leaves give the plant names such as flannel-leaf and calf's tongue. The word mullein comes from the Latin *mollis* for soft.

Mullein blooms throughout August but quickly runs out of energy for the fall. Flowering mullein is hard to find in autumn, although the huge stems stand erect for much of the winter.

Notes

20 Mushrooms are not unusual in August; we have seen many by this time, but amanitas, which are common on lawns or in woods, are worth special note.

Amanitas can have large caps of yellow, red, brown, gray, or white. They're sometimes the size of a dinner plate. The stalk usually bears a ring or annulus, and a cup or bulb can be seen at the base. The gills and the spores are white. A growth of large amanitas on the lawn is truly a beautiful sight.

These mushrooms are well known and are called by many common names including deathcap, destroying angel, and fool's mushroom, which do not acknowledge their beauty but refer instead to the mushroom's toxicity. Since amanitas can be lethal, even edible ones are best left alone.

Like other mushrooms, amanitas survive many years as underground threads (hyphae or mycelia), and picking them or knocking them down does not destroy them. Given the right conditions, amanitas will return for years.

There are two approaches to mushroom identification for those who want to pick and eat them. You can learn to identify all the poisonous mushrooms and not pick them. Or it may be safer to learn to identify a few easily recognizable species such as the morels and only pick them.

Notes

August

Green plants don't look very power-ful. But consider how plants like sow thistle can actually break up concrete once they gain a foothold in a tiny crack.

21 Yellow dandelionlike flowers have been appearing all summer. Hawkweed, cynthia, goatsbeard, and the dandelion itself are a few that we have seen. Now in August, one more, the sow thistle, takes this flower-type to greater heights.

Sow thistle bears its rayed composite flowers on a stalk, three to four feet tall. Several yellow flowers about one inch in diameter are borne above spiny leaves shaped something like those of the dandelion. Although this plant is not a true thistle, these spiny leaves give it the thistle part of its name. Pigs seem to find this plant particularly delicious, and at one time, farmers fed it to pregnant sows to increase their milk production. Probably because the white sap looks milklike, sow thistle was also given to human mothers.

Though common along roadsides, it takes advantage of breaks in concrete and often grows through cracks in sidewalks and parking lots. Blooming through all of August, sow thistle forms dandelionlike parachute seeds in the fall.

Notes

22 You may have noticed that small dead animals on the road do not remain there for long. Roadkill becomes food for several kinds of birds and mammals. A dead mouse on the lawn disappears, too, but this task is taken care of by other members of nature's cleanup crews.

A couple of insects, carrion beetles and burying beetles, quickly move in and take charge. Both use their well-developed sense of smell, seeming to come out of nowhere to find a tiny carcass in the grass. Many beetles find the dead body simultaneously, and on the carcass, mating takes place. Mating is quickly followed by egg-laying. The larvae hatch quickly, then feed on the mouse's body.

Carrion beetles have flat black-and-yellow bodies about one inch long. Burying beetles are also about one inch long but are red and black. They live up to their name and actually bury the body before depositing eggs on it. Again the larvae feed on this meat.

In both cases, the dead animal is quickly eaten and recycled into other organic material.

Next time you find a dead mouse or shrew, cover it with a plastic berry box. Check every day to see what happens to the little body. How long does it take for it to disappear?

Notes

August

Nighthawks are misnamed. Can you think of any other critters that were misunderstood and thus named incorrectly?

23 By late August, the migration that early in the month started slowly has expanded. Shorebirds line up on the beaches. Warblers pass through in waves. And each evening large flocks of nighthawks fly over.

Nighthawks, who frequently breed in the city, are well known in North America. The wings of these light brown birds are marked with white bars that are best seen on the underside. Their range extends over most of Canada and the United States; however, they winter in Central America. The long migration begins early for flocks that may contain more than one hundred individuals. With insects most abundant at dusk, the flocks actively feed as they fly by in the early evening. The bird's large, wide mouth enables it to feed on insects caught in flight.

Nighthawks are a good example of a poorly named bird. Though often flying at dusk, they are not nocturnal birds and, with no talons, certainly not hawks. While flying, they often give a nasal "peent" call. Migrating flocks soon pass, and by September, only late stragglers fly over.

Notes

24 Goldenrods begin blooming in mid-July, and for two months, the showy yellow plants grace roadsides. A highly diverse group, about eighty-five species grow in North America, and though usually thought of as a member of the meadow or field community, they also grow in bogs and forests and on cliffs and mountains.

Our most common species, the Canada goldenrod, grows to three feet in height with many lightly toothed, sharp leaves surrounding the stem. The spike of numerous yellow florets extends above the leaves and is a true composite with ray and disk flowers. Canada goldenrods develop dense clumps of many plants in meadows and roadsides. All grow from a single rootstock and continue to expand in concentric fashion, forming a clone that may be more than a century old.

Bumblebees and honeybees are quick to discover goldenrods: plants hum until fall seed formation. With a plethora of goldenrods, butterflies, moths, wasps, and flies visit too. Even the sedentary crab spider takes up its late summer hunting on the goldenrods.

Hayfever sufferers often blame goldenrod for their misery, but it's the usually unnoticed ragweed rather than the showy goldenrod that's the culprit.

Notes

August

25 In the spring, ponds echoed with the songs of mating frogs; on May evenings as many as five kinds called at once. Since then, the frogs have left and ponds are silent. There are some exceptions to this rule, however: now, in August, spring peepers and gray tree frogs begin calling again. Exactly why they call in late summer is unknown, but on August afternoons, they peep from trees as though spring has returned. No mating or even attempted mating takes place at this time, and calls emanate from the safety and seclusion of trees instead of ponds.

Besides calling, these frogs are feeding in the trees and bushes. It is not unusual to see the little brown peeper with an X on its back in our shrubs. In late summer, gray tree frogs that feed, call, and hide among the leaves are green. The young are more likely to be green, with the gray suit reserved for adults sitting on bark or buildings. Suction cups on their toes allow frogs to hold on to leaves, but they also affix themselves to glass. Indoor lights attract insects to windows, and gray tree frogs gather to hunt on this vertical, transparent plane.

Even if a frog doesn't appear on your windowpane, the insects that are attracted by lights are interesting to watch. Do the same insects appear throughout the summer? What differences do you note?

Notes

26 We recognize the huge yellow flowers and the seeds of farm field and garden sunflowers, but this diverse group has many wild species in the northland as well. All have the big yellow flowers, and although none grow to the size of the domestic sunflower, all are large.

Of the many species found in North America, two are common in the northland and bloom all of August: the tall sunflower and the woodland sunflower. Both carry three-inch-wide flower heads of numerous disk flowers surrounded by twelve to eighteen ray flowers that constantly buzz with bee activity.

The tall sunflower lives up to its name with a stately growth that may reach ten feet. The leafy stem branches at the top where many flower heads appear. The pointed leaves appear opposite each other near the ground, but alternate higher up the stem. Tall sunflowers reign supreme in meadows and along roadsides. The woodland sunflower, which is about three feet tall and grows at the edge of the woods, carries only one flower head per plant. Rough dark green leaves are opposite one another on the entire stem.

Notes

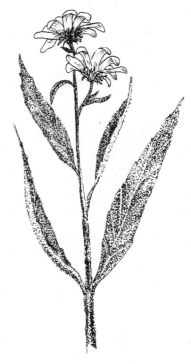

Wild sunflowers do not twist on their stalks to face the sun in the same way as cultivated varieties do. Apparently they're named for their sunshine bright blossoms, not their sun-following behavior.

August

Just as most of the paper we use begins as wood pulp, the paper nests of bald-faced hornets are made of wood fiber. If you decide to take a close look, be very cautious.

27 Large black-and-white wasps, usually called hornets, have been with us all summer. About one inch long, most of the body is black, but white markings on the side and face give them the name of white-faced or bald-faced hornets. Wasps fold their wings over the back; hornets hold their wings parallel to, not over, the body.

Colonies chew wood and leaves all summer to make oval nests that are now about a foot long. Inside, tiers of young develop, each in its own cell. Nests are begun in spring by the queen, who alone from last year's colony has survived the winter. In the protection of trees or buildings, the nest or hive now contains an exploding population of hornets and egg laying ceases. After feeding prey to young all summer, workers abandon the hive to fend for themselves, satisfying a sweet tooth with fruits and berries before dying.

Colonies consist of an egg-laying queen, sterile females called workers, and males. Workers maintain and enlarge the nest while they feed the young. Males mate with the queen. It is only the females that sting.

Notes

28 All summer, chimney swifts circled over old buildings. A close watch of their activity showed that they flew into chimneys after feeding. There they used sticks and saliva to attach their nests to the inside of the brick chimneys.

The chimney swift, a short gray bird with long wings, has been described as a flying cigar. Its long wings allow the swift to make fast flight an important part of its life; many hours each day are spent flying and feeding. A wide mouth enables them to catch insects in midair. The birds are in regular communication with each other, and twittering sounds are common. Indeed, their twittering even provides us with an easy way to locate the circling swifts. Nesting in chimneys, especially chimneys of old buildings, has made the birds common city residents.

In late August, with their families raised, swifts begin the long migration to their winter site in South America. Every afternoon and evening, the swifts feed as they fly in expanding circles. By the end of August or early September, the restless birds will move on.

A chimney, unused all summer, provides a perfect nesting place for chimney swifts. You'd better check out your chimney before starting the first fire of the fall.

Notes

August

Be absolutely sure of your mushroom identification, then be adventurous—pick some craterelles and cook them in soup. Consider surprising guests with the results of your mushroom-hunting exploits.

29 Given all the fungi that grow in the yard in late summer, it comes as no surprise that a growth of hornlike objects has appeared at the base of a maple tree. This fungus, craterellus, also known as horn of plenty, is brown, gray, or black and shaped like a horn or funnel. Although they grow in groups, each individual fungus is less than four inches across.

Dark in color and seemingly leatherlike, the thin fungus flesh is actually edible and is highly prized by many fungi fanciers who use it as a seasoning for soups. Some even claim it is better than its well-known cousins, the yellow-gold chanterelles.

Inside, the funnel is hollow; a close look at the outside reveals thin folds. The yellow-white spores are formed among these folds on small clublike structures (basidia) like those of mushrooms, but without gills.

Like many fungi, craterelles can be a bit hard to predict, and common one year, they may not appear again for years until proper conditions return. During this time, the fungus is alive underground but unseen until the black horns grow above the surface.

Notes

August

30 Big eyes, long legs, and an abdomen that extends well beyond its two wings identify the gray-brown robber fly. With its hairy body and buzzing flight, this one-inch-long insect is often mistaken for a bee.

Overwintering as larvae in the soil, the young grow and pupate in early summer, and the adults are with us for most of the summer. Both as larvae and adults, robber flies have insatiable appetites for other insects.

Hunting by the robber flies reminds one of the hunting done by birds called flycatchers. After waiting on a perch, robber flies take flight, snatching prey in midair with a typical success rate of about 15 percent. These predators use their legs to capture insects much as a dragonfly does; then, while still in flight, they paralyze the prey with a piercing bite to its back. After returning to their perch, the robber flies suck the body fluids from their captives. These voracious feeders often attack and eat insects larger than themselves, such as bees, dragonflies, grasshoppers, butterflies, and moths. Even formidable tiger beetles are devoured.

True insects have four wings and six legs, which makes it easy to differentiate them from flies with two wings and spiders with eight legs.

Notes

August

31 Asters are so common in late summer that, along with the goldenrods, they lay claim to the meadows. Like the goldenrods, asters are a diverse group. Most display a range of white to purple composite flowers that give rise to the name aster, meaning starlike.

Most of the asters grow in the meadows and roadsides, but one, the large-leaf (or big leaf) aster is a resident of mixed forests. Huge heart-shaped leaves that grow near the ground give the plant its name. Growing in groups, the asters appear in spring, and their leaves cover entire regions of the forest floor, but here in the shade only a few put forth a stem and purple flowers. Being perennials, most make food to store for another year. If a fire or other disturbance gives more sunlight to this growth, the asters respond with renewed energy, and many bloom.

Composite flowers of about twenty light purple rays surround the yellow disks, which later will become reddish. Ten to twenty of these one-inch wide flowers branch above the leafy stem. In true aster fashion, plants hang on to the flowers until late fall frosts arrive.

It's a long time from first frost to snowfall. Hardy flowers like the large-leaf aster add color to fields after delicate garden flowers have withered.

Notes

September

September

If you happen to find a feather with a large yellow midvein, it probably dropped from a northern flicker, which has also been called a yellow-shafted flicker or yellow hammer.

1 September is a time of many changes. Before this cooling month is over, frost will be prevalent; colored leaves will pull our attention toward woodlands; and the autumn migration will have reached its fulfillment.

Just as traditional as these changes is the early September appearance of migrating flickers. This brown bird has a spotted belly with a black bib and a red spot on the back of its head. It is, however, the large white rump patch, so visible in flight, that best identifies these woodpeckers.

During migration, flickers become common visitors to yards. They do two things that set them aside from other woodpeckers: they travel south in loosely knit small flocks, and they feed on the ground often as they pause en route. In September, flickers may be observed more often on the ground than in trees. They give a "flick-a, flick-a" when taking flight or a "klee-yer" from trees.

Notes

September

2 September is migration season. Although this activity is usually associated with birds, several other animals also take part in seasonal travel. Many northland bats leave for warmer climes as do a few insects, but best known is the incredible monarch flight.

Also known as milkweed butterflies, the black-and-orange monarchs have been with us since late May. They deposited their eggs on milkweed, and the gaudy black, yellow, and white caterpillars grew up with a diet of nothing but this bitter plant.

Fully developed caterpillars formed chrysalises in late summer, and adults emerged to take August or September flights to Mexico. Paper-thin but very durable wings carry them on this one-way journey. Hundreds of miles to the south, the monarchs will winter in high altitude fir trees in the Sierra Madre mountains in central Mexico. Congregating flocks are so numerous there that they turn evergreen branches orange.

Adults sip nectar from fall flowers as they pass by in September. Traveling and feeding by day, at night the monarchs roost in large groups on trees.

Some natural events, though they occur every year, are seen only occasionally. If you see a tree full of migrating monarchs, take time to marvel at the thought of these delicate butterflies and their long journey.

Notes

September

Flowers seem infinitely varied in comparison to humans who have one basic shape. Compare butter-and-eggs flowers to daisies. How many flower shapes can you find?

3 Also known as toadflax, butter-and-eggs is a familiar member of the snapdragon family imported from Europe and widely naturalized in the northland. Living in roadsides, waste places, and dry fields, the plant's long flowering season extends through summer into fall.

The two-foot stem holds many narrow leaves with flowers clustered above in a spike. Yellow flowers have the usual snapdragon shape: long thin spurs and two tightly closed lips. An orange spot on the bottom lip contributes to the name of butter-and-eggs.

Because of these closed lips, the flowers need strong insects to open and pollinate them. Bumblebees are large enough, and it is the orange spot on the flower's lower lip that invites the bees in. Once inside, bees are attracted to the nectar in the spurs, but they also transfer pollen. Closed lips keep out undesirable insects such as ants that would only take nectar and not help the flower.

As is true of many naturalized aliens, butter-and-eggs are perennial. However, they also produce seeds in brown capsules that will start new plants.

Notes

September

During late summer, we see a strange but brief insect phenomenon. Cracks in sidewalks, streets, or nearby buildings suddenly start crawling with winged insects that emerge and take to the air. Just as quickly and mysteriously, this exiting flight ends.

All summer, colonies of ants had been thriving in these cracks. In early September, the queen, who had been adding new workers (infertile females) to the colony, begins to deposit eggs of other queens (fertile females) and males. With the subsequent maturation of these ants, the colony gets restless. New winged queens climb to the surface followed by many winged males. At the surface, everyone takes flight, leaving the colony with the old queen and sterile workers who stay to survive the winter.

During the ensuing flight, mating takes place in midair, then the ants return to earth. Their purpose accomplished, mated males quickly die, and new queens, with stored sperm, set out to found new colonies. At appropriate locations, they bite off their wings and begin their families.

Because many ants make their homes in easy-to-find anthills and because they are not dangerous to humans, they make perfect subjects for observation. Instead of destroying a backyard anthill, enjoy watching the colony.

Notes

September

Why South America? Wouldn't it be easier to stop flying and spend the winter in Georgia? What instinct drives warblers to undertake this dangerous and exhausting trip?

5 Warblers are well known to us throughout the northland, and on a spring day we may spy twenty species of the singing residents and migrants. With many nesting here or further north, fall again becomes a good time for us to observe these birds.

Species recognized by their song or breeding plumage in the spring now return, but silently. They wear new attire and may look like completely different birds. The birder who claimed to have seen twenty warblers on a May day is challenged to identify the same twenty in September.

A few, such as redstarts, ovenbirds, Nashville warblers, and black-and-white warblers, look as they did early in the season, but most have become small greenish yellow birds with little variation. Fortunately, some of them carry white wing bars, eye rings, or tail markings that can help us recognize them if the nervous birds hold still long enough.

Passing flocks, called waves, comprise several species, often with chickadees and vireos acting as hosts. Together they feed, fly, and flit among trees, uttering high-pitched calls and notes as they head for their wintering grounds in the Caribbean and Central or South America.

Notes

September

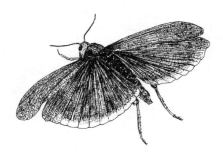

6 Insects are highly varied in their mode of maturation and although many develop from larvae appearing much different from adults (such as moths from caterpillars), some, like grasshoppers, develop from young that are merely smaller versions of adults. From early hatching, the young grasshoppers have gone through a series of molts until late-summer adulthood. Wings and reproductive parts function fully only in adults. Now, with courting and mating completed, the fields and roadsides abound with grasshopper activity. Many hop, but locusts, or Carolina grasshoppers, are more likely to fly. The term locust has been misapplied to cicadas, which are completely unrelated insects.

A disturbed two-inch-long locust may spread its hindwings and fly up to one hundred feet in open areas. Clicking noises called crepitation, believed to be territorial sounds, are often given in flight. Wings are black with a border of sharply contrasting yellow, a pattern that may cause us to mistake locusts for mourning cloak butterflies. Because of the camouflage supplied by its brown body, the locust vanishes when landing on bare ground.

When we watch with curiosity a single grasshopper, it's hard to imagine the horror that farmers feel when hordes of voracious grasshoppers begin devouring their crops.

Notes

September

Do you have the stubborn curiosity of a naturalist? Insects don't perform on demand. If you want to watch a pelecinid wasp lay its eggs, you'll need vast amounts of patience.

7 During these mild days of early September, we may see one of the strangest insects of the season. This is the egg-laying time for pelecinid wasps, which are also called ichneumon wasps, and our yards serve as good locations for this activity.

This black wasp's characteristically thin body, long antennae, and clear wings do not look unusual. It is the female's extremely long tail that makes this insect almost incredible. On her one-inch-long body, she carries a two-inch-long tube that looks like a long tail or giant stinger. This egg-laying ovipositor is neither tail nor stinger, and though it looks dangerous, it is harmless. Flying, she can barely lift the ovipositor, and when sitting, she folds it into six parts.

In late summer, the female selects the right spot on which to deposit eggs in the soil. Much of her time is spent walking over the yard finding that appropriate site; it needs to be on the larvae of developing soil insects such as May beetles or June bugs. Forcing the long ovipositor into the soil, she searches for the needed larvae. When she finds one, she lays one egg at a time; it hatches to devour the host insect.

Notes

September

8 September is the mushroom month. As northland temperatures cool and leaves change color, these fleshy growths appear in the lawns and woods. Most are saprophytic, getting nutrition from dead wood and decaying leaves; thus, they are more common in forests. Highly influenced by available moisture, populations vary from year to year.

Despite the weather variables, milk cap mushrooms seem to grow each year on the forest floor. These mushrooms contain a substance called latex that is exuded from any bruised or cut part, especially the gills. Though the latex may actually be clear or colored, it is the white, milky liquid that gives the plant its name. Even the Latin name, *Lactarius*, which means lactate or lactose, relates to the milky substance that bleeds from these mushrooms.

Never abundant, milk cap mushrooms appear in small groups in which the one- to six-inch-wide caps run the gamut of fungi colors; all bear white or yellowish spores. The caps are often funnel shaped with gills extending onto the stem. Since they usually grow in forests, it is believed that they form mutual relationships with specific trees.

Investigate the relationship between milk cap mushrooms or other mushrooms and specific trees. Do you find them near conifers, maples, oak, aspen, or do they seem to grow at random throughout the forest?

Notes

September

Your growing knowledge is giving you a fund of information for sharing. At an early fall picnic, when someone yells, "get that bug off the potato salad," explain how true bugs can be identified by their crossed wings. Perhaps you can place a stink bug on the salad so everyone can compare the two insects.

9 Though many of us refer to all insects, or any small creepy-crawly critters, as bugs, members of one group of insects are truly called that. Belonging to the order *Hemiptera*, meaning half-wing, (so named because adults cross their wings on their backs and only half shows), these insects are common in water, woods, and meadows. One of the most abundant, stink bugs, show up in September.

The one-half-inch-long bugs are usually brown, gray, or green, but some are surprisingly brightly colored. Their bodies are shield-shaped, the head holding medium-sized five-segmented antennae and large eyes. As expected, stink bugs get their name from the disagreeable odor they give off when defending themselves.

With their probing and sucking mouth parts, adults feed on plants. In early autumn, we may encounter them when gardening, berry picking, or just strolling. Besides feeding, they mate now and will soon lay eggs in preparation for the impending cold. Though bad smelling (and bad tasting), stink bugs are harmless to us, but some are predacious on other insects.

Notes

September

10 September air still holds the moisture of summer, and heavy dews are common in the chilly sunrises. In the calm of this early hour, dewdrops drape meadow plants, creating sparkling scenes. Large circular orb webs made by spiders last night now sag with moisture. Just as attractive as these aerial snares are the dew-coated funnel webs which now grace the lawns.

Not as large or delicate as the vertical webs, funnel webs are more abundant: twenty or more can easily be found in a single yard. In their droplet attire, they look like lace scattered on the lawn. The flat sheet of threads has an opening in the center, giving the webs their resemblance to funnels, and here the owner sits waiting for passing meals. A blundering insect crossing the web is quickly seized by this sedentary hunter. With poor vision, the spider relies greatly on feeling the struggling captive. The spider's fangs inject digestive venom into the prey, and with the insides of the insect thus liquefied, the spider sucks it dry. Spiders remain in these funnel webs until the cold sets in, at which time many lay eggs and die—unless they have chosen buildings such as garages and basements for their webs.

Try an experiment. Can you fool a spider by dropping a dead fly on the end of a thread into the center of a funnel web, or does the spider reject your gift?

Notes

September

11 When most of us think of migrating butterflies, we remember flights of monarchs and how these black and orange insects travel from the northland to winter in Mexico. It may come as some surprise to know that monarchs are not the only of our butterflies to migrate. Less spectacularly, a butterfly called red admiral also migrates and September is a good time to see them passing by. Migrating only to states farther south, some adults have even been known to survive a mild winter in the north.

The admiral's dark brown wings carry a great deal of red: a red bar with white spots crosses the front wings, and the hind wings are bordered with red. A pink forewing spot marks the otherwise nondescript underwings.

After spending summer in the marshes and fields, migrating adults can be found in many habitats as they pause to feed on sap, rotten fruit, or droppings. Although they are not usually flower feeders, they will occasionally sip nectar at clovers or asters. The caterpillars feed on nettles, including the abrasive stinging nettles.

Those who have walked through a patch of stinging nettles, an annoyance to farmers and hikers alike, appreciate the red admiral butterfly, whose caterpillar feeds on the plant.

Notes

September

12 Green darners, the largest of the northland dragonflies, become a common sight in September. The clear wings of these big insects span four inches. The green body between the wings is thick, extending into a long thin blue-green abdomen. This darning-needle shape and the insect's three inch length give the green darner its common name.

Huge compound eyes give these predators eyesight in nearly every direction. Such wraparound vision makes the green darners hard to catch, and it also makes them effective predators. With excellent eyesight and powerful wings that allow them to hover and fly in every direction, green darners patrol the wetlands and meadows in search of midges, caddis flies, mosquitoes, and other flying insects. Most of their victims are snatched in midair.

While many dragonflies drop their eggs on water while flying, green darners use a strong ovipositor to force eggs into plant stems near the water. By fall, the territorial adults begin to wander and are often seen flying more than a hundred feet above ground in what may be migration.

A butterfly net will help you capture a dragonfly. With care, these fascinating insects can be observed up close, then released unharmed.

Notes

September

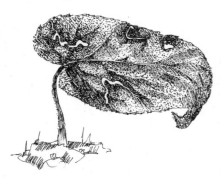

When you see foliage damaged by leaf miners, see if you can track the progress of the larva from birth to its exit from the leaf.

13 A wide variety of plant parts are eaten by insects. Whether it's roots, seeds, fruits, flower, pollen, bark, or leaves, some kind of insect will feed on it. Caterpillars, the most obvious leaf eaters, may devour their food with such intensity that they completely defoliate a tree, avoiding only the parts too hard to chew.

We do not think about leaves being eaten from the inside, but little critters called leaf miners do just this. Since leaves are virtually paper thin, it seems unbelievable that any creature could live between the upper and lower surfaces, feeding on the middle section. Mesophyll cells in the leaves, however, serve as food for insect larvae as varied as beetles, flies, wasps, and moths. As they eat their way through their youth, they excavate a patterned pathway with twists and turns that identify the species that is present in the leaf. Many tracks are long and wind over much of the leaf, while other signatures are written on small blotched regions.

During September, two woodland wildflowers, the zigzag goldenrod and the large-leaf aster, commonly carry miner autographs from the summer. Tunnels enlarging from inception to termination reveal insect growth patterns in leaves.

Notes

September

14 Salamanders, which are southern animals, are not common in the northland. We ordinarily find only two kinds here. Since both of these—the four-inch-long blue-spotted salamander and the three-inch-long red-backed salamander—live their lives under leaf litter and logs in forests, we seldom see either. Even more elusively, they do most of their feeding and moving at night. September, however, is a good time to catch sight of them, because we often move firewood, a favorite hiding place of theirs, as we prepare for winter.

Blue-spotted salamanders are mostly black with light gray-blue spots on their sides and short laterally compressed tails. Like frogs, in early spring, they breed in ponds and have even been observed to be active on March snow. Usually they are seen only in damp weather.

Red-backed salamanders are dark colored with a wide red stripe from the head to midway down the long thin tail. Two unique features are typical of these salamanders. Adults do not have gills or lungs, breathing entirely through the slimy skin, and eggs are produced in a clutch under or in a log, not in water.

You never can tell what will skitter away when you pick up a log or roll it over. Some interesting critters will never be seen unless you look into or under their hiding places. Remember to return the log to its original position.

Notes

September

To recognize all these plants as goldenrods, you will need to consult a field guide that defines the essence of goldenrodness. The same is true for many other species that have varied appearances.

15 Showy yellow flowers have been glowing in the fields, meadows, and roadsides for the last month but now, in mid-September, they begin to fade. Before they leave us, let's look at the eight kinds that we commonly see in the northland. Here, as elsewhere, goldenrods are more varied in habitat than we might anticipate.

As expected, most (five kinds) grow in open country. There we find the last to bloom and the tallest (six feet), giant goldenrod, as well as the very leafy and most common, Canada goldenrod. Two-foot-high furry types, the gray and hairy goldenrods grow there, too. A customary resident of the open prairies, stiff goldenrod, with flat oval leaves, grows sporadically in the northland.

Bogs, marshes, or wetland edges are homes for two more types: bog goldenrod, with its red stem and grass-leaved goldenrod, which has the thinnest of goldenrod leaves and which flowers in a flat-topped cluster.

A woodland species, zigzag goldenrod, has a crooked stem with its flower head at the base of broad leaves.

Notes

September

16 In keeping with the color changes of deciduous trees and shrubs in September, the hazels or hazelnuts of fence rows and woodland edges develop colors of yellow or red on their toothed leaves. This shrub is often confused with alder or is not even noticed among the larger trees.

It is not the leaf coloring that makes this shrub identifiable in fall; it's the nuts that clump on the small branches. The American hazelnut and the lesser-known beaked hazelnut both grow in the northland. Each forms its seeds in nutlike structures covered with ragged leaf bracts called husks. On the American hazelnut, the leafy husk covers the entire nut; on the beaked hazelnut, the husk grows out long and pointed.

Though they ripen in September, we may never see the mature fruits. Many animals—especially grouse, small mammals, and bears—devour them hastily, often when still green. Bears have been known to break down entire groves of these shrubs while feeding. Like other shrubs that are clones of a single plant, they will grow again from a sturdy rootstock.

If you find ripe hazelnuts, try roasting them. In texture and taste, they are similar to store-bought filberts.

Notes

September

Why is it that we think that soft, slimy creatures like slugs are repulsive? To get rid of that feeling, observe them closely and try touching them.

17 Cool, damp mornings in September give us a chance to examine members of the yard and woodland community that we usually do not see: the slugs. These little shell-less snails come out in the dampness of night or early mornings, and we see the slugs or their slime trails on streets and sidewalks until dryness and warmth force them to hide. Because of their thick coating of slime and their bad taste, slugs are able to survive in a variety of habitats including oceans, tropical rain forests, and fields. Though they are disgusting to most palates, several snakes and toads eat them willingly.

Looking much like snails that have crawled out of their shells, they have soft bodies, eyes on projected tentacles, and a single muscular foot that lays down the slime which allows them to glide over terrestrial surfaces. Most are gray-brown, and they are elastic enough to double their one-inch length. With a strong chisellike tongue, slugs feed on plant material as many northland gardeners or mushroom gatherers can testify. Soon these fall slugs will find food too hard to get, and they will move to their wintering sites under boards and logs.

Notes

September

18 Starting with sharp-shinned hawks slowly passing by in mid-August and proceeding to hardy eagles and rough-legged hawks sailing through in early December, raptor migration in the northland is long and varied with about fifteen species flying over. Except for times of hard rain or snow, virtually every day is a hawk day, but none equal the cool, partly cloudy days of mid-September when northwest winds send thousands of broad-winged hawks flying south.

After a summer in the northern forests, these midsized hawks head for wintering grounds in Central and South America. They fly in groups that increase as daytime temperatures and thermals rise. On air currents that provide lift, birds circle and soar until reaching an apex hundreds of feet high where they stream southward.

Though we can see thousands of birds in such flocks, the great heights reduce them to mere dots. Only when they fly low or rest can we observe the banded tail, spotted or barred undersides, and light wings with black tips. Within a month, broad-winged hawks will have journeyed far to the south and the great flocks of mid-September will only be memories.

A good pair of binoculars is essential for a birder. You'll use them to identify birds in flight and to better see birds that are singing high in the treetops.

Notes

September

Although it's tempting to make a pet of wild creatures, it's rarely a good decision. If you capture a critter such as a smooth green snake, observe it for a short time, then return it to a safe place in a field or forest.

19 The smooth green snake is appropriately named with an emerald green back and a white to yellow patterned belly. Because this eighteen-inch-long snake lives in meadows, marshes, and fields, it is often called a grass snake. Though it is still able to climb, the smooth green snake usually does not have the keeled scales which are found on its southern cousin, the rough green snake.

Snakes are active in the daytime, feeding on soft-bodied invertebrates such as worms, slugs, insects, and spiders. Using their coloration as camouflage, the docile smooth green snakes rarely attempt to bite humans. Though they may seem to be good pets, they seldom will eat in captivity and should be left in the wild.

With egg-laying completed in the summer, by mid-September the snakes prepare for winter. Since they are active in the daytime, it is on these fall days that we are most likely to see them. Snakes travel to hibernation sites, which are usually located below deserted anthills. There they spend winter, often in groups of more than fifty. These groups may include garter snakes or red-bellied snakes.

Notes

September

20 As adults, ant lions have four lacy wings and long thin abdomens. Except for their knobby antennae, they look like damselflies. They are weak-flying insects who feed on nectar or pollen, and their name, ant lion, seems totally inappropriate. In the world of insects, however, adults are often completely different from the young, or larvae. Ant lion larvae, often called doodlebugs, have plump hairy abdomens, short legs, and huge pincher jaws. They may spend three years in this larval form, growing to a maximum size of one-half inch in length.

Though the adult has a small appetite that is satisfied with flowers, the voracious larvae feed on insects such as caterpillars and ants. With a bit of ingenuity, they trap their game. The ant lion burrows into sandy soil, and by flicking particles with its huge jaws, it digs a conical pit. Here the predator sits with open jaws to welcome blundering ants. Because of the collapsing walls, the prey does not escape; thus the hunter is able to subdue the ant and suck out its insides.

September is a good time to look near buildings or rocky ledges to find these pits. The ant lion remains buried during winter.

When an insect is a small as the ant lion, it's difficult to fully appreciate a characteristic like its huge jaws. Bring out your magnifying glass, and you'll begin to see this critter from an ant's perspective.

Notes

September

A sweep net used to collect tibellus spiders and other critters should be made from sturdy fabric so it can be dragged through grass and bushes without damage. Try using an old pillowcase.

21 An effective way to collect meadow insects in September is to use a baglike net called a sweep net. On clear afternoons, critters climb onto plants from which they can be dislodged and knocked into the net. Sweeping for a few minutes can collect hundreds of meadow residents.

Collected critters may include bees, wasps, leafhoppers, grasshoppers, beetles, caterpillars, stink bugs, aphids, and small striped spiders about one-half inch long. These tibellus spiders have light brown bodies with a black line down the back and two dots near the end. The body is thin with an abdomen three times longer than it is wide. Though many female spiders are much larger than males, tibellus sexes are similar in size.

Because they do not make webs, these long-legged spiders rely on speed to capture insects, which are abundant in September meadows. Color patterns serve the spiders as ample camouflage. Among plant stems and leaves, they practically disappear when stretched in a straight pose. A common member of the meadow community in September, tibellus spiders will not last long in the coming cold months.

Notes

September

22 The mushrooms of September are a wide and diverse group and along with various shapes, colors, and habitats, they show different growth patterns. One of the easiest to observe now appears—a circle of marasmius mushrooms called fairy rings. The marasmius mushrooms seen on lawns, pastures, and golf courses are light brown or tan and about three inches tall.

Most mushrooms subsist on dead or decaying matter in soil. This wood, humus, or dung is often below the surface, and there, fungal threads, called mycelia, absorb the needed nutrition. If conditions are right, they send up the fruiting bodies we call mushrooms. After maturing, the fruiting bodies die and rot, but the subterranean mycelia continue to grow.

If the mycelia grow outward at the same rate in all directions and periodically (maybe annually) grow more mushrooms, the results are circles called fairy rings. Attaining a larger diameter each year, rings may continue to grow for hundreds of years. Many kinds of mushrooms can form fairy rings.

One need not be superstitious to find delightful the idea of fairies perching on mushrooms or dancing merrily within a fairy ring.

Notes

September

Look carefully at the plants that have already been blackened by early frosts. Compare them to hardy plants like the aster. Can you identify differences in the leaves, stems, or flowers?

23 Flowers of late summer, asters have been twinkling their starlike blossoms in the northland for the last month. In late September, most show little sign of fading, and many will bloom right up to the frosts. Most of us see only the white or blue asters, but actually six species are common in the northland. No doubt a meticulous botanist can find about a dozen different types in all.

Three species share blue-purple rays and yellowish disks but grow in three different habitats. Huge heart-shaped leaves, so common in mixed woods, belong to the large-leaf aster. Wetlands are home to the tallest (six feet) member of the family, the red-stemmed or swamp aster; the most common blue kind, Lindley's aster, abounds in meadows and fields. White ray flowers and yellowish disk flowers are carried on three other common asters. The flat-top aster makes its home in wetlands. In meadows and fields, we find the most common white aster: the panicled or marsh aster with flowers in long clusters. There, too, we see the shortest kind, just two feet tall, the side-flowering calico aster.

Notes

September

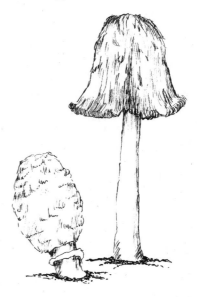

24 Many mushrooms found in September grow on decaying material in the woods, and any serious mushroom collector wanders the fall forests in search of interesting fungi. Some of these mushrooms grow on lawns, and although not as diverse as those in woods, they may be just as numerous.

One of these lawn mushrooms, coprinus, not only grows commonly in the dung of pastures but also among tree stumps or decayed matter on lawns in urban or suburban surroundings. Forming clumps, these six-inch-tall light brown mushrooms do not last long.

Coprinus is better known as shaggy mane or inky cap. The former name refers to the straggly top of these mushrooms, and the latter notes the black, inky substance formed as mature mushrooms self-digest. The caps are conical and brown, but the gills and spores are black. Self-digestion seems strange and uncommon, but in inky cap mushrooms, it is another one of nature's schemes to help with spore dispersal. Digestion of the gills exposes the spores so that they can blow away more easily. Autodigestion often consumes the entire cap and stalk; the mushroom is thus returned to the soil.

Seeds are often encased in sturdy coverings that protect them from the elements. In inky cap mushrooms, spores are protected from the process of self-digestion that destroys the rest of the mushroom.

Notes

September

We recognize some plants by their smell. Gather a variety of wildflowers and garden flowers. Blindfold people and see if they can identify the plants by their scent. They'll certainly recognize that a tansy blossom is not a rose, but will they know just what it is?

25 Goldenrods and sunflowers are not the only yellow flowers of late September's meadows and fields. The well-known tansy also grows here and sometimes takes over this domain. This persistent three-foot high transplant is a familiar sight along northland roadsides.

Formerly grown in European gardens, where it was used in cooking, cheese-making, and brewing tonic tea, this imported plant has become well established in the northland, and once it takes hold in a site, it hangs on. Flowers, rayless and looking much like buttons, cluster on flat growths above the fernlike leaves. These one-half-inch blossoms along with the leaves are odorous when crushed, giving the plant its common name of stinkweed.

Early in the season, the much-divided leaves are often mistaken for ferns. The hardy tansy grows during a long flowering season that stretches from midsummer until fall frosts. Persistent even in death, the stem remains standing throughout the winter, and it is not unusual to see a blooming tansy next to the dead stem from the previous year's growth.

Notes

September

26 Birds are mostly quiet on late September afternoons, but songs abound in meadows and fields as katydids, grasshoppers, and crickets all sing of love and home. Feeding on plants, most of these insects stay here throughout the year, but territorial field crickets may be found elsewhere too. We often hear chirps as banished males try to establish territories on our lawns and in our garages and basements.

These black one-inch-long crickets sing often during this hectic time in their lives. Like many insects, field crickets are influenced by temperature, chirping faster in warm weather, slower in cool weather. This fact has labeled field crickets living thermometers, which describes a capability even better seen in tree crickets.

Crickets hold their wings more horizontally than do grasshoppers or katydids, and males vibrate them to produce their chirps. Both males and females have spines on their abdomens called cerci, but only the female has what appears to be a tail. This tube, the ovipositor, is used to place eggs underground, safe from the winter cold. Adult crickets, so lively now, will die in the coming cold fall months.

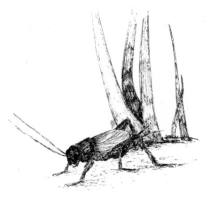

In China, crickets are kept in cages as symbols of good luck. If you decide to try caging a cricket, be sure to thoroughly wash the greens that you feed it. Residual pesticides could be very unlucky for the little critter.

Notes

September

Watch the trees in your yard and notice how different kinds show varying colors at this time.

27 Whether they are sunsets, rainbows, or northern lights, some of nature's displays are worth seeing again and again. During the last week of September, northland deciduous trees replay the autumn show that we have seen before, but willingly we may drive miles to see it again. Because of its usually bright colors, this week in September is often called peak week. After a summer of green, look for the reds of dogwood, red maple, red oak, sumac, and Virginia creeper; the oranges of cherry and sugar maple; and the yellows of ash, aspen, basswood, birch, elm, hazel, poplar, sugar maple, and willow.

Green chlorophyll used for food-making all summer breaks down in cool weather, and with it gone, yellow xanthophyll and orange carotene, always present, become visible. During clear days and cool nights, excess leaf sugars form anthocyanin, a dazzling red pigment. Though a treat for us, this panorama seems to be incidental for the trees, doing them neither good nor harm. Within two weeks, this tree-mendous spectacle will be one of our summer memories and we will look forward to next year's show.

Notes

28 Two and a half inches long and one inch wide, giant water bugs are truly huge. Not only are they large, these aquatic insects carry armored suits, their tough exoskeletons. While their hairy hind legs are well adapted to swimming, their powerful grabbing front legs are folded like pinchers, and their mouth is a short, stout, piercing beak. No wonder these critters are also called toe biters.

Giant waterbugs may be the largest insects of the northland, but with a life spent underwater in weedy ponds, they are not seen much all summer. In the water, they use their grasping legs and puncturing mouths to feed on other aquatic insects, tadpoles, and even fish. Prey are subdued with anesthetic saliva and their insides are sucked out.

Now, in fall, as cold weather moves in and temperatures in their home pond drop, these huge water bugs often emigrate from ponds to larger bodies of water, such as lakes, for winter. Their exit flights usually happen at night and may be interrupted by the presence of porch or pole lights. Getting sidetracked, these electric light bugs may buzz themselves into exhaustion.

We know that usually big critters prey on little critters. We're also pretty sure that fish eat insects. It's surprising to learn that giant water bugs sometimes eat little fish.

Notes

September

If you have an oak tree in your yard, you are fortunate. It will draw a variety of wild critters. If you don't, plant one for future generations.

29 Mainly southern trees, oaks abound in warmer parts of the United States, where more than twenty kinds can be found. Here in the northland, we see only two of these large deciduous trees: the northern red oak and the lesser-known bur oak.

The typical oak of yards, parks, and climax forests, the northern red oak is one of our tallest and strongest deciduous trees. The bright red that appears in autumn on its deeply cut and sharply pointed leaves gives this long-lived tree its name. Despite their colorful autumnal display, red oaks may be better known for their tough straight-grained wood or the numerous acorns that form biennially.

Bur oaks grow in a variety of habitats, and though often found in forests, they may also appear as solitary trees in open pastures. These trees may be as tall as red oaks, but tend to be more spreading. The leaves are deeply cut with rounded tips, but it is the acorns that appear each year only to be nearly swallowed by huge caps that make bur oaks famous.

Acorns from both types of oaks are gobbled by wildlife as varied as bears and insects. Acorn weevils and moths specialize in them; blue jays and squirrels plant many by caching them far from the tree that bore them.

Notes

September

30 Purple flowers bloomed for much of the summer, but by late September, only a few can still be found. Most of us know thistles by the many spines on their leaves and stems, but now their seeds blow in the autumn winds; what earlier were purple flowers with green prickly bracts now are fluffy white parachute seeds. The two most common thistles in northland fields, bull and Canada thistle, both reveal their seeds at this time.

Avoiding the spines, bumblebees pollinated the flowers, and the thistles used the easiest means—the wind—to disperse their seeds. These tough plants with nasty spines form soft, fluffy seeds that birds (goldfinches in particular) use for nest lining. Indeed, the late-nesting finches postpone construction until thistle down is available. There will be plenty of other wind-dispersed seeds in the fall, but thistle seeds are some of the first.

Falling on proper sites, seeds wait to germinate in spring. Perennial Canada thistles form seeds each year, while bull thistles produce only in the second year.

In spring, a patch of bare, cultivated ground will not remain bare for long. Windblown seeds such as thistle seeds will soon send up green shoots. The thistles will also send down long sturdy taproots.

Notes

October

October

If you're an angler, you know that some days the fish seem to disappear. Osprey, dependent on fish for sustenance, must be more consistent fish catchers than we are.

1 Although ospreys occasionally breed in parts of the northern United States, they most often construct their huge stick nests in the lake and river country of Canada. In fall, the cool weather begins sending them toward winter homes on the Gulf Coast and in Central America. In October, on long bent wings, this fish eagle passes through the northland.

The two-foot-long body is held aloft by wings that span five to six feet. Osprey have white undersides, brown backs, and bands of dark feathers that extend as far forward as their eyes. The tail is lightly banded. The long feathered feet have sharp talons used for catching slippery fish. Occasionally, we may hear the "kyew, kyew, kyew, kyew, kyew" call from this migrating bird.

Other raptors feed on fish, but none eat them exclusively as the ospreys do. The ospreys' journey south must take them by lakes and rivers so they will be able to feed along the way. Birds usually return to the nest they used the previous season and enlarge it. As a result, nests may reach ten feet tall.

Notes

October

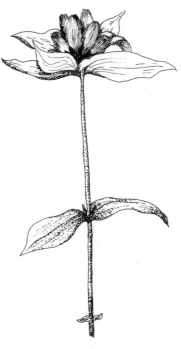

2 By the time we get to October, even the late summer wildflowers have passed their blooming and pollination stages. Now they are in seed. Only a few persist with flowers until the weather becomes cold, but after a frosty morning, we can still find some black-eyed Susans, fleabanes, clovers, asters, and, in some areas, the bottle gentians.

One of the last wildflowers to bloom, the closed or bottle gentian has a unique beauty. It blooms in the late summer in wet, undisturbed meadows, continuing to flower into October. The simple plant with opposite leaves and unique flowers may grow to two feet in height. Bottle gentian is one of the few flowers to bloom without opening. The petals, a deep purple-blue, even while closed are a great addition to the fall flora. The one-inch-wide blossoms are composed of five petals, but we never see the insides.

Held tightly shut, the blossoms can be entered only by large strong insects, such as bumblebees, for nectar and pollination. The purple perennial, which may be the last wetland flower to bloom, remains late in the season.

From the human point of view, honeybees are more significant than bumblebees, but many plants are dependent on the sturdy bumblebee for pollination.

Notes

October

Luminescent mushrooms such as honey mushrooms don't give off enough light to make them easily visible on a dark night, but if you discover a clump during daylight hours, return after dark and look for a faint glow.

3 Large clusters of honey mushrooms now seem to be exploding from the bases of trees in parks and woods throughout the area. Nearly all are growing on dead oak, maple, or birch trees, but a few parasitize live trees.

Cap colors vary from tan to gold to dark brown, and they may be sticky or dry. Scales and black hairs are scattered on the caps. Light colored gills are attached to the stem and white spores drop from between the gills. Often these spores fall on other caps of the tightly packed mushrooms. Honey mushrooms stand nearly six inches high with caps reaching about four inches across. The stalks are rough and fibrous and usually have a ring or annulus around them. Clusters, which contain twenty or more of these highly variable mushrooms, may be common one year but difficult to find the next.

As is true of other mushrooms, mycelial threads remain in the wood substrate, and each year, if the situation is right, fruiting bodies containing spores will grow again. Under some conditions, these mycelia are luminescent and can add a little glow to the night in a northland autumn forest.

Notes

October

4 Meadow mushrooms, probably the most collected mushrooms in North America, usually emerge in groups, but occasionally they appear alone in lawns, pastures, cemeteries, golf courses, baseball fields, and meadows. The three-inch-wide caps are initially white but become brown with age. Pink gills mature to dark purple-brown and drop chocolate-brown spores. The white stalk often has a thin annulus or ring left from the veil that covered the opened cap.

Most common in fall, meadow mushroom growths usually follow rains and cool weather and may form fairy rings in lawns and fields at this time. These mushrooms are closely related to the cultivated mushrooms of pizza fame. Many fungus fanciers claim that the wild type taste better than their store-bought cousins.

Unfortunately, the dangerous destroying angel mushrooms also grow in fall on lawns and meadows and also have an annulus on the stalk with a cap similar to meadow mushrooms. Destroying angel mushrooms differ by having white gills, white spores, and a cup at the base of their stalk. Only careless pickers would confuse them.

Because of the similarities between amanitas and meadow mushrooms, you should take a class before you go on a mushroom-hunting expedition.

Notes

October

In autumn, young ruffed grouse compete with their elders for territory. In spring, they will compete for mates. This competition between young and old is common in nature.

5 Permanent residents of our woods, ruffed grouse are with us all summer, although they usually remain unseen. Their nests, built in late spring on the forest floor, went undetected, and our sporadic summer sightings were limited to a passing bird feeding along woods' edges or at road crossings.

Now, in the fall, grouse make two changes in their lives. The chicks that for the past season traveled and fed with their mother have become too large for the home territory and therefore take flight in an annual dispersal. The five to ten young fly off in all directions to fend for themselves and claim land. These flights bring the birds out of seclusion, and they may now be spotted on roads or in yards. Finding a feeding and wintering site is not easy: travel, predation, and weather combine to make this a time of great loss of life among the grouse population.

Established males, threatened by these young ones who suddenly drop in, defend their territories by drumming. At first this sound, which ordinarily heard in the spring, seems out of place, but the older birds drum with some regularity from a favorite log to secure their homes. Fall days periodically take on this sound of spring.

Notes

October

6 With a heavy dew or fog in early October, late spider webs glisten their silken threads holding visible droplets of moisture. On a cool morning, we may spy a few orb webs in the meadow, funnel webs in the yard, and many sheet webs in trees, bushes, and tall grasses along the forest edge.

The name sheet webs may imply that they are merely flat platforms, and although some are, most are shapely and constitute an amazing formation of numerous threads. Two such constructions common in autumn are worthy of note. The tiny bowl and doily spider, one-fourth inch long, makes a web shaped like a bowl. The filmy dome spider, also one-fourth inch long, constructs its web like a dome. The results are webs with bowls turned in opposite directions. Both spiders are dark with yellow abdominal patterns; each hides under its bowl. Insects flying through this network of threads hit them and fall down to where the owners wait. Prey are subdued and eaten at this site. These webs will not be constructed much longer this fall, but the hardy spiders continue to be seen for another month as they prepare for winter as adults.

You can probably identify several kinds of spider webs: orb, funnel, and sheet. Next time you see a web, try to give a name to its structure.

Notes

October

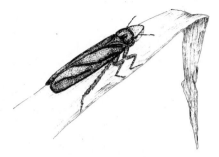

A hand lens will help you get a close look at a tiny leafhopper. A hand lens, held close to the eye, gives clear, steady magnification.

7 By mid-October, nearly all meadow plants have gone to seed or died in the frosts. Yet in the warmth of an Indian summer afternoon, a myriad of insects can still be found here. Most abundant of these are tiny insects with pointed heads and big eyes: the leafhoppers. About one-fourth inch long, most are green or brown.

More than two thousand species of leafhoppers live in North America. Endowed with piercing mouths, each kind feeds on the sap of a particular plant. In the meadow, the chosen plants seem to be goldenrods, asters, and grasses.

Antennae on these leafhoppers are short, but their hind legs, which they use to hop among the meadow plants, are long. Their folded wings lie parallel to each other over their bodies. In some species, these wings are striped and brightly colored. Though able to fly, leafhoppers are not likely to do so.

Most of the meadow insects that appear so active this afternoon will soon die in the coming cold, but not leafhoppers. These insects winter as adults on the ground among plant litter. Their hardiness helps to explain their abundance.

Notes

October

8 Perhaps no time of year is like early October when it comes to seeing sparrow species. Between the lingering summer residents and the passing migrants, the northland woods and meadows hold so many that on virtually any day at least ten kinds can be seen. Alone or in flocks, sparrows are now here in large numbers, and for once during the year, we cannot ignore the brown birds that look so similar.

Many resident sparrows are gone, but some streaked ones remain: song sparrows in yards, savannah sparrows in meadows, and Lincoln sparrows in bogs. Unstreaked birds include the chipping sparrows in yards, swamp sparrows in wetlands, and white-throated sparrows in forests.

Breeding in northern forests and on the tundra but now passing through and pausing here are an impressive number of species: white-crowned sparrows (white on the head, but not on the throat); American tree sparrows (who wear a large dark chest spot); fox sparrows (reddish brown with spots); and Harris sparrows (whose black face and throat of summer are now only black markings).

It is possible, but less likely, that we will also glimpse the clay-colored sparrows, vesper sparrows, and LeConte's sparrows in this busy season.

If you can't yet identify all the sparrows, you can at least describe them. Note the back and breast color, any bars that may appear on the tails or wings, spots or streaks, and the presence or absence of a cap.

Notes

October

During a long migration, an omnivorous bird like the Lapland longspur appears to have an advantage over birds with a more limited diet.

9 After a summer in the tundra, Lapland longspurs pause here as they pass through on their way to a winter on the prairies and fields to the south of us. The six-inch-long birds appear to be in no hurry to reach wintering sites and often remain in suitable locations for many days.

They travel in mixed flocks, sharing the fields with other birds such as sparrows, horned larks, and snow buntings. In its winter plumage, a lapland longspur has a reddish brown back and nape, a streaked belly, and a tail bordered with white feathers. During breeding season, the male sports a black face and chest, but the colors have faded by now. A very long hind toe claw, as big as the toe itself, gives longspurs their name.

Here in the fields, longspurs seek meals of seeds and any available insects to sustain them for the remainder of their migration. Looking much like sparrows, they can be distinguished by the rattling "ticky-tick-tew" or the musical "teew" call notes, often given while the birds are in flight. In October they are slow to move on, but they are usually gone by the time snow covers the northland.

Notes

October

10 Most of the meadow flowers that bloomed in summer or fall have gone to seed. However, the pearly everlasting is now in seed and, without changing much from its flowering days, still gets plenty of notice.

Flowers are borne on clusters above the leafy stalks. Though everlastings are composites, its flowers are all disks, no rays, and there are separate plants for male and female blossoms. Male flowers have yellow centers, females white, but both are surrounded by white bracts. Abundant thin, hairy leaves fill the stem. Now, in October, the plants look much as they did in August. Clusters of balled seeds, similar to the flowers, still stand on leafy stems, even though the leaves are turning brown or gray.

Since this perennial does not wilt or break apart quickly after being picked and dried, pearly everlasting is often gathered and used for winter bouquets. Maybe this is why the two-foot-tall plant of dry meadows, roadsides, and pastures is called everlasting.

Pick some stems of pearly everlasting and add them to a bouquet of other dried flowers. A spritz of hair spray will keep most flowers from dropping.

Notes

October

The green canopy that spreads over us and the bright wildflowers at our feet can blind us to the many interesting fungi that are present throughout the forest. Now that leaves have dropped, if you begin looking, you may see the slender combed fungi.

11 Iciclelike spines suspended from white delicate growths on trees and rotten logs add a strange beauty to the October woods. The bodies of these toothed fungi are soft and delicate and are said to be delicious by those who have sampled them. Up to a foot long, they can be found growing on damp wood of forest trees, dead or alive.

Both types of toothed fungi living in northland forests are white and grow on deciduous trees such as maple, birch, or oak, but they differ in their shapes and lifestyles. The teeth or spines are actually structures that the fungi use to disperse spores from their fruiting bodies.

Comb tooth fungus, also called coral or comb hericium, branches extensively, and each branch is covered with delicate spines or teeth. Growing only on dead trees, the branching structures can get quite large and may form small colonies. Bearded-tooth fungus has a growth of larger spines developing from the unbranched body that gives it the long icicle appearance. Bearded-tooth, also called lion's mane or old man's beard, can be found on dead or living trees in late summer or fall.

Notes

October

The rate of tree cricket chirps can be used to estimate the temperature. The rule is that the number of chirps in fourteen seconds added to forty equals the temperature in degrees Fahrenheit.

12 Most of us recognize crickets as the dark chirping insects that call in fields and meadows and occasionally indoors in late summer. These black ground crickets overshadow the quieter tree crickets who also reside in the northland. Tree crickets are mostly light green with long antennae and huge clear oval wings that fold flat over their abdomen.

As we might expect from the name, they may be found in trees or bushes of the forests, but many also live in the meadows. Whereas tree crickets are silent by day and sing at night, the meadow inhabitants sing both day and night. The male's continuous trill speeds or slows with the ambient temperature.

Males lift their wings when singing, and though this helps with sound resonation, it also releases a pheromone that attracts females. Apparently, since females cannot hear the chirps, calls are territorial and aimed at other males. Adult tree crickets will lay eggs in branches before dying in the cold.

Notes

October

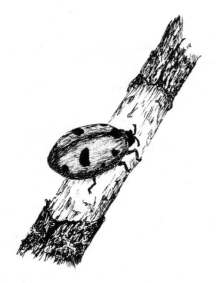

If you want to introduce a reluctant young child to the pleasures of insect observation, start with the ladybug. Most children are willing to let a ladybug walk on their hand.

13 Also known as ladybird beetles, the red ladybugs with black spots are some of the better-known and best-loved insects. Different kinds of ladybugs can be identified by the varying number and arrangement of their spots. They are considered to be beneficial insects since both larvae and adults feed on aphids.

To deal with winter, ladybugs take a rather unusual approach. Usually insects choose one of four ways to cope with winter: dying after laying eggs, hibernating, migrating, or staying active. Ladybugs appear to do two of these. In September and October, adults migrate to hibernating sites. They travel, sometimes long distances, to reach these locations. Some ladybugs, however, remain in the northland, where they readily hibernate with other species.

Hibernating under logs, leaves, or similar debris, the quarter-inch-long insects form aggregates of hundreds or thousands. In a torpor, they survive winter. A few species winter alone, and some, like the two-spotted ladybug, come indoors, which explains why we see them in autumn at windows. In the spring, ladybugs will return to warm-weather sites.

Notes

October

14 The northland is not home to many snakes: only two kinds are common here—the well-known striped garter snake and the lesser-known, but maybe just as abundant, red-bellied snake. Extending from head to tail on the latter, the red colors cover far more of the undersides than just the belly. This ventral pigment, shading from bright red to orange-yellow, explains the snake's common name, copper-belly. The snake's back is colored in shades of brown ranging from very light to almost black, and four narrow lines run the length of its body. These small snakes seldom exceed a length of twelve inches.

Red-bellied snakes live farther north than most snakes and are found in many areas of Canada. These snakes, common in woods and bogs, forage under leaves and logs for slugs, snails, earthworms, and insect larvae. Like garter snakes, they give live birth.

Now, during the mild days of October, we may see more of these elusive snakes than at any other time of the year as they travel over trails and roads to their hibernating sites in deserted ant mounds or building foundations.

Before killing a red-bellied snake, think about its diet. It eats many of the critters that would otherwise devour your garden. And it's harmless to humans, so why not let it live.

Notes

October

Autumn's fallen leaves provide a protective mulch on the forest floor where they eventually become a rich humus that will nourish woodland plants and flowers.

15 Because of their annual color show, trees get more attention in early October than at any other time. Each year we watch the return of the brilliant autumn colors; reds followed by or concurrent with yellows. Along with this dazzling display, one of nature's ironies is played out in October. In response to colder temperatures and less daylight, trees drop the very same organs that made food for them all summer and provided the energy for growth. Most northland deciduous trees spend five months each year with leaves and seven months without. Keeping leaves, although replacements will have to be grown next year, is not good for their survival.

Shedding leaves is an adaptation to winter. With their extensive surface area, leaves would catch more snowfall than the trees could support. However, the main reason trees drop leaves is that leaves are the source of moisture loss, and in the cold, dry air of winter this process would cause the plants to die of desiccation. So after trees reclaim leaf chlorophyll, a group of cells forms a wall called an abscission or separation layer. With little or nothing holding the leaf on the tree, a brisk wind, rain, or even its own weight makes it fall.

Notes

16 Almost everyone finds a mid-October walk in northland forests to be a pleasant experience. The brilliant leaf color alone would make the walk great, but changing foliage is not the only thing happening among the plants. At the base of stumps and logs and even fairly high up on tree trunks, groups of light golden-brown pholiota mushrooms can be seen.

Some of the most beautiful of the fall mushrooms, the pholiotas, grow on deciduous trees, their rotten logs, or nearby soil. The caps are about four inches across, sticky, and full of bumpy growths called scales, some of which are quite sharp. Scales are scattered over the cap but also can be found in the ring or annulus on the stalk. The golden-brown gills, under the cap, are attached to the stalk; rusty-brown spores form and fall from these gills.

The mushrooms are not large, but among the many kinds of pholiotas, they are some of the largest. Being saprophytes, they are dependent on moisture and rotten wood. When both are available, as often happens in the woods of mid-October, pholiotas become common.

To humans, decaying food is dangerous, but most fungi live on decaying vegetation. You can expect to find pholiota mushrooms on rotting wood.

Notes

October

When we compare one thing to something else, we gain understanding. We can guess, for instance, that the Milbert's tortoise shell butterfly has mottled wings.

17 Orange and black decorations are common in homes and schools during this month, and one of the last butterflies of the season, the Milbert's tortoise shell, fits into the general decor. These two-inch-long butterflies have dark wings with a thick yellow-orange band. A few spots of blue added to the hind wings make the butterflies one of the northland's most colorful specimens.

Milbert's tortoise shell butterflies stay active in the fall sunlight, visiting hardy flowers and sipping tree sap until late in the month. The spread-wing pose on leaves, buildings, or roads during clear October days is a splendid addition to this lovely time. The adults will hibernate in buildings and tree hollows or behind bark.

Found in much of Canada, Milbert's tortoise shells are basically northern butterflies. In warm weather they seek homes in moist pastures and edges of forests. They deposit their eggs on nettles, and the caterpillars feed almost exclusively on the leaves of these plants. The chrysalises are formed in summer, and the butterflies emerge as adults any time from mid-July to early September.

Notes

October

18 Insects—so common in the meadow all summer and early fall—now begin to disappear in the frosty days of mid-October. After chilly nights, however, if afternoon temperatures rise, many survivors will appear. Among them are some predators that are still active: spiders, dragonflies, and assassin bugs.

Assassin bugs, which have rough brown bodies, elongated heads, folded antennae, and pointed beaks, are rightly named. Adults do late-season hunting by sitting on plant stems or hardy flowers and catching prey with their grasping front legs. Piercing victims with their beaks, they suck them dry.

To some people, all insects are bugs, but members of the order *Hemiptera* are the true bugs. Adults fold their wings over their back allowing only half to be seen (hemi means half). Both young and adults are predaceous.

At one-half to one inch long, assassin bugs are a dominant predator in the October meadow. They seem invincible as they hunt in the afternoon sunlight. However, they and their insect prey will soon succumb to the chill.

People often attribute human characteristics to animals. You can see that in the assassin bug's name. It is, of course, just a hungry bug, not a vicious killer.

Notes

October

The harvestman's willingness to lose a limb in order to save its life seems almost unimaginable to humans. Other creatures, however, share that sometimes useful characteristic.

19 Because they have eight legs, harvestmen, or daddy longlegs, are mistakenly called spiders. However, spiders have two body parts, the front cephalothorax and the rear abdomen; the harvestmen have these two joined to form what appears to be a single body part. Their small oval bodies have extremely long, thin, and flexible legs.

The name harvestmen comes from the phenological observation that these insects are more common during harvest times. Though the validity of this conclusion varies in different localities, it is a fairly good observation. Southern species may winter as adults while northland species do not. They are active now, laying eggs behind bark; the adults will soon succumb to cold.

These active critters stalk around feeding on plant juices and dead insects. Departing from a sap and scavenger diet, a few kinds prey on live insects. Clawed appendages (pedipalps) in front of the head are used for feeding. The long legs are of interest in two ways. Only six of the eight legs are used for walking: the second pair are used as antennae to feel. When caught by the legs, harvestmen can, in a process called autotomy, lose them at will and escape.

Notes

October

20 The northland's tiniest owls put on quite a show for us when they migrate south in October. Saw-whet owls are only eight inches long and fit comfortably in our hand. They wear blotchy streaks below, are dark above, and have no ear tufts.

During most of the year, we seldom see or hear this little resident of the deep forests. The owls are nocturnal and, because they are small, are likely to be located by hearing their calls, not by sight. Their song is a mellow whistle note, "too, too, too, too"; it is repeated many times, often a hundred or more per minute. Saw-whet owls get their name from the raspy call note that sounds like a saw being sharpened on a whet stone.

Though not a flocking bird, at peak migration times, like now, many saw-whets pass by, heading south. Banding stations have caught more than one hundred saw-whet owls in a single night. They fly low during their nocturnal migration, preying on small mammals along the way. Daytime roosts during migration or in winter are in dense evergreens. Sometimes we discover their gray-white regurgitated pellets at these sites.

If a bird hides so well that it is rarely seen, you might name it for its call. That's how the saw-whet owl got its name.

Notes

October

Take a sketch pad along on an autumn walk. Look for just one type of plant, bird's nest fungus, for instance. Sketch it in all its variations, and you will really begin to know it.

21 Brown and less than half an inch high, bird's nest fungus would not be noticed were it not for two conditions: it commonly grows on wood chips, which are often used for trails and gardening, and when mature, it looks like a little bird's nest complete with a set of eggs.

Bird's nest fungus is related to the puffballs, and like them, it has devised a unique method for dispersing its spores. The bird's nest is a cuplike growth that often sits on a small stalk. It remains closed in youth, but opens when mature to reveal a "clutch" of several (often as many as ten) "eggs." These eggs, correctly called peridoles, are composed of spores and, with the help of some raindrops, will get thrown from the fungus. Cups are shaped so that rain drops will send the eggs considerable distances, up to seven feet. This explains why the fungus is also known as splash cup.

Bird's nest fungus grows in colonies, and the mycelia winds among wood chips, sticks, nut shells, vegetable debris, humus, and dung. The fungus is quite common in the moist decay of autumn, but usually goes undetected.

Notes

22 Maybe it is because we call conifers evergreens that many people have the mistaken notion that they do not shed their leaves or needles. Leaves do fall from these trees, but instead of dropping all their needles at once, pine and most other conifers shed only part of them at a time. This is why pine trees have some yellow needles mixed with the green ones each fall. Of course, the northland has a notable exception. Tamarack is our only deciduous conifer: an evergreen that is not always green. In the fashion of other deciduous trees, tamaracks put on a colorful show before the annual needle drop.

The middle of October belongs to the tamaracks. Almost on cue, tamaracks, or larch, wait until other deciduous trees have had their show. Then, when the reds of maple, cherry, and sumac and the yellows of aspen, poplar, and birch have passed, the yellow-golds of tamarack take over. This conifer of bogs and swamps gets attention for a week until the one-inch-long needles fall. Perhaps it is the poor soil in these habitats that causes the clustered needles to fall leaving tiny cones behind.

Keep track of the coming and going of tamarack color. Does it occur every year in October? In the same week of October? How does this event relate to temperature and rainfall?

Notes

October

If you find a dead red skimmer, examine its wings carefully with a hand lens or magnifying glass. What can you determine about the structure of these transparent wings.

23 A clear, mild late October day brings out many critters—as well as many of us—to take advantage of the sunlight. After a chilly night, temperatures may rise to the forties or fifties. In sunny places, we may find a few frost survivors such as flies, grasshoppers, spiders, or red dragonflies.

Dragonflies of one species or another have been with us since spring, but now we see only the last of the adults sitting in the sun to stay warm and avoid being frozen to death. One of these late-season dragonflies, the red skimmer, has a long thin red abdomen and a dark thorax between the four clear wings.

As is true of other dragonfly young, the red skimmer young live in water and spend winter there. Though adults scatter to the fields and meadows, they, too, are never far from water. Earlier in the fall, eggs were deposited individually in a tandem flight on the water's surface. The female gently touched the water with her abdomen and placed the eggs there. Mating and egg-laying done by now, the red skimmers try to stay warm and feed on those insects which are still active, but soon they will succumb to the frosty nights.

Notes

October

To see the floating threads of ballooning spiders, look toward (never at) the sun. Try to find the traveling spider.

24 Indian summer days after mid-October seem to bring a bit of magic with them. Clear, calm days with warm temperatures reaching into the midfifties are welcomed by all—ourselves included—but spiders make the best use of this time. Many baby spiders hatch in late summer, and for the last two months, they have been molting and growing. They are still small, and must molt several times before reaching adulthood. During the mild October days, these tiny spiders take advantage of rising thermals to travel making this the greatest spider dispersal time.

Young spiders and small adults travel by air. To do this, they climb a branch, a post, or even a blade of grass, lift their abdomen, and throw out silken thread. As the lengthening silk floats off, it carries the spider with it. Most ballooning spiders travel only short distances, but some have been known to travel hundreds of miles. Ballooning happens during much of the year, but on these days, when the leaves are off the trees and the afternoon sun is low, we see travel threads appearing everywhere. These days filled with silk are sometimes called the season of gossamer days.

Notes

October

If you're out bird watching, carrying your binoculars, and come upon some cup fungi, turn the binoculars upside down. You'll find that, when held close to the fungi, they will magnify and let you see details like the eyelashes.

25 Fungal cups are common in the fall forest, and some even persist until the arrival of snow. Brown, black, orange, yellow, red, and blue-green cups can all be found. Two distinct and noticeable fungi of the October woods are red-orange eyelash cups and blue-green stain.

The former, a small fungus about a half-inch in diameter, which grows on rotten logs, is easy to overlook. If it were not for its bright red-orange color, we would not see it. Groups of eyelash cups on damp decaying logs or on nearby soil are likely to catch our attention, but the tiny eyelashes themselves are harder to discern. When the cup opens and forms a disk at maturity, the margins are fringed with eyelashlike brown hairs that most of us need magnification to see. They may help protect the spores forming inside the cups.

In autumn, wet, rotten logs on the forest floor often display a blue-green stain that looks like spilled ink. This pigment comes from mycelia that subsequently form one-fourth-inch-wide blue-green cups on tiny stalks. These fertile growths hold spores on their surface and function as fruiting bodies for this stained fungus.

Notes

October

26 With leaves gone from the trees, we find it easier to see some small critters of late October. Hardy butterflies, moths, and spiders that would be lost in foliage are now visible, and we can see the aerial dances that take place along the edges of meadows and forests during these afternoons and evenings.

Many small insects appear to be swarming, but when we examine them a bit more closely, we see a rising-falling pattern. The small insects are about the size of mosquitoes and are often inaccurately called by that name. Instead, they are gnats, midges, March flies, and crane flies. During these flights, they are not interested in biting us. Indeed, nearly all lack the mouth parts to bite us even if they wanted to do so. As members of the order *Diptera*, all have only two wings instead of the usual four, but those two wings are powerful enough to keep them in flight for a long time.

Instead of a massive autumn insect attack, what we witness on late October days is the dancing display flight usually done by male insects. In these flights, they battle each other for females and mate with them. Eggs are deposited in water before it freezes.

List the northland insects that actually bite, sting, or otherwise harm humans. It's a short list, isn't it? Most insects have little interest in people.

Notes

October

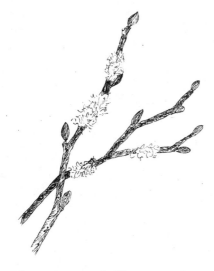

Many critters exude fibrous strands —spiders, caterpillars, even woolly alder aphids. The fibers spun for cocoons can be respun by humans into useful threads. Their original purpose, however, was predation or protection.

27 For most of the year, alders are hardly even noticed. They are the small weedy trees along the edges of wetlands and roadsides. For most of the year, too, aphids share the same anonymity. They are the small green wingless insects that live on plant stems, sucking sap and giving honeydew to ants. Now, after the trees drop their leaves, overlooked aphids on overlooked alders team up to present a roadside scene we can not overlook. Woolly alder aphids form large populations on branches of alders, where they feed on sap. What makes them obvious is the long white strands of waxy material the aphids produce from their abdomen that make them look like a cottony or woolly fungus. The one-eighth-inch-long insects form a tight colony that remains in one place while feeding. Apparently, the woolly growth deceives predators and protects the colony.

As with many insects, their life cycles are a bit complex. Some of these aphids survive winter on alders, while others go to maples. In either case, the woolly colonies linger through much of the chilly autumn and may still be on the alders after snow covers the ground.

Notes

28 In the chilly evenings of late October, we do not expect to see active insects, but in our car headlights or fluttering at the windows are the late-season moths. A huge and diverse group is found even among these thirty-five degree moths, but two general kinds exist. Linden loopers (or winter moths) and fall cankerworm (or spanworm) are commonly seen on these evenings. Though adults are evident now, both types are named for their larval stages when, as inchworms, they lived on maple, oak, apple, cherry, or basswood. Now, as adults, the moths have undeveloped mouths: they cannot eat and survive only on stored food from the larval stage.

Each species varies from light brown, or nearly white, to dark gray. Fall cankerworm is a bit darker. Only the males fly; wingless females of both kinds are hidden on the ground.

Sensing the chilly air, these moths find that now is a season of few predators and a good time in their short lives to mate and lay eggs. Constantly shivering their wings, they are able to stay warm and remain active on these cold nights.

It's hard to believe that these moths can remain active in these chilly temperatures. Watch their shivering wings to see how they do this.

Notes

October

Don't try to eat highbush cranberries fresh, they're much too bitter. Use them for jelly. Berries that are inedible fresh often make tasty preserves.

29 In late October, those trees still holding berries become obvious. Sumac's purple berries, mountain ash's orange clusters, and crab apples all appear now. Perhaps brightest and most juicy of all, highbush cranberries hang from small trees. The fruit's resemblance to the bog cranberry gives this little tree its name. It is actually a king of viburnum.

Only ten feet tall, the shrubby trees get little attention until these berries appear. Now we notice it along roadsides, in wet areas, and scattered in forests. Berry pickers gather the fruits and make one of the best-tasting jellies in the northland. Trees produce brightly colored berries so that birds will notice and eat them, thereby spreading the seeds; but highbush cranberries often linger on trees through fall, giving the impression that not many critters eat the sour fruits.

Last summer the highbush cranberry held white flowers in a flat umbel growth, similar to the berry cluster now present. Unlike other viburnums—nannyberry and arrowwood—highbush cranberry has maplelike three-lobed leaves.

Notes

October

30 Late October is a good time for us to turn over a few logs and see how some critters are preparing for winter. Offering a shelter from cold, desiccation, and predators, the logs provide a rather stable environment, and many kinds of animals thrive here.

An early-hibernating hornet or wasp has chosen this site to prolong the life of her colony. Nearby, a few slugs and land snails, like the ones on sidewalks and lawns just a few weeks ago, have also become inactive.

Many other critters here are still active. Earthworms draw back at the incoming light when the log is over-turned. As long as the ground is not frozen, they remain mobile. Sow bugs, also called wood lice or pill bugs, form groups or roll up in self defense. They are one of the few terrestrial crustaceans. Among them are centipedes and millipedes. Predaceous centipedes have two legs on each body segment while the scavenger millipedes have four. Both may be called thousand-leggers. A strange insect, the earwig, lives here too. With abdominal pincers that look like calipers, the mother defends her eggs with her life.

If you know nothing about insects, turn over a log and you will only see bugs. With just a bit of knowledge, you'll be able to identify one insect, then another, and another.

Notes

October

If bumps on your lawn suggest that moles are tunneling underground, look for another culprit. Star-nosed moles live only in wetlands.

31 Moles are well-known tunneling animals of lawns, parks, and golf courses, but the northland's only mole tunnels in none of these sites. The star-nosed mole lives in wetlands, usually low areas near lakes and streams.

The mole's five-inch-long body ends in a hairy three-inch-long tail. Large claws for burrowing tip the front feet. It is the twenty-two fleshy projections, or tentacles, on the nose (eleven on either side of the nostrils) that give the critter its name. Since moles have tiny eyes, they may use these tentacles to help feel as they dig.

In late October, the moles prepare for the coming cold. Because they live in wetland homes, they tend to be more active on the surface than below it. Sometimes in fall, we find dead, but unmarked, bodies of star-nosed moles that make us wonder about the cause of death. In this time of peak population, some may disperse and starve.

Star-nosed moles do not cease movement in winter, remaining active day and night. They swim well and can pursue aquatic prey even under the ice. In snow, they travel above or below the surface, but always stay near water.

Notes

November

November

With care, mosses can be transplanted to terrariums where they provide a velvety green carpet if kept moist.

1 Though they have been with us all year and in most cases, for many years, mosses blend into the forest floor and are not even noticed by us. In late October or early November, however, after the leaves fall and before the snow covers, nothing hides the mosses, and we see how abundant these tiny plants are. In many woods, it seems that all midsize or large trees have green carpets surrounding their base, and nearby soil, logs, and rocks are coated with these leafy lilliputians.

Getting down for a closer look, we see that these minute plants have a stem, green leaves, and elliptical and pointed spore capsules. Most form capsules during warm weather and continue to carry them through winter. These containers grow off a single leafy stalk or from prostrate branching stems. A moss called hairy-cap is a giant among the mosses, reaching a height of four inches. With its shape and color, it is often said to look like a miniature evergreen tree. Soon the mosses will be covered, but beneath the snow, they will pass winter in relative warmth and remain green.

Notes

2 Many of us recognize lichens as the flat, crusty, blue-green, yellow, or brown growths seen on rocks and trees. We do not expect them to stand upright or be colorful. However, now, in early November, before snow covers their one-inch-tall bodies, we can see bright red British soldier lichens growing on a variety of substrata. Also known as the matchstick, or redcap, lichen, the lichen's red fruiting body is responsible for it being called British soldier. The vertical yellow-green lichen body is branched, with the spore-holding red fruiting bodies on top.

Overshadowed by the green of summer and soon buried under winter's snow, these showy lichens appear briefly on humus, soil, rotting logs, wood piles, and fence posts throughout the northland. The bright red British soldier lichens do not grow alone: greenish bodies of other lichens are nearby. Some have similarly shaped, but lighter, fruiting bodies, others look like minute golf tees, trumpets, or cups (one is called pixie cup), and still others are just green stalks. All have the algae and fungi needed for these diverse and hardy organisms to survive winter.

When the woods are drab and brown, tiny bright red British soldier lichens are as delightful to see as the first spring wildflowers.

Notes

November

Woolly bear caterpillars are said to forecast the weather. Do you know, and perhaps believe in, any other natural weather prognosticators?

3 We know most insects better as adults than as larvae, but with the familiar woolly bear caterpillars, we would be hard pressed to find, or even name, the adults. These two-toned caterpillars are young isabella moths, a kind of tiger moth. The elusive two-inch-long adults have yellow-orange wings and bodies with black abdominal bands.

In the fall, throughout the northland, we regularly see the hairy caterpillars as they cross roads and sidewalks long after other insects are gone. In their quest for food, the larvae search for late-blooming asters, clovers, and sunflowers in fields and meadows. Besides meals, they seek winter resting sites; unlike most other moths or butterflies, they hibernate as caterpillars. Typically, isabella moths have two generations per year. It is only the caterpillars of the second generation that need to cope with the cold.

Some people have endowed the woolly bear caterpillars with weather-prophesying capabilities. They all have a reddish brown band centered between black at either end. Some say that the blacker their bodies, the colder the winter. Actually, color patterns are a response to growth, not cold; with each molt, the colored bands change slightly in size.

Notes

_____

_____

_____

_____

_____

November

4 Wood ferns stood up to thirty inches tall in the summer, but because of the nearby growths of lady fern, ostrich fern, cinnamon fern, interrupted fern, and bracken, we hardly even noticed them. With the coming of shorter days and the chill of fall, the leaves of other ferns faded to brown, but the wood ferns stayed green, and now we can finally see them.

Only the polypody fern of cliffs and rocky hillsides joins the wood fern in staying green among other November forest flora. Throughout the long winter, buried under snow, some wood ferns retain their color, while others fade. Most, however, will still be green if dug up in December.

Wood ferns have characteristically long feathery leaves called fronds. These contain many divided leaflets and subleaflets above a twelve-inch tall stalk. On wood ferns, the lowest leaflets have a very long first subleaflet. Sterile empty fronds grow near the light-spotted fertile ones. The underside dots, or sori, are seen under magnification to be C-shaped capsules with many spores.

Wood fern spores are so tiny, they can only be seen under magnification. Ferns reproduce by spores just as dandelions reproduce by seeds. Many spores are extremely hardy, remaining dormant for years until environmental conditions are right for new growth to begin.

Notes

November

Reindeer moss is not a moss; it's a lichen. When you observe plants, try to place them in the correct general category by asking yourself a few questions: Is this a conifer or a deciduous tree, a flowering plant or a fern, a moss, or a lichen?

5 Looking like masses of tiny branching bushes, gray or greenish clumps of reindeer lichen are common in the tundra and in far northern forests. They are eaten by caribou or reindeer and may erroneously be called reindeer moss. We also see these lichens in the northland, where, like other growth on the November forest floor, they will soon be blanketed by snow for the winter months.

The lichens comprise colonies of many fine-branching and intertwining bodies. Growing on the forest floor, the clumps seem barely attached to the soil and are readily knocked loose by bumps or wind gusts. In their habitat of sandy soil, pine forests, humus, or rocky open areas, reindeer lichens dry out greatly. In this state they become brittle and crumble underfoot, but when remoistened, they become spongy, soft, and quite palatable to hungry herbivores.

The clumps may reach up to four inches in height and a foot in diameter. The multibranched bodies are composed of the symbiotic algae and fungi seen in all lichens. Fungi hold moisture, and in the sunlight, algae make food. Spores form in tiny capsules on the lichen branch tips.

Notes

November

6 Given the freeze-thaw conditions of early November and the wet snows that cover everything one day and melt a few days later, trees and logs are often wet. Such conditions bode well for the appearance of hardy brown or black jelly fungi. Growing in thick colonies on rotting deciduous logs, especially oak, the one-inch-wide fungal bodies fuse to form large, thick masses up to a foot long. Repeated drying forms a hard, solid fruiting body that becomes soft and slimy when moist—hence its name.

Fungal bodies remain on logs and dead branches all year. However, during the summer, they are less likely to be seen, and in winter, they are dry and frozen. So now, as they slime up in the rains and wet snows of autumn, is the time to see (or feel) them in the bare forests. The jelly fungus begins as a nearly colorless body but becomes dark brown or black with age. These jelly masses are not likely to be confused with other fungi and certainly not with mushrooms, but they form spores in a manner similar to that of the mushrooms. The black, yucky jelly growths produce white spores.

When the weather is dry, see if you can identify a jelly fungus. Check it again after a rain. Were you correct?

Notes

November

If you want to attract brown creepers and other insect-eating birds to your feeder, be sure to provide suet.

7 Small, solitary, and camouflaged, brown creepers are not likely to be seen unless they move or give their high-pitched calls. Birds sometimes have inaccurate or cumbersome names, but the brown creeper seems to be appropriately named. The five-inch-long birds are brown on the back and tail, with white underneath and above the eyes. They feed by creeping up trees in a spiral route starting from the base, then flying to other trees and repeating this ascent. In the upward treks, brown creepers often give "seee" call notes that help us locate them. A stiff tail braces the bird during these climbs, while a curved beak probes under bark for insects.

Though common in the northland, brown creepers breed in the boreal forests. Those here in November may winter with us, but more likely, they are late migrants and will keep going to sites south and east of here. Bark insects provide the nutritious meals needed in this cool month, and their days are spent locating and eating such critters. Usually they feed alone, but they may flock with nuthatches and kinglets. Wintering creepers will occasionally visit feeders for suet.

Notes

November

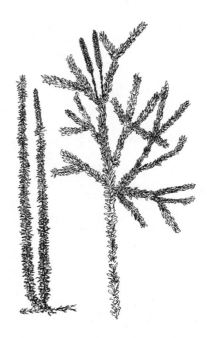

8 In November, woods are basically gray and brown, so individual green plants stand out against the neutral background. Besides a plethora of mosses, a few leafy green plants, and wood ferns, small evergreen club mosses abound in many colonies. Also known as ground cedars, ground pines, running pines, or princess pines, these club mosses often look like little trees only three to six inches tall. Connected by underground spreading stems, most appear to have little spikelike growths on top; these give the club to club moss. Common in northland woods, nearly ten kinds can be found growing here—all of which stay green under the snow throughout winter. Most common in conifer forests, these northern plants are also found in the northland's mixed forests. They range from single spikes looking like big mosses to branched and treelike growths.

Branching rhizomes, or stems, are their usual method of spreading, and this process accounts for the colonies. Clubs that top the stems contain spores that ripen and disperse in autumn winds. Tiny and tinder-dry, these spores were formerly used to provide explosive ignition in fireworks, photographic flashes, and magicians' flames.

Club mosses such as princess pine are often gathered for holiday wreaths. Before picking any greens, ask yourself whether you are damaging the environment in any way.

Notes

November

If you destroy cobweb spiders along with their webs, you will have to deal with the insects those webs would have caught.

9 In the cold weather of November, spider webs have become only a memory. On dew-drenched September mornings, webs were scattered all over the yard, but now the only ones we see are those from spiders that have moved indoors. In these warmer places, they build their webs, and spend the season.

Funnel webs of the house spider are common in corners of garages and porches; the long-legged cellar spider spins its few threads in the basement and attic; but perhaps the most common is the network of silk from cobweb spiders. While many spiders spin large, elaborate webs, those of the cobweb spinners are the series of irregular lines that we see in corners, heating ducts, window sills, garages, basements, or attics. There the spiders sit upside down with the patience of sedentary hunters.

The gray-brown cobweb maker is so common in human dwellings that it is known as the domestic spider. Its cousin, the northern spider—more likely found among trees and rocks—has a black abdomen with white markings. Both of these quarter-inch-long spiders appear dead as they sit and wait for weeks in their webs to catch indoor insects.

Notes

10 Many of us think of puffballs as the brown, ball-like growths on stumps and logs that explode in clouds of spores when stepped on. These certainly are puffballs, but this fungi group is much more varied. Ranging in size from marbles to melons, they are found on forest soil, lawns, driveways, sand, or logs. Puffballs may look like golf balls, pears, or stars. They grow alone or form groups, and many are edible. Puffballs are fungi that produce numerous spores in ball-shaped cases. When the fungus reaches maturity, the outer skin ruptures at the top, causing it to look and act like a tiny volcano. Every bump, step, raindrop, or wind gust can release a mass of spores.

Fall is a good time to see puffballs, and the four that grow in the northland are worth noting. Pear-shaped puffballs are common on rotten logs and nearby soil. Spiny white golf-ball types are often seen in lawns. Giant white puffballs grow in fields, pastures, cemeteries, or along streams, and though watermelon sized, they are edible when newly formed. Earthstars, common under conifers, start out like other puffballs, but the folding outer skin gives them their star shape.

When a puffball reaches maturity, experiment with it. Tap it lightly; slice it open; dust the spores into a terrarium. Will they grow for you?

Notes

November

A tiny deer mouse perched on a bookshelf is charming, but you'd better caulk your cabin's cracks. As their numbers increase, their charm decreases.

11 Mice of many species look similar; often we need to see their tail lengths to tell them apart. Jumping mice have tails much longer than their bodies; those of voles and lemmings are very short; and deer and white-footed mice have medium-sized tails about equal to their body length. Deer and white-footed mice both live in the northland. With their large eyes and ears, they are well adapted to nocturnal activities. Omnivores, they feed on nuts, seeds, buds, berries, insects, and carrion while living on the ground or in trees. To most of us, the two mice look identical because of their brown backs, light undersides, and four-inch-long bodies. Deer mice, however, tend to have longer tails and are usually residents of boreal forests; the slightly shorter white-footed mice are more common in deciduous forests.

European house mice are pests in urban areas throughout the country, but in northland rural settings or cabins, deer mice are traditional guests, albeit uninvited. In fall, some move indoors, and in many homes, the influx of deer mice is as regular as the first snowfall.

Notes

12 Long-eared and short-eared owls nest in the northland and also show up as regular, though never abundant, fall migrants. These relatives are about the same size and share similar names. Nevertheless, the sibling owls live quite different lives.

To casual observers, fifteen-inch-tall long-eared owls and twenty-two-inch tall great horned owls may look alike because each has feather tufts above the head. Though long-ears hold the tufts much more towards the center of the head than the great horns, it is the size of the tuft that distinguishes the two. Long-eared owls reside in northern conifer forests but winter through much of the country—often far south. In their daytime roosts, they stay close to tree trunks and fluff up their feathers when threatened.

Breeding in prairies, marshes, dunes, and on the tundra, short-eared owls are residents of open country where they hunt from the air, often during daylight. When not flying, these birds are usually seen perched on short poles, muskrat houses, duck blinds, or even on the ground. We can see the small ear tufts only when the owls are near.

Birds can be identified by their size, shape, coloring, call, and flight pattern and also by their habits. One way to distinguish long-eared and short-eared owls, for instance, is by the time of day that they hunt.

Notes

November

We call the soft brown critters flying squirrels, but really they glide from tree to tree. Bats, on the other hand, are mammals that truly fly.

13 Appropriately equipped with huge eyes, flying squirrels are the most nocturnal of the northland squirrels; they are virtually never seen during the day. Fluffy, soft gray-brown fur helps them stay warm and active throughout the winter, but it is their flat tail and the folds of skin that extend from front to hind legs that give them their gliding ability.

The smaller relatives, southern flying squirrels, live in deciduous forests and feed on nuts and insects. The northern species live in coniferous forests where it eats fruits, seeds, fungi, bird eggs, and even flesh.

Because of their quiet nocturnal lives, most of us notice their presence only when they decide to reside in our homes or cache food indoors with us. Many home and cabin owners have found unused drawers, boots, or coat pockets stashed with a flying squirrel's treasures.

In November's early darkness, we may notice their high-pitched chirps emanating from nearby woods or we may be fortunate enough to watch as they twist and turn in their tail-rudder glide among the trees. However, since they cache food in trees, not on the ground, we are not likely to see their tracks in snow.

Notes

November

14 Among the fallen leaves and brown meadow plants of mid-November, we sometimes find a growth of green hollow sticks. These horsetails, or scouring rushes, are common along northland river banks, lake shores, damp shaded slopes, and wet woods, but some may also be found in drier places such as road cuts and meadow edges.

These simple evergreen plants can grow to three feet tall. The hollow stems seen in November stand through early snows and may keep this pose all winter. Plants are unbranched, but like bamboo, they have gray bands at intervals on stems where tiny teethlike leaves grew. Since they can be pulled apart and reassembled at these junctions, horsetails are sometimes called puzzle plants.

Though some horsetails stand tall and green through the winter, others bleach to light colors and collapse on the forest floor. These deciduous types have many branches, which give them a feathered, or taillike, appearance. Without flowers, these fern relatives developed spores in stem-top cones earlier in the season. During winter, horsetails are among the few plants that remain green in the snow.

Horsetails are also called scouring rushes because their stems contain abrasive silica.

Notes

_____

_____

_____

_____

November

15 Milkweed's pink flowers, borne in ball-shaped clusters, bloomed in the heat of midsummer. At that time these tough plants with the bitter white juice stood along roadsides and meadows where they attracted myriads of insects and spiders. Best known of these are the milkweed bugs, monarchs, and skipper butterflies.

The insects moved on as cold temperatures moved in, and now the brown plants still stand but hold five or six pods in place of the flowers. Fat at the bottom, pointed at the top, the rough follicles split open during October's dry clear days, revealing rows of tightly packed seeds. In the winds of autumn and early winter, they loosen, spread tufts of white hairs, and drift over open spaces like tiny parachutes. The open seed pods are usually empty by midwinter. This enchanting wind dispersal spreads the seeds, but most will not germinate. Undeterred, the hardy milkweed lives on in its branching rootstock.

Fluffy-filled milkweed pods are very photogenic at this time. When the seeds disperse, they can be used in floral arrangements.

Notes

16 Rough-legged hawks, one of the largest and most northern hawks in North America, are often seen in November over fields and other open country as they move through to winter in similar southern sites.

Rough-legged hawks are about the size of their well-known cousins, the red-tailed hawks, but they can be distinguished in several ways. They are usually not as dark above or light below as the red-tailed hawks. They have a black belly and black wing spots, but it is the large dark tail band that is their identifying feature.

Alone or in small groups, these hawks hunt the open country, often hovering over meadows in their quest for food. Until they move on, we may see rough-legged hawks flying and hovering or perched low in open areas. They are the only hawk to breed on the tundra where, faced with a limited supply of trees, they nest on the ground. There they feed on rodents and other small mammals that have fluctuating population cycles. In lean years, they need to fly further for adequate food.

We read of the lemmings and their rush to the sea. Rough-legged hawks and other reptiles find easy pickings during these mass migrations, but when they are over, the tundra can be a hungry place to live.

Notes

November

Shrubs, bushes, brush—the leafy green plants that aren't quite trees but certainly aren't wildflowers seem hard to identify. The common buckthorn, however, defines itself with its long-lasting leaves.

17 When northland trees dropped their leaves in October, a few did not respond with the rest, holding their greens to the end of the month. Eventually, weeping willows and lilacs gave in and bared their branches, but in the woods, another tree resisted until now. The common buckthorn stands only about fifteen feet tall, but by remaining green for the last month, it has finally been noticed by hikers.

Though some buckthorns are native to North America, it is the common buckthorn, an immigrant, that grabs our attention in the autumn. Apparently, this native of Europe and Asia thrives in northland woods but has not become acclimated enough to drop its three-inch-long glossy leaves with other trees in October; it does so in November. The shade-tolerant trees do well in the forest's understory. Sharp, stout spines that grow on the tips of branches and twigs add the word thorn to the name of the tree.

Not only do we notice the leaves at this time, but we also note the quarter-inch dark berries. The waxwings and grosbeaks find them now, too, and will continue to eat them throughout the coming cold months.

Notes

18 Though only two feet tall, these shrubs of the open woods, thickets, and meadows are rarely ignored. In early summer, they graced their habitats with large pink flowers, and in midfall, we saw the burrlike insect galls on their spiny stems. Now, as the snows begin to cover the northland, the bushes hold many half-inch-long fleshy red fruits known as hips. They have a limited resemblance to their large cousins, the apples.

Rose hips contain large seeds in their flesh. The hips and the seeds within them are eaten by many birds, and both small mammals and wild-food fanciers are quick to sing the praises of these fruits as well. They are said to be so rich in vitamin C that three rose hips have an amount of that vitamin equal to that of an orange or from six to twenty times that found in a glass of orange juice. Some claim that now, after the frosts, is a prime time to pick rose hips to be steeped in hot water for tea. They can also be boiled into jelly (with apples and pectin) or candy, or eaten raw. For the more ambitious, hard boiling and sweetening can produce rose hip syrup or butter.

Rose hips are so flavorful that they are the main ingredient in many herb teas—even one that is supposedly peach flavored.

Notes

November

Because our favorite edible fruits and berries—strawberries, raspberries, cherries, apples—are red, be careful to caution children that not all red berries are edible.

19 With the coming of winter holidays, we often see ornaments made of holly. The sharp evergreen leaves and red berries make this a common seasonal decoration. These leaves and berries come from the American holly, a tree native to southeastern United States; but in the northland, we have our own holly that also displays its red berries now.

The simple oval leaves persisted until late October on this shrubby tree of wetland areas along streams, ponds, swamps, and lakes, but since they dropped, the red berries of the northland's winterberry holly have become visible.

As a way of attracting animals, especially birds, trees display fruits and berries in bright colors. This is certainly true of this little holly that we would not notice without its red berries. The berries are eaten by birds and small mammals, but they are not recommended for human consumption: their ingestion can cause vomiting, diarrhea, and stupor. Though these berries catch our attention in November, they do not remain on this small tree much longer. Unlike the berries of some southern hollies, they are gone by midwinter.

Notes

We expect predators to prey on other species: birds on rodents, fish on insects. But often they prey on their own, so we shouldn't be surprised that northern shrikes eat other birds.

20 From the far north, they arrive here in October. Perched alone in semiopen country, northern shrikes spend the winter hunting in the northland. The shrikes have gray backs, black wings and tail, and a black mask or patch just below the eyes. The white on their undersides and wings is very apparent when they fly.

The robin-sized birds act like raptors, though they are really a type of songbird. Summering in northern Canada and Alaska, they feed on small mammals, birds, and insects. Until snow covers the northland, they continue to hunt small mammals, but the white blanket gives shelter to these little critters, and shrikes switch to a diet of birds. This explains why they are often seen around feeders.

Shrikes have hooked beaks to tear their prey, but because they have no talons, they cannot hold their victims as the raptors do. To compensate for this, shrikes impale their prey on thorns of hawthorn and buckthorn or use barbed wire. There they are able to pull their prey apart (thus earning their name of butcher birds) or leave it for later snacking.

Notes

November

Consider planting a patch of cheerful sunflowers next spring. You'll enjoy them next summer, and in the fall, birds such as evening grosbeaks will relish their seeds.

21 When nuthatches and juncos visit bird feeders, they are alone and silent; we hardly notice their presence. But when evening grosbeaks arrive, we all take note.

Looking similar to giant goldfinches, the eight-inch-long birds are yellow and black with white wing patches that are readily seen as they fly. They spend the winter in noisy, gregarious flocks that take over the feeders. With huge bills, they crack and gobble hordes of sunflower seeds and scatter even more with their active feeding habits. Whoever came up with the saying "eats like a bird" was not watching a flock of evening grosbeaks. Indeed, keeping the flock well fed can be quite a challenge for the bird feeder owner. Apparently, grosbeaks make rounds, visiting many feeders. When not devouring sunflower seeds, they do quite well on a diet of other seeds and berries.

Whether at feeders or in nearby trees, the noisy birds constantly give "cleer, clee-ip, peer" calls but become quiet suddenly as the flock moves on. Though grosbeaks are common through November in the northland, wintering flocks will fly far south and east of here.

Notes

November

If you approach quietly from down-wind you may get quite close to critters like the beaver that have poor eyesight.

22 All summer beavers remained active at their lodges and dam sites. Because of rains and the growth of their families, the beavers needed to enlarge and replace much of their woody structures. In winter, they will be secluded within the lodge under the snow. Here, usually in family units of four to ten, the beavers stay warm and well-fed and live an inactive life when compared to their work during the warmer months.

Now, in November, when the freeze sets in, we can see their winter preparations. These brown mammals, the largest rodents in North America, have poor eyesight, and we may be able to watch undetected as they stock their caches. To beat the freeze-up, beavers may even work in the daytime. Limbs of alder, aspen, birch, and willow are cut, brought to water, and cached at a convenient spot. After ice covers the pond, the beavers can go from lodge to cache without surfacing.

During November beavers may venture over the ice, giving us a rare opportunity to see their tracks in the new snow. Webbed feet and a flat dragged tail tell of the beaver's presence.

Notes

November

To get the most out of a winter walk, purchase a track field guide. You'll never see many forest critters, but when you can identify their tracks, you'll know they were around.

23 Sometimes all the variables that make for good tracking come together, giving us excellent conditions in which to find many clear tracks. Although snow, now newly covering the ground, will be here several months, perhaps no time is better than late November for some northland tracking.

The recently frozen ground holds the snow well, and the snow is wet, shallow, and shows clear footprints. Not only does the snow cooperate, so do the track makers. November is still warm enough to see autographs of critters that will hibernate or tunnel later in the winter.

In the meadows and fields, we see tracks of red fox, coyote, deer, skunk, vole, and shrew. In the woods appear red fox, wolf, deer, moose, skunk, mouse, shrew, weasel, marten, fisher, bobcat, snowshoe hare, gray squirrel, red squirrel, chipmunk, bear, porcupine, and grouse tracks. Over at the marsh, we find raccoon, mink, otter, star-nosed mole, muskrat, and beaver tracks. Not only are the kinds of tracks varied, so are the gaits and patterns. Each day we can read stories written in footprints and discover the nocturnal lives of the critters around us.

Notes

November

2 4 By late November, days are chilly and nights are cold. Our first snows have come, gone, and come again. With the ground frozen and the lakes freezing, the cold breath of winter has settled in. For the black bear, this chill means getting settled and going to sleep. All fall the bears have been preparing for winter by building body fat from a diet of fruits, berries, roots, insects, and meat. By now the critters are fat enough to sleep, and they need to locate a suitable place to hibernate. In the snow, bears wander through their territories to find proper dens. Though caves are preferred, they are not common here, so fallen trees, stump hollows, or conifers may serve as substitutes. Within a few weeks, before the really bitter cold and deep snow arrive, the bears will be asleep.

November offers one of our few opportunities to find the tracks of this large mammal in the snow. Bears walk with a slightly pigeon-toed gait, tracks of their hind feet partially covering the front ones. In wet snow, toe claws are easy to see, and the four-by-six-inch hind feet are impressive. Even the smaller front feet leave a four-by-four inch track. Soon these tracks will be covered by snow or will melt into oblivion, but fortunately, we can see them this one time.

If you're very lucky, you may be able to track a bear to its den. It wouldn't be wise to disturb it.

Notes

November

Do you have any instinctual responses to decreasing daylight or to colder temperatures? To what are pine siskins responding when they choose to fly south or remain in the northland?

25 In November, northlanders look for omens of the coming winter. Perhaps the frozen ground, lake freeze-up, and early snows give promise of what is in store for us in the months ahead. November can also be the time to tell whether or not this will be a pine siskin winter.

Breeding in coniferous forests, these five-inch-long streaked brown cousins of the goldfinches often nest in parts of the northland. In fall, they form wintering flocks that soon head to the south. During some years these flocks may travel as far as the gulf states, while in other years, they remain here as wintering finches. Pine siskins come to bird feeders, but they are late to arrive and may share the stage with wintering goldfinches or redpolls. Though siskins wear yellow, theirs is not as pronounced as the goldfinches' color, and their lack of a red throat or face separates them from the streaked redpolls.

As November progresses, we may see pine siskin flocks of fifty or more birds in woods, roadsides, or weedy meadows where they feed on seeds and regularly give their rising buzzy "shreeeee" call.

Notes

26 In summer, bald eagles nest in the northland; in winter many eagles congregate along the Mississippi River or in various National Wildlife Refuges; but it is now, in late November, that the migrating bald eagles pass over in largest numbers. Most of us have no trouble recognizing the adults with their three-foot-long dark bodies, white heads and tails, and wings that span nearly seven feet. Young bald eagles are often the same size as the adults, but because they lack similar head and tail patterns they may be misidentified as their cousins, the golden eagles. Immature eagles do not have the white feathers of the adults, but they do carry light patterns under their wings and tails.

The cold and snows of autumn send the eagles south from their northern nesting sites in the forested lake country. Flocks may form during these migration flights, and a drive through the northland at this time can offer us some impressive sights of eagles. Though a few eagles choose to winter this far north, most go south to rivers and wetlands where they feed on fish and dead water birds. This fact makes November, before they have gone to wintering sites, the best time for northlanders to see flocking bald eagles.

Notes

Bald eagles were on their way to extinction a few years ago. DDT, an insecticide that was applied to farm fields, ran off into streams and lakes. The DDT was absorbed by the smallest organisms, then was concentrated as it moved through the food chain. Bald eagles ate it when they ate fish and laid eggs with fragile shells. The eagles are making a comeback now that DDT has been banned.

November

27 Sumac, a shrubby little tree, called for little attention until the arrival of fall colors. Then, from old fields, fencerows, roadsides, swamp margins, and forest edges, they painted their compound leaves with a rich bright red and then bowed out and faded

As if that moment of fame were not enough, they now hold tight clusters of red-purple berries. The tiny hairy one-eighth-inch berries contain large seeds and do not seem edible—but such is not the case. The berries are eaten by wintering birds, and nearly every northlander who has sampled wild foods has heard of Indian lemonade. Red sumac berries, steeped in water for the proper time and then sweetened, make a tasty pink lemonade substitute that rivals the store-bought type. Prolonged steeping, however, can cause a bitter taste to permeate the drink.

The northland has two sumacs, smooth and staghorn, that live in similar habitats. Smooth sumac lacks the hairy stems of staghorn, which look to some people like deer antler velvet.

Enter your wild foods kitchen and begin a test project. Prepare several pints of water, some boiling, some cold. Place washed sumac berries in each container. Refrigerate some; place others in the sun. Test by tasting at ten minutes, twenty minutes, then every half hour until the flavor seems right. Record the procedure that was most effective for making sumacade.

Notes

November

28 The largest, most common, and most frequently seen shrew of the northland is the short-tailed shrew, but other tiny shrews also live here. Collectively, the other four kinds are sometimes called long-tailed shrews. All have ranges which stretch over much of the north; the masked and arctic shrews live as far north as the Arctic Ocean. Pygmy and water shrews stay a little further south.

Masked and pygmy shrews are extremely tiny; the pygmy is often proclaimed to be the smallest mammal in North America. Its two-inch-long gray body weighs about the same as a dime. The masked shrew is slightly larger and probably the most common of these four, but looks identical to the pygmy. Water and arctic shrews are bicolored. Both are light underneath, and while the water shrew is gray above, the arctic is black and brown. Largest of the four, three-inch-long water shrews live in wetlands.

Now in the snow of late November, we may see their tiny tunnels or even the shrews themselves as they search for food. Shrews need to eat regularly day and night to survive winter.

Extremely high metabolism makes the shrews always in a hurry and always hungry. Their insatiable appetites need to be satisfied all winter.

Notes

November

29 Though it grew to be five feet tall in summer and had rather attractive pink-purple flowers and huge rhubarblike leaves, burdock gets more notice in autumn than it did then. Along roadsides and waste places where this native of Europe has become well established, its flowers, leaves, and stem all turn brown in the cold, and we now see (or may feel) the fruits.

Burdock gives us an example of seeds that are adapted to dispersal by animals. Some plants attract animals with bright-colored fruits and berries. The animals eat the seeds, which pass through their digestive tracts and are planted where they fall. Burdock, however, grabs on for a ride. Its fruits are tenacious burrs that are covered with hooked barbs. These half-inch-long burrs are so effective that a November walk through a field nearly always brings us back with a few uninvited hitchhikers. The seeds are deep within the burrs, but as we, or our pets, pull off the burrs, we open them and spread the seeds. Burdock is another example of plants which outsmart animals. The plants are so good at seed dissemination that often by midwinter they are devoid of all seeds.

Apparently Velcro™ was modeled after burdock fruits. They certainly cling to clothing just as tightly as the hooked side of the fastener.

Notes

30 Most autumn and winter woods wanderers have seen a three-inch-wide fan-shaped fungus growing on logs, dead trees, or wounded live ones. Colored in concentric zones of white, cream, yellow, brown, red, or blue-green, this little shelf fungus grabs our attention. This zoned pattern is responsible for its common name, turkey tail, and the various colors add *versicolor* to its Latin name.

With a surface of alternating velvety hairs and smooth tissue, the stalkless leathery body has a texture unexpected in shelf fungi. The fungus is pliable and soft in moist weather, but dries in the winter air. Its underside is white and is filled with minute pores. Its multicolored caps are slow to decay and have actually been used for ornaments— including earrings and necklaces.

Rare on conifers, turkey tail commonly sprouts from deciduous trees. There it grows in rows, tiers, shelving masses, overlapping clusters, or even circular rosettes. It persists all year but is easiest to see in the bare forest. A late fall walk in the woods is likely to reveal turkey tail on trees near the snow.

Turkey tail varies widely in color. Note the colors that you observe and determine whether they bear any relationship to the tree on which the fungi are growing.

Notes

December

December

Most mink garments are constructed from ranch-bred mink pelts. The wild mink in the northland keep theirs all winter.

1 Mink, ranging through most of North America, are one of the most widespread members of the weasel family. These dark mammals are capable of living on land, but we never find them far from water. Common along lakes, marshes, or streams, they den under roots, rocks, hollow logs, streambanks, or in old muskrat houses. During their night hunts, they pursue muskrats, rabbits, squirrels, fish, snakes, frogs, waterfowl, and other aquatic animals.

Except for some light color on the chin, the entire pelt of this sixteen-inch-long mustelid is black or dark brown. The eight-inch-long tail is also dark but not as bushy as that of its cousins, the martens or the fishers.

Because of an early December freeze-up, minks are likely to be seen now: they may hunt during the day as well as at night, and ice and snow cover can send them out of the wetlands for their meals. Light snow on early winter ice makes for great tracking, and each day we can check the progress of these and other wandering hunters. In weasel family fashion, two-print tracks of minks lope through the wetlands and often lead to water.

Notes

December

2 While cross-country skiing in early December, we may see a few critters on the snow that we do not expect to encounter. With the temperature hovering between twenty-five and thirty-five degrees, many small animals travel over the surface, including caterpillars, leafhoppers, spiders, and many quarter-inch-long insects with long legs and clear wings that look a bit like mosquitoes. These are the winter crane flies.

Wings folded over their dark bodies, they show up clearly on the snow. During mild days, the males fly in a rising-falling pattern, and occasionally we may even observe a mating pair on the snow surface. Larvae develop in decaying vegetable matter, and unlike that of most other insects, the adult stage is in late fall and early winter. No doubt, cold causes problems, but the scarcity of insect-eating predators is an advantage.

Like other crane flies, they have only two clear wings, with short stubby halteres in place of the second pair. These structures are thought to help in stabilizing flight. Though they are related to and look like mosquitoes, winter crane flies cannot bite.

The winter crane flies again illustrate the ability of insects to live in varied conditions.

Notes

December

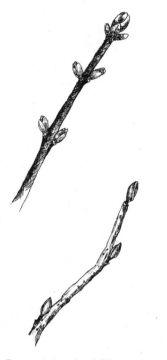

Recognizing the difference between alternate and opposite bud arrangements will help you identify leafless trees in winter.

3 It is a long way from these dark days of December to the bright days of spring, but deciduous trees are prepared for it already. Actually, they have been prepared since they dropped their leaves a couple of months ago, forming new buds on their twigs. Though the buds look like nothing more than bumps now, there is a bit of next spring tucked into the tiny contents of each. Even in winter, buds may open to reveal folded green leaves. In the warmth and longer days of next spring, these leaves will emerge. Northlanders wishing to speed up the seasons have brought twigs indoors to force buds to open early. This can be done later in winter, but not now. Apparently, buds need an extended exposure to cold.

Winter buds vary, and with a little practice, we can learn to recognize different kinds. All have a terminal, or apical, bud on the tip and lateral, or axial, buds on the sides. Some trees such as ash, maple, dogwood, and elder have lateral buds across from or opposite each other. However, most northland trees such as oak, cherry, elm, birch, aspen, poplar, alder, willow, hazel, basswood, and sumac have buds staggered in an alternating pattern.

Notes

December

4 The huge five-foot tall fronds of ostrich fern graced shaded wet areas all summer. In fall, these long plumes faded and turned brown, and by November only the large tough rootstocks and shorter fertile fronds could be seen. Because the huge green fronds of ostrich ferns are sterile, they must also grow these additional fertile structures. In early December, snow covers nearly all that remains of the ostrich ferns except the two-foot fronds, which continue to stand all winter.

Dwarfed by the long green leaves, these brown structures with a similar leaf shape have been hidden in their midst since summer. Instead of green leaflets, they hold a network of long spore capsules off the midvein. Other ferns usually have these spore capsules, called sori, under the fronds.

Now, helped by the snow cover, we see just how common these ferns are in wooded wet areas. Typically, December snows are not deep enough to cover the knee-high fertile fronds, and walking here, we can feel the rootstocks beneath the snow. Though they produce many spores and form new colonies from these fertile fronds, established ostrich ferns spread by their rootstocks.

Unless you look closely at ostrich fern fronds, you may not realize that you are seeing spore capsules rather than dried leaflets.

Notes

December

When you see golden-crowned king-lets or other birds eating insects that they find under bark, look for some yourself. Pull off a few flakes of bark and see if you can gather enough bugs for a bird's dinner.

5 Usually, it is the high-pitched "see-see-see" calls in the tops of conifers that attract us to tiny golden-crowned kinglets. The birds are only four inches long and, with gray bodies and white wing-bars, not very showy. Only the male's golden crown and the female's yellow add a bit of color to their bodies.

They flit quickly among the branches with blurred, nervous wing movements. These golden-crowns are summer breeders in the boreal forests of Canada. Their cousins, the ruby-crowned kinglets, summer with them but stay further south in the cold weather. Occasionally, in the northland, we see the diminutive birds flitting through trees in December.

The small flocks are constantly calling high-pitched notes as they move through chilly branches. Despite the cold, they are able to find and exist on a diet of nutritious insects, adults and larvae, that they pull from cracks and from behind bark. During long frigid winter nights, the small birds congregate in sheltered areas to survive, but in the more severe cold of midwinter, most will move further south.

Notes

December

6 In early December, tree leaves are long gone, and buds will not be opening for months, but on the twigs of small shrubby willow trees, we see interesting growths. They look familiar, but out of place. There, on the willows, are what appear to be pine cones. About one inch long, these structures have the same shape and overlapping scales as real cones. Instead of finding seeds under the scales, however, we find many insects.

Known as willow-cone galls, these phenomena are the results of eggs deposited by tiny insects in the tree's terminal buds last summer. The plant responded with huge swellings that expanded to form these cones. Deep down in their centers sleep the larvae of the gnats that caused all this. In fall they entered a torpor in an attempt to survive winter and emerge in spring as adults.

The gnats that cause these cones to develop often share them with plenty of uninvited guests. In one study, more than five hundred insects were taken from twenty-three willow-cone galls; only fifteen were the original gnats.

Compare your sharp eyes to those of scientists. How many insects can you find in a willow-cone gall? Be sure to use a hand lens.

Notes

December

Many parasitic plants live on their hosts without killing them. If the black knot fungus kills the chokecherry tree, it destroys its source of nourishment and support.

7 Bearing spikes of white flowers last spring and bitter purple berries in late summer, chokecherry trees attracted bees, birds, and people. Now, in winter, we notice these small trees again, but in a different way. Chokecherry is susceptible to the growth of a parasitic fungus called black knot. Up to twelve inches long and an inch thick, the hard black fungus is easy to see on the bare tree branches of December.

Black knot begins by entering a crack or wound, causing an expanded swelling on the affected twigs or branches. This canker creates a longitudinal break in the bark that is soon covered by black fungal growth. As the fungus grows on diseased branches, the branches are bent at odd angles and its outer portions die. The whole branch can die—even the entire tree in extreme cases. Apparently, fungus mycelia penetrate into the tree's growth cells. Within the dark fungal tissue, many fruiting bodies develop, and spores are formed in small sacs called asci.

Black knot is present all winter, and we can readily see how common it is in the northland. In some woods, it appears that most chokecherries are affected by it.

Notes

December

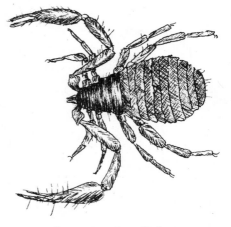

8 Common residents of soil and leaf litter communities, pseudoscorpions are usually not seen in these habitats. It is only when we happen upon these tiny animals in our houses that we become aware of their presence.

Pseudoscorpions get their name from the long pincers these tiny critters have. Their bodies are seldom over a quarter-inch long, and they do not have the long tail of true scorpions. Pseudoscorpions live in houses all over the world, including the northland, but despite their misleading name, they are totally harmless.

With flat bodies, they fit into cracks and openings that we do not even see. By walking forwards, backwards, or sideways, pseudoscorpions are able to survive in these tiny places and feed on mites, clothes moths, carpet beetle larvae, book lice, and other minute insects. Indoors, they remain active all winter—doing much of their hunting at night; we sometimes surprise them when we turn on the morning light. This is most common in the bathroom, where we may see them on walls or trapped in sinks as they search for prey and moisture.

Pseudoscorpions bear little resemblance to spiders, but they, along with true scorpions, mites, and ticks, are all arachnids. Their segmented bodies are divided into two regions; the anterior bears four pairs of legs.

Notes

December

Mosquitoes aren't the only critters that enter homes on firewood. Sit by the fire and strip the bark off a few pieces of wood. Do you find insects, their tracks, or their eggs?

9 Winter is one time of the year when northlanders expect to be without mosquitoes. Yet even now, in the dark days of December, we may encounter these insects.

In the life cycle of the mosquito, larvae and pupae develop in open water—usually in ponds, lakes, or marshes, but perhaps in just a puddle—until adults emerge. Males feed on plant sap and nectar, but females need blood protein from humans or other animals to help fertilized eggs form.

Different species emerge throughout the warm weather; one kind, the house mosquito, continues to reproduce until the weather becomes too cold. Adults of the last brood hibernate, often choosing sleeping sites behind bark or in cracks of wood. If they happen to select a stick of firewood for hibernating, the mosquitoes (and we) may be in for a surprise. When firewood is taken into the house, light and warmth wake the critters, and we get live winter mosquitoes. Females carrying fertilized eggs seek a meal of blood, and in a house, they have a limited number of animals to get it from. Even if they do get blood, it will be hard to find a place for their eggs.

Notes

December

10 A December snowfall that stops by late afternoon sets the stage for us to check out the activity of nocturnal mammals. By the next morning, this new blanket has fresh autographs written by hare, mice, shrews, deer, raccoons, and ermine. The ermine's small two-print pattern of tracks looks like two of our fingertips in snow.

Except for the ends of their three-inch-long tail, short-tailed weasels wear a white coat for winter and are known as ermines. Only they and snowshoe hares enter the northland winter with such a coat, and the eight-inch-long ermines are the only predator that changes its coat from season to season.

These solitary nocturnal hunters are seldom seen, and were it not for their tracks, we might not know that they live with us. Enjoying a diet of small mammals, ermine spend much of winter beneath the snow pursuing their prey. They often cache food under logs and roots and in rodent burrows. In early winter snows, however, they lope over meadows, streams, marshes, and forests. Following their trail can be a workout for us as they jump, zigzag, circle, double-back, and tunnel throughout the terrain.

Next time you see the tracks of an ermine or some other critter, take time to follow them just as far as you can. You can learn a lot about the animal's winter lifestyle.

Notes

December

If you look at bird beaks, you will get clues about their diet. Pine grosbeaks can crack seeds with their large beaks. Other birds have long pointed beaks for extracting insects from holes. Look for other variations.

11 Sometimes during December, we have visits at the feeder from birds that are about the size of robins, but are pinkish rose in color and have thick bills. Gray-brown birds of similar size and shape accompany them in a small flock. Both brightly colored male and drab female pine grosbeaks have dark tails with white wing bars on the dark wings. These birds are quite tame and easy to get close to.

Pine grosbeaks are residents of the boreal forests and do not migrate far from their northern homes. Some do not get this far south all winter. Although we may only see a few of these large bright birds in early winter, December is perhaps the best month to find them. While here, they frequently leave the conifers to visit bird feeders.

Using their large beak (grosbeak means big beak), they feed on seeds such as sunflower seeds at bird feeders, and also on the fruits and berries that are still available such as mountain-ash and crab apple. Pine grosbeaks are usually silent while sitting and feeding, but in flight they give the "pui pui pui" call and occasionally, a musical "chee vli."

Notes

December

12 By early December, the northland has received some snow, and in these dark days, much more is forecast. With severe cold not yet with us, some of the small critters that winter under the snow are now moving on its surface. Among these are several kinds of wolf spiders.

These brown or black spiders are usually seen on the ground, where they hunt at night without making webs. With excellent eyesight and impressive speed, they capture their prey.

Wolf spiders are with us all year, but on mild December days, with a temperature near freezing and a few inches of snow cover, we are likely to see them active in the daytime. The wetland wolf spiders need to learn to cope with freezing water and ground in early winter; to handle these changes, they walk over the snow in search of shelter and prey. They are not alone: as these spiders of the wetlands move about, residents of the meadows and woods are traveling too. Indeed, the snow on a mild December day may become a highway for spiders and insects. With a little looking, we can see several kinds during an hour's walking or skiing.

After a fresh white snowfall, wolf spiders and other small black critters stand out against the white snow. Pause to examine the little black specks.

Notes

December

When you plant trees in your yard, you may want to select a mountain-ash. It will draw birds, and it also provides year-round color.

13 Most trees produce seeds and fruits that ripen in late summer or fall and by December are only a memory. A few, such as hawthorn, buckthorn, and crab apple, last far into the winter, but perhaps the best known and most colorful of these winter berries are those of the mountain-ash.

It must be the compound pinnate leaves that adds the word ash to this tree's name, since nothing else links this tree to the true ashes. Mountain-ash has about fifteen toothed leaflets on its long leaves.

In the northland, we have two native mountain-ash trees and one that was introduced from Europe. All have winter berries that delight us as well as birds such as the waxwings and the grosbeaks. Small and shrubby, American mountain-ash with its little red berries grows on rocky hills and along streams and swamps, while the larger showy mountain-ash is fairly common in boreal forests. The introduced European mountain-ash is probably best known: it has been planted in many yards and parks. Midsized trees bear umbels of white flowers in spring and now display clusters of the long-lasting orange-red berries.

Notes

14 To many of us, mice are small mammals that all look alike. However, using the size of the tail as a distinguishing feature, we can put them into three basic groups. Jumping mice have tails much longer than their bodies; deer and white-footed mice have body-length tails; and voles have tails that are less than half the length of their bodies. Voles can also be recognized by their small eyes and ears and by their dark fur. They stay active all winter. Boreal red-backed voles of the damp forests and bogs and meadow voles of the meadows and fields are the two most common voles in the northland.

Also known as meadow or field mice, meadow voles counteract their long list of predators by being highly prolific. One female had seventeen litters in just one year while in captivity. They make networks of ground-level tunnels that are used all year. With routes that crisscross the yards, meadows, and fields, they spend winter under the snow in relative warmth, feeding on grasses and seeds. When their tunnels open onto our paths, we can see on the snow their tiny footprints, which show that they walk rather than hop. Nearby, you may spy the openings to their ventilation shafts.

Because voles remain active throughout the year, they are easy prey for hungry birds and carnivorous mammals. You may see marks on the snow that show a life and death struggle, one almost surely lost by the little vole.

Notes

December

When porcupines are in the area, be sure to store tools and canoe paddles carefully. Their sweat-soaked handles hold salt that is irresistible to porcupines.

15 Equipped with long sticky quills, porcupines are not likely to be confused with other mammals, yet their name means pig with spines. Far from being pigs, porcupines are arboreal rodents that feed on buds, small twigs, and the inner bark of trees. Conifers are their first choice, but they will eat deciduous trees as well. Fond of salt, they also gnaw plywood and varnished boards.

During summer, porcupines are solitary, but to keep warm in winter, they may den with others in tree hollows and stumps, or under outbuildings. Oval scats (droppings) litter the region of a well-used den.

These porcupines are in a greater hurry in winter than they were in summer. They plod through snow leaving a pigeon-toed, foot-dragging pattern. In wet snow, the long claws show well. They make trails between dens and feeding sites, using the same trails until they need to find another source of food.

December is a good time to follow their tracks and get a look at these quilled neighbors. Although porcupines usually feed at night, they can sometimes be seen during the day in trees where they remain through chill and wind until they are finished eating.

Notes

16 Occasionally, on chilly December mornings, we discover a companion in the bathroom. There, in the bathtub, sits a brown spider with long hairy legs. The half-inch-long body is lost among these legs, which make the spider look twice its size. The spider has what appears to be two tails.

Known as house spiders, these funnel-web makers live in houses, garages, and basements. It is common to find their snares in corners or cracks in any of these buildings. Most are brown with a few gray stripes on the backside. All have long spinnerets that look like tails and are used for web making. Males and females are nearly the same size.

These spiders remain indoors all year, and they may live for several years. Apparently, in cold weather, they search the house at night for water and new hunting sites and appear to find both in the bathroom. However, the smooth sides of the bathtub trap them if they should blunder into it. We come along in the morning and see these harmless critters caught there.

A dilemma. Should you wash it down the drain or carefully place it back in a corner? Why not err on the side of mercy and save the harmless house spider from drowning.

Notes

December

Considering that bird identification is often difficult, rejoice when you can declare confidently, "that's a snowy owl." You don't have to tell your companions that the bird's white feathers gave you a pretty good clue.

17 Breeding in the northern tundra, two-foot-long snowy owls do a couple of things we do not expect of owls: in the land of the midnight sun, they hunt during the day, and because they live north of the tree line, they nest on the ground. In both cases, the tundra does not give them any other choice.

In late fall, migrating snowy owls arrived in the northland, and many remain with us for the winter. Here they continue their habit of day hunting in the open prairies, fields, marshes, and beaches. Often they are seen perched on the ground, or on haystacks, stumps, fence posts, utility poles, or buildings.

The adult owls are light in color, and old males are nearly pure white. The young have dark bars and spots and may look like other owls. Both the adults and the immature birds have yellow eyes and feathered feet with large talons. Their summer diet consists of tundra birds and mammals, especially lemmings. These mice have cyclic populations, and some years depleted numbers cause snowy owls to travel further south than usual. During such years, they have been seen as far south as Alabama.

Notes

18 Because they grow out flat from trees and logs, we call them shelf fungi. Many kinds exist in the northland, and though varying in shape, size, and color, they are usually harder (often like wood) and last longer than other fungi. It is interesting to note that the shelf grows parallel to the ground and if a tree holding a shelf fungus falls on its side, the fungus continues to grow, but at a right angle to its original orientation—still parallel to the ground. Three common shelf fungi that are easy to see in December are artist fungus, horse hoof fungus, and birch polypore fungus.

Artist fungus can live for fifty years and reach a diameter of two feet as it grows on dead deciduous trees. The woody gray-brown upper surface has rings with rounded ridges. The white lower surface bruises quickly, and markings here produce pictures or prints. Horse hoof fungus is the shape and size of a horse's hoof. The gray woody body with brown below persists on birch, poplar, and maple. The birch polypore fungus is smooth and white on top, but browns with age. Growing in a kidney, or semicircular shape, the fungus winters on white birch trees.

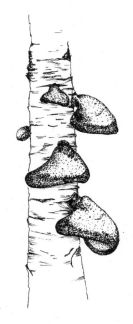

How could you design an experiment that would answer the following question: Do shelf fungi, which grow parallel to the ground, respond to gravity, light, or something else? Considering how slowly fungi grow, you might need considerable time to conduct your experiment.

Notes

December

River otters appear to take pleasure in their swoops and slides. If you find their toboggan marks, perhaps you will see them at play.

19 A streamlined body with a rich dark-brown pelt, silvery underparts, and a thick fifteen-inch-long tail characterizes the river otter, the most aquatic and largest member of the northland's weasel family. The thirty-inch-long river otters live near water just about anywhere in North America. They are at home in rivers, lakes, ponds, marshes, and even on the ocean coasts.

Because of December's freeze-up of lakes and rivers, we are more likely to see otters traveling over ice or land now than at any other time. They lope in the characteristic weasel-family gait, leaving a gap of fifteen to twenty inches between their three-inch-long paw prints. Wherever and whenever possible, the otters slide on their bellies through the snow. It is their eight- to ten-inch-wide toboggan marks that identify these wandering predators.

Their thick fur seems to handle these snow slides well, and even an occasional dip through holes in the ice does not slow them down. Such cold swims are important to their winter survival. Although they feed on other critters, fish is their staple food. The ample, but not deep, snow cover makes mid-December a good time for us to look for this aquatic mammal.

Notes

December

20 Along with cold and darkness, the snow buntings appear in December. Flocks of the tundra-nesting birds began arriving here in October and although many go further south to the prairies, others stay with us, appearing completely at home in snowy fields.

Varying in number from year to year, they may gather in flocks of more than a hundred or less than twenty, but the gregarious birds always deal with winter in groups. Occasionally, horned larks and longspurs join them.

To cope with wind, cold, and drifting snow, wintering flocks feed on weed seeds as they spend the season in fields or on shores and roadsides. They have been known to bury themselves in snow to survive the deepest chills.

Typically, we see snow bunting flocks when they fly up from along the roadsides, giving a rough purring "brrt" call as we pass by. After making a few circles, the seven-inch-long white birds settle down again, continuing their search for food. The birds may not stay all winter, so now is the time to see these living snowflakes.

Why do some plants hold their seeds throughout winter? Probably because it's beneficial for their seeds to fall on moist spring ground. What's good for the plants, however, also is good for seed-eating birds like the snow buntings. They need a massive amount of seeds to survive the winter.

Notes

December

People have strong feelings about blue jays. Some find their behavior boorish; others are charmed by their cocky ways.

21 Some birds, such as swallows, respond to cold weather by migrating. Others, like the black-capped chickadees, travel little, if at all, in the cold. A few birds seem to cope with winter by sending some of their species to the south while others remain. Among these are the blue jays.

During September and early October, their south-bound migrating flocks were passing by. These flocks became large: at peak travel time, we could see hundreds in a single day. The migrants scattered through much of the southern and eastern United States for the winter months.

Others chose to stay behind, and many blue jays become regular visitors at bird feeders during the northland winter. Forming small groups, they continue the aggressive behavior they exhibited in the warmer months, and their raucous "jeeah" or "queedle, queedle" calls sound in the cold.

Some studies suggest that all the young birds move south in the fall along with many adults and that it is only other adults that stay here for the winter. Whatever the case may be, these blue-crested birds do well in winter and are expanding their range north.

Notes

December

22 The pine marten, with a yellowish brown back blending into a black tail and a pale buff breast, is one of the northland's most handsome mammals. Although they are permanent residents of boreal forests, they are so seldom seen that only their tracks in the snow tell of their presence.

Like other members of the weasel family, pine martens are mostly carnivores, eating squirrels, mice, shrews, hare, and birds, although they also eat various fruits. They den in trees or among rocks. Though other mammals of their species climb trees, none can match the pine marten's skill. Sixteen inches long with a bushy eight-inch-long tail, pine martens are midsized among the northland mustelids—large compared to weasels and mink, but small when seen with fishers and otters.

Late December snows provide good conditions for checking the progress of these nocturnal hunters. Active pine martens explore the forest floor, logs, hollows, and trees. Their two-print patterns, often appearing at two-foot intervals, show that they leap through the woods. Seeing their tracks is common on northland outings, but seeing the elusive pine martens themselves is rare.

Rodents reproduce so prolifically that without carnivores, they would overrun fields and forests. Follow the pine marten's tracks and look for recent kills.

Notes

December

A hint of green in midwinter cheers us more than a forest filled with green in midsummer. Scan the vertical face of cliffs for polypody ferns, mosses, and lichens.

23 On rocky hills in southern states, ferns grow that remain green all winter and so are commonly called Christmas ferns. We do not have that particular evergreen fern, but on the northland's shaded rocky cliffs, another fern also keeps its green color all year. The polypody fern uses its spreading rhizomes to send out roots to hold on to the rocky substrate that it commonly frequents.

Polypody, also called rock-cap or comb fern, has fronds less than a foot long that grow in the typical fern shape. A single midvein has long thin leaflets but displays no other branching. The small fern fronds are deep green in color.

Growing on steep rocks can be difficult, but with little competition from other plants and sheltered from severe weather, the polypody fern not only survives but actually lives a long life. Its tough, leathery leaves help it cope with the problem of desiccation in winter's arid air. Though evergreen, the fern keeps growing new leaves to replace the old ones that die. Spore capsules are formed in clumps underneath the fronds, mainly toward the top.

Notes

December

24 We are more likely to take notice of conifers in December than in June. If you touch the tips of their needles, you will find that spruce needles are pointed and sharp; the needles of balsam fir and hemlock are flat and blunt.

Known as balsam fir, but usually called balsam, this conifer grows to become a medium-sized tree with four-inch-long cones. Common in mixed forests, it grows in association with maples, aspen, and birch. The upper surface of the one-inch-long needles is dark green, the lower surface, light green. The needles remain on the tree for nearly ten years.

Hemlock is more common in the eastern states: its western limit of growth is the western Great Lakes. Hemlock is a large tree with tiny cones. Its stands often dominate regions of the forest. Growing along lake shores and streams, and near swamps, it thrives in cool, moist environments among deciduous trees. The flat needles, about one-half-inch long, dark green above, light green below, remain on the tree three years.

Because it has needles that stay attached to the twigs, balsam fir serves as an excellent decorative tree.

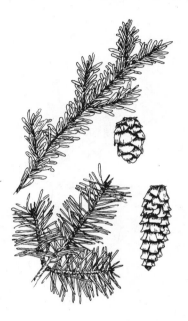

Balsam fir, spruce, and pine are commonly raised on tree farms, cut, and sold as Christmas trees. No matter which tree your family prefers, be sure to give it lots of water.

Notes

December

Seeing the sharp needles, we can use the saying, "When you are all spruced up, you are looking sharp," to differentiate spruce from other conifers.

25 Perhaps no other trees are more attractive in winter than the pyramidal evergreens we know as spruce. With ranges that extend across the northern United States and Canada, black spruce and white spruce make up huge parts of the boreal forests. Each has long-lasting sharp needles that completely surround the stems.

The tree's pointed shape is an adaptation to reduce snow accumulation. Closely spaced branches, however, hold enough snow to keep the ground around the tree's base clear, and many critters take advantage of this. Owls, grouse, hare, deer, and songbirds use the spruce for shelter, although only spruce grouse and snowshoe hare eat the needles.

Black spruce, smaller and more pointed than white, bears half-inch-long needles. A resident of poorly drained swamps and bogs, it often grows near tamarack. White spruce, bearing one-inch-long needles, lives in forests, hillsides, and old fields, which it often shares with aspen, birch, and balsam.

Notes

26 Mistletoe, a plant that we often use as an ornament this time of year, does grow wild in the southern states. There, the evergreen plant attaches to a tree branch, commonly sycamore or American elm. A parasite, it absorbs nutrients from its host. The foot-tall plant, which carries white berries, persists for the winter and is regarded as a symbol of love and peace.

In the northland, we also have a mistletoe. Although it, too, is a tree parasite, it differs from southern mistletoe in many ways. Dwarf mistletoe, also called witch's broom, appears as a dark growth in the branches of spruce trees; black spruce is most susceptible to it. A fungus, it sends mycelia into living tree cells to obtain nutrition. It can become a large mass, but usually clusters of dwarf mistletoe are less than a foot in diameter. If, during our winter walks, ski treks, or other outings, we see a growth in spruce branches that looks like a bunch of intertangled twigs, we might think witch's broom is a better name for this plant than dwarf mistletoe. Because it's a parasite, we're not likely to think of it as a symbol of love and peace, though neither it nor southern mistletoe appear harmful to host trees.

Friends may think you're an eccentric but knowledgeable botanist if you hang a bunch of dwarf mistletoe in an archway and attempt to steal a holiday kiss.

Notes

December

If you are traveling in moose territory, it's essential to boil drinking water drawn from ponds and streams. Moose host a parasite that can make humans ill.

27 Very long legs and powerful muscles allow moose, the largest of the deer family, to move at ease in the northland's deep snow of late December. Thirty inches of snow would stop deer or send them to their yards but do not seem to bother these huge animals.

Although their diet consisted mainly of aquatic plants during the warmer months, moose now feed on browse for the winter. When the ponds and lakes freeze over, moose move among the foliage. There they dine on the twigs of conifers such as cedar and balsam as well as on those of deciduous trees such as willow, aspen, alder, dogwood, birch, and mountain maple. Their dietary needs may overlap with those of the deer, but the mobile and powerful moose are not deterred by this.

Except for the cows with their calves, moose tend to winter alone. You will know if they are in the area because they leave huge hoof prints the size of saucers in deep snow; the prints of their dew claws show clearly. Strides of two feet are common, and they often drag their toes. Feeding at dusk and dawn, moose bed down among the browse, leaving ice-coated sites that tell of their presence. With the rutting season long gone, the bulls now drop their huge antlers.

Notes

December

28 The red-breasted nuthatch often acts like its larger cousin, the white-breasted nuthatch; it travels down trees headfirst while hunting for insects in cracks and holes in the bark. Unlike its cousin, however, the five-inch-long red-breasted nuthatch is a resident of coniferous forests where it also feeds on seeds it forces from cones. Typically, it caches its treasures in tree nooks and crannies.

In the northland, these tiny birds visited earlier in the fall as they passed by on their way to winter homes in southern states. In December, however, we find that a few hardy red-breasted nuthatches are spending the winter with us. They frequently visit bird feeders, looking for sunflower seeds, peanut butter, and suet. Although they are the tiniest birds at the feeder, they are often aggressive toward larger birds.

Red-breasted nuthatches have a blue-gray back and a black cap. A black line extends through the eye area with a white line above it. Their undersides are rusty red, the males' brighter than those of the females. The "ank" and "enk" calls are higher pitched than those of the white-breasted nuthatch.

Peanut butter is a nutritious food for birds such as the red-breasted nuthatch. Mix it with seeds before serving it to the birds.

Notes

December

White-breasted nuthatches, along with most northland birds, will survive winter without the food provided at bird feeders. But feeding birds in your backyard makes their lives easier and yours more pleasurable.

29 In December, white-breasted nuthatches are among the most common guests at bird feeders; their visits are exceeded only by those of chickadees and blue jays. At feeders, the six-inch-long birds sample suet, peanut butter, and sunflower seeds. Often they fly with sunflower seeds to the bark of nearby trees where they take a characteristic pose, head down and out, and with strong bills, crack open the seeds. Indeed, this behavior gives the birds their name. Nuthatch is derived from nut hack, and they do hack the nuts and seeds.

Along with their white breasts, these nuthatches have white faces, black caps, bluish-gray backs, and, under their tails, some chestnut feathers. The low-pitched "yank yank" calls may be given any time of the year as the birds feed and travel headfirst down the trees.

Permanent residents of the northland, as well as most of the eastern United States, they are consistent feeder visitors. In fact, they visit feeders so often that they appear to need for winter survival the food that humans provide. Actually, during their bark searching, they find plenty of nutritious insects.

Notes

December

30 Timber wolves and coyotes both live in the northland. While the national range of the wolf has shrunk, that of its smaller cousin, the coyote, is growing. Formerly a prairie resident, the coyote now is found throughout the whole country. Being highly adaptable, it lives well among people, often going undetected. However, one place the coyote avoids is the home territory of wolves.

Also known as brush wolves, coyotes are about the size of small collies. It is hard to tell a small wolf from a large coyote, but you can if you look for the coyote's long rusty ears and legs. Though not as gregarious as wolves, coyotes may travel and hunt with their young until midwinter. Now, with the breeding season due to begin in January, the yearlings will disperse.

During December, most coyotes travel and hunt alone, but on moonlit nights, we may hear several "yapping" together. Coyote tracks look similar to those of dogs, and only their gait can separate the two. Cunning coyotes leave a clean, narrow trail, while the domestic dog's trail is erratic. Wandering and hunting at night, coyotes survive winter by being able to eat anything and live anywhere.

Adaptable critters such as the coyote ensure the survival of their species because they can survive in a variety of habitats, withstand temperature variations, and eat whatever is available.

Notes

December

Your hearing is not nearly as acute as the great gray owl's, but it's probably better than you think. Find a stump; sit down and listen intently. You'll hear much more than you did when you were crunching noisily through the snow.

Notes

31 Although most great gray owls reside in far northern forests and bogs, some do nest in the northland. Yet, we seldom see these huge owls except in the winter when they often leave the heavy forests to hunt in open country.

Two feet long and possessing a wing span of five feet, great gray owls reign as North America's largest owl. The gray-brown body has a long tail, a rounded head with rings around the yellow eyes, and a black chin. Great gray owls hunt over bogs and forest clearings in winter and may be active during the day as well as at night. Typically, we see them perched on trees, posts, or utility poles as we drive along winter roads. Such an impressive bird demands our attention, and more than one motorist has stopped for a longer look. The birds will often tolerate the presence of humans, which allows us to closely observe them from parked cars or even to approach them on foot.

Great gray owls hear incredibly well; they are able to determine the location of a mouse in its burrow more than a foot beneath the snow surface. In a silent flight, they plunge into the snow for their prey. Masses of fluffy feathers help to cushion the impact.